The 12th IAAF World Athletics Championships

Berlin 15 - 23 August 2009

Complete Results & Athletes Reference

Silverthorn Press　　　　　　　　　　　　　　　　　　Simon Barclay

2009 edition
© 2011 by Simon Barclay. All rights reserved

ISBN 978-1-4477-5685-9

World Athletics Championships 2009 - Berlin

Contents

	Page
Previous Championships	4
Event World & Championship Records prior to Berlin:	
Men	5
Women	6
Previous Championship Gold Medal Performances:	
Men	7
Women	8
New World and Championships Records Set	9
Participating Nations and Number of Athletes	10
Medal Table	11
Events:	
100m	12
200m	20
400m	26
800m	31
1500m	36
5000m	41
10000m	44
Marathon	45
3000m Steeplechase	49
100m/110m Hurdles	52
400m Hurdles	56
High Jump	60
Pole Vault	64
Long Jump	70
Triple Jump	76
Shot Put	82
Discus	88
Hammer	94
Javelin	100
Heptathlon Events	106
Heptathlon Final Table	117
Decathlon Events	118
Decathlon Final Table	134
20km Walk	135
50km Walk	137
4x100m Relay	138
4x400m Relay	141
Athlete Index and Previous Championship Appearances	143

World Athletics Championships

Championship	Year	Dates	Host Nation	Countries	Athletes
1st	1983	7 - 14 August	Helsinki, Finland	153	1355
2nd	1987	28 August - 6 September	Rome, Italy	159	1451
3rd	1991	23 August - 1 September	Tokyo, Japan	167	1517
4th	1993	13 - 22 August	Stuttgart, Germany	187	1689
5th	1995	5 - 13 August	Gothenburg, Sweden	191	1804
6th	1997	1 - 10 August	Athens, Greece	198	1882
7th	1999	20 - 29 August	Seville, Spain	201	1821
8th	2001	3 - 12 August	Edmonton, Canada	189	1677
9th	2003	23 - 31 August	Paris, France	198	1679
10th	2005	6 - 14 August	Helsinki, Finland	191	1688
11th	2007	25 August - 2 September	Osaka, Japan	197	1800
12th	2009	15 - 23 August	Berlin, Germany	202	1984

Records at the start of the Championships - MEN

Event	World Record	Mark	Year	Championship Record	Mark	Year
100m	Usain Bolt (Jamaica)	9.69	2008	Maurice Greene (United States)	9.80	1999
200m	Usain Bolt (Jamaica)	19.30	2008	Tyson Gay (United States)	19.76	2007
400m	Michael Johnson (United States)	43.18	1999	Michael Johnson (United States)	43.18	1999
800m	Wilson Kipketer (Denmark)	1:41.11	1997	Billy Konchellah (Kenya)	1:43.06	1987
1500m	Hicham El Guerrouj (Morocco)	3:26.00	1998	Hicham El Guerrouj (Morocco)	3:27.65	1999
5000m	Kenenisa Bekele (Ethiopia)	12:37.35	2004	Eliud Kipchoge (Ethiopia)	12.52.79	2003
10000m	Kenenisa Bekele (Ethiopia)	26:17.53	2005	Kenenisa Bekele (Ethiopia)	26:49.57	2003
Marathon	Haile Gebrselassie (Ethiopia)	2:03:59	2008	Jaouad Gharib (Morocco)	2:08:31	2003
3000m Steeplechase	Saif Saaeed Shaheen (Qatar)	7:53.63	2004	Moses Kiptanui (Kenya)	8:04.16	1995
110m Hurdles	Dayron Robles (Cuba)	12.87	2008	Colin Jackson (Great Britain)	12.91	1993
400m Hurdles	Kevin Young (United States)	46.78	1992	Kevin Young (United States)	47.18	1993
High Jump	Javier Sotomayor (Cuba)	2.45	1993	Javier Sotomayor (Cuba)	2.40	1993
Pole Vault	Sergey Bubka (Ukraine)	6.14	1994	Dmitri Markov (Australia)	6.05	2001
Long Jump	Mike Powell (United States)	8.95	1991	Mike Powell (United States)	8.95	1991
Triple Jump	Jonathan Edwards (Great Britain)	18.29	1995	Jonathan Edwards (Great Britain)	18.29	1995
Shot Put	Randy Barnes (United States)	23.12	1990	Werner Günthör (Switzerland)	22.23	1987
Discus	Jürgen Schult (East Germany)	74.08	1986	Virgilijus Alekna (Lithuania)	70.17	2005
Hammer	Yuriy Sedykh (Soviet Union)	86.74	1986	Ivan Tsikhan (Belarus)	83.89	2005
Javelin	Jan Železný (Czech Republic)	98.48	1996	Jan Železný (Czech Republic)	92.80	2001
Decathlon	Roman Šebrle (Czech Republic)	9026	2001	Tomáš Dvořák (Czech Republic)	8902	2001
20km Walk	Vladimir Kanaykin (Russia)	1:17:16	2007	Jefferson Pérez (Ecuador)	1:17:21	2003
50km Walk	Denis Nizhegorodov (Russia)	3:34:14	2008	Robert Korzeniowski (Poland)	3:36:03	2003
4x100 Relay	Jamaica	37.10	2008	United States	37.40	1993
4x400 Relay	United States	2:54.29	1993	United States	2:54.29	1993

Records at the start of the Championships - WOMEN

Event	World Record	Mark	Year	Championship Record	Mark	Year
100m	Florence Griffith Joyner (United States)	10.49	1988	Marion Jones (United States)	10.70	1999
200m	Florence Griffith Joyner (United States)	21.34	1988	Silke Gladisch-Möller (East Germany)	21.74	1987
400m	Marita Koch (East Germany)	47.60	1985	Jarmila Kratochvílová (Czechoslovakia)	47.99	1983
800m	Jarmila Kratochvílová (Czechoslovakia)	1:53.28	1983	Jarmila Kratochvílová (Czechoslovakia)	1:54.68	1983
1500m	Qu Yunxia (China)	3:50.46	1993	Tatyana Tomashova (Russia)	3:58.52	2003
5000m	Tirunesh Dibaba (Ethiopia)	14:11.15	2008	Tirunesh Dibaba (Ethiopia)	14:38.59	2005
10000m	Wang Junxia (China)	29:31.78	1993	Berhane Adere (Ethiopia)	30.04.18	2003
Marathon	Paula Radcliffe (Great Britain)	2:15:25	2003	Paula Radcliffe (Great Britain)	2:20:57	2005
3000m Steeplechase	Gulnara Samitova-Galkina (Russia)	8:58.81	2008	Yekaterina Volkova (Russia)	9:06.57	2007
110m/100m Hurdles	Yordanka Donkova (Bulgaria)	12.21	1988	Ginka Zagorcheva (Bulgaria)	12.34	1987
400m Hurdles	Yuliya Pechonkina (Russia)	52.34	2003	Kim Batten (United States)	52.61	1995
High Jump	Stefka Kostadinova (Bulgaria)	2.09	1987	Stefka Kostadinova (Bulgaria)	2.09	1987
Pole Vault	Yelena Isinbayeva (Russia)	5.05	2008	Yelena Isinbayeva (Russia)	5.01	2005
Long Jump	Galina Chistyakova (Soviet Union)	7.52	1988	Jackie Joyner-Kersee (United States)	7.36	1987
Triple Jump	Inessa Kravets (Ukraine)	15.50	1995	Inessa Kravets (Ukraine)	15.50	1995
Shot Put	Natalya Lisovskaya (Soviet Union)	22.63	1987	Natalya Lisovskaya (Soviet Union)	21.24	1987
Discus	Gabriele Reinsch (East Germany)	76.80	1988	Martina Hellmann (East Germany)	71.62	1987
Hammer	Tatyana Lysenko (Russia)	77.80	2006	Mihaela Melinte (Romania)	75.20	1999
Javelin	Barbora Špotáková (Czech Republic)	72.28	2008	Osleidys Menéndez (Cuba)	71.70	2005
Heptathlon	Jackie Joyner-Kersee (United States)	7291	1988	Jackie Joyner-Kersee (United States)	7128	1987
20km Walk	Olimpiada Ivanova (Russia)	1:25:41	2005	Olimpiada Ivanova (Russia)	1:25:41	2005
4x100 Relay	East Germany	41.37	1985	United States	41.47	1997
4x400 Relay	Soviet Union	3:15.17	1988	United States	3:16.71	1993

Gold Medal Performances in each Championships

Event		1983	1987	1991	1993	1995	1997	1999	2001	2003	2005	2007	2009
100m	Men	10.07	9.93	9.86 WR	9.87	9.97	9.86	9.80 CR	9.82	10.07	9.88	9.85	9.58 WR
200m	Men	20.14	20.16	20.01	19.85 CR	19.79 CR	20.04	19.90	20.04	20.30	20.04	19.76 CR	19.19 WR
400m	Men	45.05	44.33	44.57	43.65	43.39 CR	44.12	43.18 WR	44.64	44.77	43.93	43.45	44.06
800m	Men	1:43.65	1:43.06 CR	1:43.99	1:44.71	1:45.08	1:43.38	1:43.30	1:43.70	1:44.81	1:44.24	1:47.09	1:45.29
1500m	Men	3:41.59	3:36.80	3:32.84 CR	3:34.24	3:33.73	3:35.83	3:27.65 CR	3:30.68	3:31.77	3:37.88	3:34.77	3:35.93
5000m	Men	13:28.53	13:26.44	13:14.45 CR	13:02.75	13:16.77	13:07.38	12:58.13 CR	13:00.77	12:52.79	13:32.55	13:45.87	13:17.09
10000m	Men	28:01.04	27:38.63 CR	27:38.74	27:46.02	27:12.95 CR	27:24.58	27:57.27	27:53.25	26:49.57 CR	27:08.33	27:05.90	26:46.31 CR
Marathon	Men	2:10:03	2:11:48	2:14:57	2:13:57	2:11:41	2:13:16	2:13:36	2:12:42	2:08:31 CR	2:10:10	2:15:59	2:06:54 CR
3000m Steeplechase	Men	8:15.06	8:08.57	8:12.59	8:06.36 CR	8:04.16 CR	8:05.84	8:11.76	8:15.16	8:04.39	8:13.31	8:13.82	8:00.43 CR
110m Hurdles	Men	13.42	13.21	13.06	12.91 WR	13.00	12.93	13.04	13.04	13.12	13.07	12.95	13.14
400m Hurdles	Men	47.50	47.46 CR	47.64	47.18	47.98	47.70	47.72	47.49	47.25	47.30	47.61	47.91
High Jump	Men	2.32	2.38 CR	2.38 CR	2.40	2.37	2.37	2.37	2.36	2.35	2.32	2.35	2.32
Pole Vault	Men	5.70	5.85 CR	5.95 CR	6.00 CR	5.92	6.01 CR	6.02 CR	6.05 CR	5.90	5.80	5.86	5.90
Long Jump	Men	8.55	8.67 CR	8.95 WR	8.59	8.70	8.42	8.56	8.40	8.32	8.60	8.57	8.54
Triple Jump	Men	17.42	17.92 CR	17.78	17.86	18.29 WR	17.85	17.59	17.92	17.72	17.57	17.74	17.73
Shot Put	Men	21.39	22.23 CR	21.67	21.97	21.47	21.44	21.79	21.87	21.69	21.73	22.04	22.03
Discus	Men	67.72	68.74 CR	66.20	67.72	68.76 CR	68.54	69.08 CR	69.72 CR	69.69	70.17 CR	68.94	69.43
Javelin	Men	89.48	83.54 CR	90.82	85.98 CR	89.58	88.40	89.52	92.80 CR	85.44	87.17	90.33	89.59
Hammer	Men	82.68	83.06 CR	81.70	81.64	81.56	81.78	80.24	83.38 CR	83.05	83.89 CR	83.63	80.24
Decathlon	Men	8666	8680	8812 CR	8817 CR	8695	8837 CR	8744	8902 CR	8750	8732	8676	8790
20km Walk	Men	1:20:49	1:20:45 CR	1:19:37 CR	1:22:31	1:19:59	1:21:43	1:23:34	1:20:31	1:17:21	1:18:35	1:22:20	1:18:41
50km Walk	Men	3:43:08	3:40:53 CR	3:53:09	3:41:41	3:43:42	3:44:46	3:47:54	3:42:08	3:36:03	3:38:08	3:43:53	3:38:35
4x100 Relay	Men	37.86 WR	37.90	37.50 WR	37.48	38.31	37.86	37.59	38.47	38.06	38.08	37.78	37.31 CR
4x400 Relay	Men	3:00.79	2:57.29 CR	2:57.53	2:54.29 WR	2:57.32	2:56.65	2:58.91	2:58.19	2:58.96	2:56.91	2:55.56	2:57.86

Event		1983	1987	1991	1993	1995	1997	1999	2001	2003	2005	2007	2009
100m	Women	10.97	10.90 CR	10.99	10.82 CR	10.85	10.83	10.70 CR	10.82	10.93	10.93	11.01	10.53
200m	Women	22.13	21.74 CR	22.09	21.98	22.12	22.32	21.77	22.52	22.38	22.16	21.81	22.02
400m	Women	47.99 WR	49.38	49.13	49.82	49.28	49.77	49.67	49.86	48.89	49.55	49.61	49.00
800m	Women	1:54.68	1:55.26	1:57.50	1:55.43	1:56.11	1:57.14	1:56.68	1:57.17	1:59.89	1:58.82	1:56.04	1:55.45
1500m	Women	4:00.90	3:58.56 CR	4:02.21	4:00.50	4:02.42	4:04.24	3:59.53	4:00.57	3:58.52 CR	4:00.35	3:58.75	4:03.74
3000m	Women	8:34.62	8:38.73	8:35.82	none	none	none	none	none	none	none	none	none
5000m	Women	none	none	none	8:28.71 CR	14:46.47 CR	14:57.68	14:41.82 CR	15:03.39	14:51.72	14:58.59 CR	14:57.91	14:57.97
10000m	Women	none	31:05.85	31:14.31	30:49.30 CR	31:04.99	31:32.92	30:24.56 CR	31:48.81	30:04.18 CR	30:24.02	31:55.41	30:51.24
Marathon	Women	2:28:09	2:25:17	2:29:53	2:30:03	2:25:39*	2:29:48	2:26:59	2:26:01	2:23:55 CR	2:20:57 CR	2:30:37	2:25:15

* marathon course was short by 400m.

Event		1983	1987	1991	1993	1995	1997	1999	2001	2003	2005	2007	2009
3000m Steeplechase	Women	none	none	none	none	none	none	none	none	none	9:18.24 CR	9:06.57 CR	9:07.32
100m Hurdles	Women	12.35	12.34 CR	12.59	12.46	12.68	12.50	12.37	12.42	12.53	12.66	12.46	12.51
400m Hurdles	Women	54.14	53.62 CR	53.11 CR	52.74 WR	52.61 WR	52.97	52.89	53.34	53.22	52.90	53.31	52.42 CR
High Jump	Women	2.01	2.09 WR	2.05	1.99	2.01	1.99	1.99	2.00	2.06	2.02	2.05	2.04
Pole Vault	Women	none	none	none	none	none	none	4.60 WR	4.75 CR	4.75	5.01	4.80	4.75
Long Jump	Women	7.27	7.36 CR	7.32	7.11	6.98	7.05	7.06	7.02	6.99	6.89	7.03	7.10
Triple Jump	Women	none	none	none	15.09 WR	15.50 WR	15.20	14.88	15.25	15.18	15.11	15.28	14.95
Shot Put	Women	21.05	21.24 CR	20.83	20.57	21.22	20.71	19.85	20.61	20.63	20.51	20.54	20.44
Discus	Women	68.94	71.62 CR	71.02	67.40	68.64	66.82	68.14	67.10	67.32	66.56	66.61	65.44
Javelin	Women	70.82	76.64 CR	68.78	69.18	67.56	68.78	67.09	69.53 CR	66.52	71.70 WR	67.07	67.30
Hammer	Women	none	none	none	none	none	none	75.20 CR	70.65	73.33	75.10	74.76	77.96 CR
Heptathlon	Women	6714	7128 CR	6672	6837	6651	6739	6861	6694	7001	6887	7032	6731
10km Walk	Women	none	44:12.00 CR	42:57.00 CR	42:59	42:13.00 CR	42:55.49	none	none	none	none	none	none
20km Walk	Women	none	none	none	none	none	none	1:30:50 CR	1:27:48 CR	1:26:52 CR	1:25:41 CR	1:30:09	1:28:09
4x100 Relay	Women	41.76	41.58 CR	41.94	41.49 CR	42.12	41.47 CR	41.92	42.32	41.78	41.78	41.98	42.06
4x400 Relay	Women	3:19.73	3:18.63 CR	3:18.43	3:16.71 CR	3:22.29	3:20.92	3:21.98	3:20.65	3:22.63	3:20.95	3:18.55	3:17.83

New Records Set in Berlin 2009

World Records (3)

Event	Mark	Athlete	Country
100m (m)	9.58	Usain Bolt	Jamaica
200m (m)	19.19	Usain Bolt	Jamaica
Hammer (w)	77.96	Anita Włodarczyk	Poland

Championship Records (8)

Event	Mark	Athlete	Country
100m (m)	9.58	Usain Bolt	Jamaica
200m (m)	19.19	Usain Bolt	Jamaica
10000m (m)	26:46.31	Kenenisa Bekele	Ethiopia
Marathon (m)	2:06:54	Abel Kirui	Kenya
3000m SC (m)	8:00.43	Ezekiel Kemboi	Kenya
4x100m (m)	37.31	Steve Mullings, Michael Frater, Usain Bolt, Asafa Powell	Jamaica
Hammer (w)	77.96	Anita Włodarczyk	Poland
400m Hurdles (w)	52.42	Melaine Walker	Jamaica

Participating Nations (202) & Numbers of Competitors (1984)

Afghanistan (2)
Albania (1)
Algeria (6)
American Samoa (2)
Andorra (2)
Anguilla (2)
Antigua and Barbuda (2)
Argentina (6)
Armenia (2)
Australia (38)
Austria (5)
Azerbaijan (1)
Bahamas (15)
Bahrain (10)
Bangladesh (1)
Barbados (4)
Belarus (26)
Belgium (23)
Belize (1)
Benin (2)
Bermuda (1)
Bhutan (1)
Bolivia (2)
Bosnia and Herzegovina (1)
Botswana (5)
Brazil (30)
British Virgin Islands (1)
Brunei (1)
Bulgaria (11)
Burkina Faso (2)
Burundi (2)
Cambodia (1)
Cameroon (3)
Canada (31)
Cape Verde (2)
Cayman Islands (2)
Central African Republic (2)
Chile (4)
China (32)
Chinese Taipei (2)
Colombia (11)
Comoros (2)
Congo (2)
Democratic Republic of the Congo (2)
Cook Islands (2)
Costa Rica (3)
Croatia (5)
Cuba (34)
Cyprus (4)
Czech Republic (22)
Denmark (3)
Djibouti (1)
Dominica (1)
Dominican Republic (6)
Ecuador (10)
Egypt (4)
El Salvador (2)
Equatorial Guinea (2)
Eritrea (8)
Estonia (18)
Ethiopia (38)
Federated States of Micronesia (1)
Fiji (2)
Finland (20)
France (78)
French Polynesia (2)
Gabon (2)

Gambia (2)
Georgia (2)
Germany (85)
Ghana (3)
Gibraltar (1)
Great Britain (51)
Greece (21)
Grenada (6)
Guatemala (2)
Guinea (2)
Guyana (3)
Haiti (2)
Honduras (2)
Hong Kong (1)
Hungary (12)
Iceland (2)
India (6)
Indonesia (2)
Iran (2)
Iraq (2)
Ireland (17)
Israel (4)
Italy (37)
Côte d'Ivoire (2)
Jamaica (46)
Japan (57)
Jordan (2)
Kazakhstan (14)
Kenya (43)
Kiribati (2)
Kuwait (2)
Kyrgyzstan (2)
Laos (2)
Latvia (15)
Lebanon (2)
Lesotho (2)
Liberia (3)
Libya (2)
Lithuania (15)
Luxembourg (1)
Macau (1)
Macedonia (1)
Madagascar (2)
Malawi (2)
Malaysia (2)
Maldives (2)
Mali (2)
Malta (1)
Marshall Islands (1)
Mauritania (2)
Mauritius (3)
Mexico (18)
Moldova (6)
Monaco (1)
Mongolia (2)
Montenegro (2)
Morocco (22)
Mozambique (2)
Myanmar (2)
Namibia (4)
Nauru (2)
Netherlands (11)
Netherlands Antilles (2)
New Zealand (16)
Nicaragua (2)
Niger (1)
Nigeria (25)

Northern Mariana Islands (2)
North Korea (6)
Norway (17)
Oman (1)
Pakistan (2)
Palau (2)
Palestine (2)
Panama (3)
Papua New Guinea (2)
Paraguay (1)
Peru (4)
Philippines (2)
Poland (42)
Portugal (30)
Puerto Rico (5)
Qatar (9)
Romania (17)
Russia (106)
Rwanda (3)
Saint Kitts and Nevis (7)
Saint Lucia (1)
Saint Vincent & the Grenadines (2)
Samoa (2)
San Marino (2)
São Tomé and Príncipe (2)
Saudi Arabia (12)
Senegal (4)
Serbia (9)
Seychelles (2)
Sierra Leone (2)
Singapore (2)
Slovakia (13)
Slovenia (13)
Solomon Islands (2)
Somalia (1)
South Africa (24)
South Korea (19)
Spain (51)
Sri Lanka (2)
Sudan (9)
Suriname (2)
Swaziland (2)
Sweden (23)
Switzerland (11)
Syria (2)
Tajikistan (2)
Tanzania (10)
Thailand (1)
Togo (2)
Tonga (2)
Trinidad and Tobago (20)
Tunisia (5)
Turkey (12)
Turkmenistan (2)
Turks and Caicos Islands (1)
Tuvalu (2)
Uganda (12)
Ukraine (54)
United Arab Emirates (2)
United States (160)
U.S. Virgin Islands (2)
Uruguay (3)
Uzbekistan (6)
Vanuatu (2)
Venezuela (2)
Vietnam (2)
Zambia (5)
Zimbabwe (6)

Medal Table

Rank	Nation	Gold	Silver	Bronze	Total
1	United States	10	6	6	22
2	Jamaica	7	4	2	13
3	Kenya	4	5	2	11
4	Russia	4	3	6	13
5	Poland	2	4	2	8
6	Germany	2	3	4	9
7	Ethiopia	2	2	4	8
8	Great Britain	2	2	2	6
9	South Africa	2	1	0	3
10	Australia	2	0	2	4
11	Bahrain	2	0	1	3
12	Cuba	1	4	1	6
13	China	1	1	2	4
14	Norway	1	1	0	2
15	Spain	1	0	1	2
16	Barbados	1	0	0	1
16	Croatia	1	0	0	1
16	New Zealand	1	0	0	1
16	Slovenia	1	0	0	1
20	France	0	1	2	3
20	Trinidad and Tobago	0	1	2	3
22	Bahamas	0	1	1	2
23	Japan	0	1	1	2
24	Canada	0	1	0	1
24	Cyprus	0	1	0	1
24	Czech Republic	0	1	0	1
24	Eritrea	0	1	0	1
24	Ireland	0	1	0	1
24	Panama	0	1	0	1
24	Portugal	0	1	0	1
24	Puerto Rico	0	1	0	1
32	Estonia	0	0	1	1
32	Mexico	0	0	1	1
32	Qatar	0	0	1	1
32	Romania	0	0	1	1
32	Slovakia	0	0	1	1
32	Turkey	0	0	1	1
	Total	**47**	**48**	**47**	**142**

Men's 100m

Qualification for quarter-finals: first three in each heat plus the next four fastest finishers.

Heat 1   15 August 2009

Position	Lane	Athlete	Country		Time
1	6	Michael Frater	Jamaica	Q	10.30
2	4	Arnaldo Abrantes	Portugal	Q	10.41
3	2	Shintaro Kimura	Japan	Q	10.47
4	7	Simone Collio	Italy		10.49
5	5	Matic Osovnikar	Slovenia		10.52
6	3	Béranger Aymard Bosse	Central African Republic		10.55
7	8	Jack Iroqa	Solomon Islands		10.98
	1	Dominic Carroll	Gibraltar		DNF

Heat 2   15 August 2009

Position	Lane	Athlete	Country		Time
1	4	Darvis Patton	United States	Q	10.26
2	6	Emanuele Di Gregorio	Italy	Q	10.35
3	2	Masashi Eriguchi	Japan	Q	10.38
4	5	Barakat Al-Harthi	Oman		10.41
5	8	Stefan Schwab	Germany		10.50
6	1	Liqat Ali	Pakistan		10.64
7	3	Oumar Bella Bah	Guinea		11.20
	7	Delivert Arsene Kimbembe	Congo		DNS

Heat 3   15 August 2009

Position	Lane	Athlete	Country		Time
1	8	Martial Mbandjock	France	Q	10.28
2	6	Obinna Metu	Nigeria	Q	10.38
3	3	Asafa Powell	Jamaica	Q	10.38
4	4	Aziz Ouhadi	Morocco		10.40
5	2	Derrick Atkins	Bahamas		10.44
6	5	Ivano Bucci	San Marino		11.24
7	7	Leon Mengloi	Palau		11.60

Heat 4   15 August 2009

Position	Lane	Athlete	Country		Time
1	6	Dwain Chambers	Great Britain	Q	10.18
2	1	Olusoji Fasuba	Nigeria	Q	10.31
3	5	Monzavous Edwards	United States	Q	10.32
4	8	Ben Youssef Meité	Ivory Coast		10.41
5	3	Shehan Abeypitiyage	Sri Lanka		10.53
6	7	Wilfried Bingangoye	Gabon		10.62
7	2	Mohamed Faisal	Brunei		11.12
8	4	Masoud Azizi	Afghanistan		11.79

Heat 5   15 August 2009

Position	Lane	Athlete	Country		Time
1	6	Daniel Bailey	Antigua & Barbuda	Q	10.26
2	8	Jaysuma Saidy Ndure	Norway	Q	10.35
3	4	Adrian Griffith	Bahamas	Q	10.37
4	5	Tobias Unger	Germany		10.42
5	2	Adrian Durant	US Virgin Islands		10.46
6	7	Jurgen Themen	Surinam		11.24
7	3	Yondan Namelo	Federated States of Micronesia		11.78

Men's 100m (continued)

Heat 6 — 15 August 2009

Position	Lane	Athlete	Country		Time
1	6	Christophe Lemaître	France	Q	10.23
2	3	Marc Burns	Trinidad & Tobago	Q	10.39
3	4	Dariusz Kuć	Poland	Q	10.46
4	1	Ryan Moseley	Austria		10.58
5	8	Franklin Nazareno	Ecuador		10.71
6	5	Chi Ho Tsui	Hong Kong		10.77
7	2	Mohamed Masudul Karim	Bangladesh		11.32
8	7	Quaski Itaia	Nauru		11.76

Heat 7 — 15 August 2009

Position	Lane	Athlete	Country		Time
1	4	Andrew Hinds	Barbados	Q	10.30
2	8	Simeon Williamson	Great Britain	Q	10.34
3	6	Ronald Pognon	France	Q	10.35
4	7	Martin Keller	Germany	q	10.35
5	5	Ángel David Rodríguez	Spain	q	10.39
6	1	Basílio de Moraes	Brazil		10.54
7	3	Denvil Ruan	Anguilla		11.31
8	2	Soulisack Silisavadymao	Laos		11.66

Heat 8 — 15 August 2009

Position	Lane	Athlete	Country		Time
1	5	Samuel Francis	Qatar	Q	10.21
2	6	Emmanuel Callander	Trinidad & Tobago	Q	10.24
3	7	Churandy Martina	Netherlands Antilles	Q	10.26
4	8	Daniel Grueso	Colombia	q	10.27
5	1	Rolando Palacios	Honduras	q	10.28
6	3	Fernando Lumain	Indonesia		10.76
7	4	Hussain Haleem	Maldives		11.00
8	2	Suwaibou Sanneh	Gambia		11.02

Heat 9 — 15 August 2009

Position	Lane	Athlete	Country		Time
1	3	Usain Bolt	Jamaica	Q	10.20
2	2	Gerald Phiri	Zambia	Q	10.30
3	5	Egwero Ogho-Oghene	Nigeria	Q	10.30
4	8	Bryan Barnett	Canada		10.42
5	4	José Carlos Moreira	Brazil		10.55
6	7	Aisea Tohi	Tonga		11.32
7	6	Okilani Tinilau	Tuvalu		11.57

Heat 10 — 15 August 2009

Position	Lane	Athlete	Country		Time
1	6	Richard Thompson	Trinidad & Tobago	Q	10.36
2	1	Tyrone Edgar	Great Britain	Q	10.42
3	3	Simon Magakwe	South Africa	Q	10.54
4	7	Aziz Zakari	Ghana		10.57
5	2	Idrissa Sanou	Burkina Faso		10.74
6	4	Mhadjou Youssouf	Comoros		10.89
7	8	Desislav Gunev	Bulgaria		11.07
8	5	Nooa Takooa	Kiribati		11.74

Men's 100m (continued)

Heat 11 15 August 2009

Position	Lane	Athlete	Country		Time
1	8	Tyson Gay	United States	Q	10.16
2	6	Kim Collins	St Kitts & Nevis	Q	10.28
3	3	Fabio Cerruti	Italy	Q	10.36
4	7	Kemar Hyman	Cayman Islands		10.59
5	4	Carlos Jorge	Dominican Republic		10.73
6	2	Aaron Victorian	American Samoa		11.37
7	5	Tiraa Arere	Cook Islands		11.55

Heat 12 15 August 2009

Position	Lane	Athlete	Country		Time
1	3	Michael Rodgers	United States	Q	10.25
2	2	Naoki Tsukahara	Japan	Q	10.28
3	8	Adam Harris	Guyana	Q	10.35
4	4	Ramon Gittens	Barbados		10.47
5	6	Cédric Nabe	Switzerland		10.51
6	5	Danny D'Souza	Seychelles		10.92
7	1	Phillip Poznanski	Marshall Islands		11.97
8	7	Clayton Kenty	Northern Mariana Islands		12.29

Qualification for semi-finals: first three in each quarter-final plus the next fastest finisher.

Quarter-Final 1 15 August 2009

Position	Lane	Athlete	Country		Time
1	3	Dwain Chambers	Great Britain	Q	10.04
2	4	Richard Thompson	Trinidad & Tobago	Q	10.08
3	5	Martial Mbandjock	France	Q	10.22
4	6	Emanuele Di Gregorio	Italy		10.26
5	8	Adam Harris	Guyana		10.39
6	7	Arnaldo Abrantes	Portugal		10.40
7	2	Martin Keller	Germany		10.40
8	1	Masashi Eriguchi	Japan		10.45

Quarter-Final 2 15 August 2009

Position	Lane	Athlete	Country		Time
1	6	Michael Rodgers	United States	Q	10.01
2	7	Tyrone Edgar	Great Britain	Q	10.04
3	4	Naoki Tsukahara	Japan	Q	10.15
4	5	Gerald Phiri	Zambia	q	10.16
5	8	Egwero Ogho-Oghene	Nigeria		10.19
6	1	Simon Magakwe	South Africa		10.71
	2	Christophe Lemaître	France		DSQ
	3	Daniel Grueso	Colombia		DSQ

Quarter-Final 3 15 August 2009

Position	Lane	Athlete	Country		Time
1	1	Asafa Powell	Jamaica	Q	9.95
2	3	Darvis Patton	United States	Q	10.05
3	8	Marc Burns	Trinidad & Tobago	Q	10.12
4	5	Kim Collins	St Kitts & Nevis		10.20
5	6	Samuel Francis	Qatar		10.20
6	4	Olusoji Fasuba	Nigeria		10.25
7	7	Ronald Pognon	France		10.27
8	2	Shintaro Kimura	Japan		10.54

Men's 100m (continued)

Quarter-Final 4 15 August 2009

Position	Lane	Athlete	Country		Time
1	6	Tyson Gay	United States	Q	9.98
2	5	Michael Frater	Jamaica	Q	10.09
3	3	Jaysuma Saidy Ndure	Norway	Q	10.16
4	4	Andrew Hinds	Barbados		10.23
5	1	Adrian Griffith	Bahamas		10.28
6	7	Obinna Metu	Nigeria		10.36
7	8	Fabio Cerutti	Italy		10.37
8	2	Ángel David Rodríguez	Spain		10.39

Quarter-Final 5 15 August 2009

Position	Lane	Athlete	Country		Time
1	3	Daniel Bailey	Antigua & Barbuda	Q	10.02
2	4	Usain Bolt	Jamaica	Q	10.03
3	7	Monzavous Edwards	United States	Q	10.15
4	8	Churandy Martina	Netherlands Antilles		10.19
5	5	Simeon Williamson	Great Britain		10.23
6	2	Rolando Palacios	Honduras		10.24
7	6	Emmanuel Callander	Trinidad & Tobago		10.27
8	1	Dariusz Kuć	Poland		10.38

Qualification for the Final: first four in each semi-final.

Semi-Final 1 16 August 2009

Position	Lane	Athlete	Country		Time
1	6	Usain Bolt	Jamaica	Q	9.89
2	4	Daniel Bailey	Antigua & Barbuda	Q	9.96
3	3	Darvis Patton	United States	Q	9.98
4	8	Marc Burns	Trinidad & Tobago	Q	10.01
5	5	Michael Rodgers	United States		10.04
6	1	Martial Mbandjock	France		10.18
7	2	Jaysuma Saidy Ndure	Norway		10.20
8	7	Tyrone Edgar	Germany		DSQ

Semi-Final 2 16 August 2009

Position	Lane	Athlete	Country		Time
1	5	Tyson Gay	United States	Q	9.93
2	4	Asafa Powell	Jamaica	Q	9.95
3	3	Richard Thompson	Trinidad & Tobago	Q	9.98
4	6	Dwain Chambers	Great Britain	Q	10.04
5	7	Michael Frater	Jamaica		10.14
6	2	Monzavous Edwards	United States		10.14
7	1	Gerald Phiri	Zambia		10.19
8	8	Naoki Tsukahara	Japan		10.25

FINAL 16 August 2009

Position	Lane	Athlete	Country		Time
GOLD	4	Usain Bolt	Jamaica	WR	9.58
SILVER	5	Tyson Gay	United States		9.71
BRONZE	6	Asafa Powell	Jamaica		9.84
4	3	Daniel Bailey	Antigua & Barbuda		9.93
5	8	Richard Thompson	Trinidad & Tobago		9.93
6	1	Dwain Chambers	Great Britain		10.00
7	2	Marc Burns	Trinidad & Tobago		10.00
8	7	Darvis Patton	United States		10.34

Women's 100m

Qualification for quarter-finals: first three in each heat plus the next five fastest finishers.

Heat 1 — 16 August 2009

Position	Lane	Athlete	Country		Time
1	2	Lucimar Aparecida de Moura	Brazil	Q	11.41
2	4	Shelly-Ann Fraser	Jamaica	Q	11.41
3	5	Marion Wagner	Germany	Q	11.49
4	3	Yomara Hinestroza	Colombia	q	11.61
5	6	Paulette Zang Milama	Gabon		11.74
6	8	Balpreet Kaur Purba	Singapore		12.30
	7	Yvonne Bennett	Northern Mariana Islands		DNS

Heat 2 — 16 August 2009

Position	Lane	Athlete	Country		Time
1	4	Kerron Stewart	Jamaica	Q	11.31
2	8	Vida Anim	Ghana	Q	11.38
3	3	Ivet Lalova	Bulgaria	Q	11.48
4	5	Chisato Fukushima	Japan	q	11.52
5	6	Ahamada Feta	Comoros		11.80
6	2	Fatou Tiyana	Gambia		12.22
7	7	Dana Abdul Razak	Iraq		12.38

Heat 3 — 16 August 2009

Position	Lane	Athlete	Country		Time
1	6	Carmelita Jeter	United States	Q	11.22
2	5	Virgil Hodge	St Kitts & Nevis	Q	11.47
3	4	Rakia Al-Gassra	Brunei	Q	11.49
4	2	Carol Rodríguez	Puerto Rico		11.64
5	7	Halimat Ismaila	Nigeria		11.74
6	3	Yah Soucko Koïta	Mali		12.16
7	8	Rosa Mystique Jones	Nauru		13.42

Heat 4 — 16 August 2009

Position	Lane	Athlete	Country		Time
1	4	Debbie Ferguson-McKenzie	Bahamas	Q	11.26
2	5	Verena Sailer	Germany	Q	11.29
3	6	Oludamola Osayomi	Nigeria	Q	11.49
4	8	Sónia Tavares	Portugal		11.64
5	2	Ivana Rožhman	FYR Macedonia		12.60
6	7	Sorai Bella Reklai	Palau		13.75
7	3	Muqimyar Robina	Afghanistan		14.74

Heat 5 — 16 August 2009

Position	Lane	Athlete	Country		Time
1	4	Aleen Bailey	Jamaica	Q	11.29
2	2	Evgeniya Polyakova	Russia	Q	11.41
3	6	Myriam Soumaré	France	Q	11.45
4	8	Ayanna Hutchinson	Trinidad & Tobago	q	11.54
5	3	Ani Khachikyan	Armenia		12.30
6	7	Alice Khan	Seychelles		12.64
7	5	Mariama Bah	Guinea		13.33

Women's 100m (continued)

Heat 6   16 August 2009

Position	Lane	Athlete	Country		Time
1	3	Veronica Campbell-Brown	Jamaica	Q	11.34
2	7	Ezinne Okparaebo	Norway	Q	11.35
3	8	Semoy Hackett	Trinidad & Tobago	Q	11.36
4	4	Sheniqua Ferguson	Bahamas	q	11.57
5	2	Gloria Diogo	São Tomé & Príncipe		11.78
6	5	Philaylack Sackpraseuth	Laos		13.42
7	6	Asenate Manoa	Tuvalu		13.75

Heat 7   16 August 2009

Position	Lane	Athlete	Country		Time
1	3	Lauryn Williams	United States	Q	11.36
2	7	Tahesia Harrigan	British Virgin Islands	Q	11.39
3	6	Nataliya Pohrebnyak	Ukraine	Q	11.54
4	4	Momoko Takahashi	Japan	q	11.75
5	8	Martina Pretelli	San Marino	q	12.65
6	2	Terani Faremiro	French Polynesia		12.96
7	5	Tioiti Katutu	Kiribati		14.38

Heat 8   16 August 2009

Position	Lane	Athlete	Country		Time
1	3	Chandra Sturrup	Bahamas	Q	11.28
2	4	Anna Geflikh	Russia	Q	11.47
3	7	Guzel Khubbieva	Uzbekistan	Q	11.63
4	6	Serafi Anelies Unani	Indonesia	q	12.05
5	2	Elis Lapenmal	Vanuatu	q	13.11
6	5	Savannah Sanitoa	American Samoa		14.23
	8	Blessing Okagbare	Nigeria		DNS

Heat 9   16 August 2009

Position	Lane	Athlete	Country		Time
1	7	Kelly-Ann Baptiste	Trinidad & Tobago	Q	11.42
2	5	Muna Lee	United States	Q	11.44
3	6	Eleni Artymata	Cyprus	Q	11.47
4	8	Courtney Patterson	US Virgin Islands		11.88
5	3	Pia Tajnikar	Slovenia		11.88
6	2	Pauline Kwalea	Solomon Islands		13.67
7	4	Beatriz Mangue	Equatorial Guinea		14.03

Qualification for semi-finals: first three in each quarter-final plus the next 4 fastest finishers.

Quarter-Final 1   16 August 2009

Position	Lane	Athlete	Country		Time
1	5	Kerron Stewart	Jamaica	Q	10.92
2	3	Chandra Sturrup	Bahamas	Q	11.06
3	8	Semoy Hackett	Trinidad & Tobago	Q	11.37
4	1	Guzel Khubbieva	Uzbekistan		11.43
5	6	Ezinne Okparaebo	Norway		11.44
6	4	Evgeniya Polyakova	Russia		11.52
7	7	Ivet Lalova	Bulgaria		11.54
8	2	Yomara Hinestroza	Colombia		11.76

Women's 100m (continued)

Quarter-Final 2 16 August 2009

Position	Lane	Athlete	Country		Time
1	5	Lauryn Williams	United States	Q	11.06
2	3	Aleen Bailey	Jamaica	Q	11.12
3	4	Tahesia Harrigan	British Virgin Islands	Q	11.21
4	6	Vida Anim	Ghana	q	11.34
5	7	Eleni Artymata	Cyprus	q	11.37
6	1	Ayanna Hutchinson	Trinidad & Tobago	q	11.40
7	2	Chisato Fukushima	Japan		11.43
8	8	Myriam Soumaré	France		11.45

Quarter-Final 3 16 August 2009

Position	Lane	Athlete	Country		Time
1	4	Veronica Campbell-Brown	Jamaica	Q	10.99
2	6	Debbie Ferguson-McKenzie	Bahamas	Q	10.08
3	3	Muna Lee	United States	Q	11.13
4	5	Verena Sailer	Germany	q	11.26
5	7	Anna Geflikh	Russia		11.46
6	1	Nataliya Pohrebnyak	Ukraine		11.49
7	8	Rakia Al-Gassra	Brunei		11.51
8	2	Sónia Tavares	Portugal		11.55

Quarter-Final 4 16 August 2009

Position	Lane	Athlete	Country		Time
1	5	Carmelita Jeter	United States	Q	10.94
2	6	Shelly-Ann Fraser	Jamaica	Q	11.02
3	3	Kelly-Ann Baptiste	Trinidad & Tobago	Q	11.05
4	4	Lucimar Aparecida de Moura	Brazil		11.44
5	8	Virgil Hodge	St Kitts & Nevis		11.51
6	1	Oludamola Osayomi	Nigeria		11.55
7	2	Sheniqua Ferguson	Bahamas		11.59
8	7	Marion Wagner	Germany		11.64

Qualification for the Final: first four in each semi-final.

Semi-Final 1 17 August 2009

Position	Lane	Athlete	Country		Time
1	6	Shelly-Ann Fraser	Jamaica	Q	10.79
2	4	Kerron Stewart	Jamaica	Q	10.84
3	5	Lauryn Williams	United States	Q	11.01
4	3	Debbie Ferguson-McKenzie	Bahamas	Q	11.03
5	7	Kelly-Ann Baptiste	Trinidad & Tobago		11.07
6	2	Verena Sailer	Germany		11.24
7	8	Tahesia Harrigan	British Virgin Islands		11.34
8	1	Ayanna Hutchinson	Trinidad & Tobago		11.58

Semi-Final 2 17 August 2009

Position	Lane	Athlete	Country		Time
1	4	Carmelita Jeter	United States	Q	10.83
2	3	Veronica Campbell-Brown	Jamaica	Q	11.00
3	5	Chandra Sturrup	Bahamas	Q	11.01
4	6	Aleen Bailey	Jamaica	Q	11.16
5	8	Muna Lee	United States		11.18
6	1	Vida Amin	Ghana		11.43
7	7	Semoy Hackett	Trinidad & Tobago		11.45
8	2	Eleni Artymata	Cyprus		11.49

Women's 100m (continued)

FINAL 17 August 2009

Position	Lane	Athlete	Country	Time
GOLD	3	Shelly-Ann Fraser	Jamaica	10.73
SILVER	4	Kerron Stewart	Jamaica	10.75
BRONZE	5	Carmelita Jeter	United States	10.90
4	6	Veronica Campbell-Brown	Jamaica	10.95
5	8	Lauryn Williams	United States	11.01
6	2	Debbie Ferguson-McKenzie	Bahamas	11.05
7	7	Chandra Sturrup	Bahamas	11.05
8	1	Aleen Bailey	Jamaica	11.16

Men's 200m

Qualification for quarter-finals: first three in each heat plus the next five fastest finishers.

Heat 1   18 August 2009

Position	Lane	Athlete	Country		Time
1	4	Shawn Crawford	United States	Q	20.60
2	2	Roman Smirnov	Russia	Q	20.85
3	3	Brian Dzingai	Zimbabwe	Q	20.97
4	6	Adam Harris	Guyana		21.28
5	1	Aaron Armstrong	Trinidad & Tobago		21.38
6	7	Khalil Al-Hanahneh	Jordan		21.98
	5	Dwain Chambers	Great Britain		DNS
	8	Jaysuma Saidy Ndure	Norway		DNS

Heat 2   18 August 2009

Position	Lane	Athlete	Country		Time
1	4	Brendan Christian	Antigua & Barbuda	Q	20.81
2	2	Aleixo-Platini Menga	Germany	Q	20.84
3	7	Charles Clark	United States	Q	20.87
4	1	Ben Youssef Meité	Ivory Coast	q	20.93
5	8	Omar Jouma Bilal Al-Salfa	United Arab Emirates	q	20.94
6	3	Niko Verekauta	Fiji		21.43
7	6	Amr Ibrahim Mostafa Seoud	Egypt		21.44
	5	Desislav Gunev	Bulgaria		DNF

Heat 3   18 August 2009

Position	Lane	Athlete	Country		Time
1	5	Steve Mullings	Jamaica	Q	20.62
2	6	Paul Hession	Ireland	Q	20.66
3	8	Kenji Fujimitsu	Japan	Q	20.69
4	3	David Alerte	France	q	20.72
5	4	Khalid Idrissi Zougari	Morocco		21.24
6	2	Franklin Nazareno	Ecuador		21.84
	7	Gerald Phiri	Zambia		DNS

Heat 4   18 August 2009

Position	Lane	Athlete	Country		Time
1	8	Marlon Devonish	Great Britain	Q	20.92
2	5	Ramil Guliyev	Azerbaijan	Q	21.12
3	7	Marek Niit	Estonia	Q	21.21
4	3	Nathaniel McKinney	Bahamas		21.26
5	6	Joel Redhead	Grenada		21.37
6	1	Ronalds Arajs	Latvia		21.38
7	2	Sibusiso Matsenjwa	Swaziland		21.93
8	4	Andrew Hinds	Barbados		22.60

Heat 5   18 August 2009

Position	Lane	Athlete	Country		Time
1	5	Usain Bolt	Jamaica	Q	20.70
2	8	Rondell Sorrillo	Trinidad & Tobago	Q	20.74
3	4	Sam Effah	Canada	Q	20.80
4	2	Sandro Viana	Brazil		21.18
5	6	Eddy De Lepine	France		21.23
6	7	Hitoshi Saito	Japan		21.38
	3	Obinna Metu	Nigeria		DNS

Men's 200m (continued)

Heat 6   18 August 2009

Position	Lane	Athlete	Country		Time
1	7	Alonso Edward	Panama	Q	20.71
2	4	Marc Schneeberger	Switzerland	Q	20.76
3	5	Emmanuel Callander	Trinidad & Tobago	Q	20.81
4	2	Ihor Bodrov	Ukraine		21.00
5	6	Hamed Hamdan AlBishi	Saudi Arabia		21.00
6	3	Ramon Gittens	Barbados		21.33
7	8	Vyacheslav Muravyev	Kazakhstan		21.48

Heat 7   18 August 2009

Position	Lane	Athlete	Country		Time
1	2	Martial Mbandjock	France	Q	20.65
2	5	Marco Cribari	Switzerland	Q	20.80
3	4	Rolando Palacios	Honduras	Q	20.83
4	6	Kim Collins	St Kitts & Nevis	q	20.83
5	8	Alexander Kosenkow	Germany		20.99
6	7	Ángel David Rodríguez	Spain		21.37
7	3	Tyson Gay	United States		DNS

Heat 8   18 August 2009

Position	Lane	Athlete	Country		Time
1	1	Jared Connaughton	Canada	Q	20.82
2	8	Shinji Takahira	Japan	Q	20.86
3	2	Stéphane Buckland	Mauritius	Q	21.00
4	6	Patrick van Luijk	Netherlands		21.05
5	4	Fanuel Kenosi	Botswana		21.75
6	5	Nikolai Portelli	Malta		22.11
7	7	Gabriel Mvumvure	Zimbabwe		22.67
	3	Arnaldo Abrantes	Portugal		DNS

Heat 9   18 August 2009

Position	Lane	Athlete	Country		Time
1	6	Robert Hering	Germany	Q	20.64
2	3	Wallace Spearmon	United States	Q	20.66
3	7	Gavin Smellie	Canada	Q	20.71
4	4	Thuso Mpuang	South Africa	q	20.91
5	5	Ramone McKenzie	Jamaica		20.97
6	2	Seth Amoo	Ghana		21.04
	8	Churandy Martina	Netherlands Antilles		DNS

Qualification for semi-finals: first three in each quarter-final plus the next four fastest finishers.

Quarter-Final 1   18 August 2009

Position	Lane	Athlete	Country		Time
1	3	Usain Bolt	Jamaica	Q	20.41
2	2	David Alerte	France	Q	20.51
3	4	Martial Mbandjock	France	Q	20.55
4	8	Charles Clark	United States	q	20.55
5	5	Rondell Sorrillo	Trinidad & Tobago	q	20.58
6	1	Kim Collins	St Kitts & Nevis		20.84
7	6	Marc Schneeberger	Switzerland		20.91
8	7	Gavin Smellie	Canada		21.27

Men's 200m (continued)

Quarter-Final 2 18 August 2009

Position	Lane	Athlete	Country		Time
1	3	Shawn Crawford	United States	Q	20.37
2	6	Marlon Devonish	Great Britain	Q	20.66
3	8	Rolando Palacios	Honduras	Q	20.69
4	7	Shinji Takahira	Japan		20.69
5	4	Roman Smirnov	Russia		20.72
6	1	Omar Jouma Bilal Al-Salfa	United Arab Emirates		20.97
	5	Jared Connaughton	Canada		DQ
	2	Brian Dzingai	Zimbabwe		DNF

Quarter-Final 3 18 August 2009

Position	Lane	Athlete	Country		Time
1	4	Steve Mullings	Jamaica	Q	20.23
2	7	Ramil Guliyev	Azerbaijan	Q	20.40
3	6	Paul Hession	Ireland	Q	20.48
4	3	Brendan Christian	Antigua & Barbuda	q	20.58
5	8	Emmanuel Callander	Trinidad & Tobago	q	20.62
6	5	Aleixo-Platini Menga	Germany		20.68
7	1	Ben Youssef Meité	Ivory Coast		20.78
8	2	Stéphane Buckland	Mauritius		21.33

Quarter-Final 4 18 August 2009

Position	Lane	Athlete	Country		Time
1	6	Alonso Edward	Panama	Q	20.33
2	4	Wallace Spearmon	United States	Q	20.44
3	3	Robert Hering	Germany	Q	20.58
4	5	Marco Cribari	Switzerland		20.81
5	1	Thuso Mpuang	South Africa		20.87
6	7	Kenji Fujimitsu	Japan		20.97
7	8	Sam Effah	Canada		20.97
8	2	Marek Niit	Estonia		DNS

Qualification for the Final: first four in each semi-final.

Semi-Final 1 19 August 2009

Position	Lane	Athlete	Country		Time
1	3	Usain Bolt	Jamaica	Q	20.08
2	5	Alonso Edward	Panama	Q	20.22
3	6	Shawn Crawford	United States	Q	20.35
4	4	David Alerte	France	Q	20.45
5	7	Robert Hering	Germany		20.52
6	2	Rondell Sorrillo	Trinidad & Tobago		20.63
7	8	Rolando Palacios	Honduras		20.67
8	1	Brendan Christian	Antigua & Barbuda		20.79

Men's 200m (continued)

Semi-Final 2   19 August 2009

Position	Lane	Athlete	Country		Time
1	5	Wallace Spearmon	United States	Q	20.14
2	3	Steve Mullings	Jamaica	Q	20.26
3	2	Charles Clark	United States	Q	20.27
4	4	Ramil Guliyev	Azerbaijan	Q	20.28
5	7	Martial Mbandjock	France		20.43
6	8	Paul Hession	Ireland		20.48
7	6	Marlon Devonish	Great Britain		20.62
8	1	Emmanuel Callander	Trinidad & Tobago		20.70

FINAL   20 August 2009

Position	Lane	Athlete	Country		Time
GOLD	5	Usain Bolt	Jamaica	WR	19.19
SILVER	6	Alonso Edward	Panama		19.81
BRONZE	4	Wallace Spearmon	United States		19.85
4	8	Shawn Crawford	United States		19.89
5	3	Steve Mullings	Jamaica		19.98
6	7	Charles Clark	United States		20.39
7	1	Ramil Guliyev	Azerbaijan		20.61
8	2	David Alerte	France		20.68

Women's 200m

Qualification for quarter-finals: first three in each heat plus the next six fastest finishers.

Heat 1   19 August 2009

Position	Lane	Athlete	Country		Time
1	8	Simone Facey	Jamaica	Q	22.83
2	2	ChaRonda Williams	United States	Q	23.08
3	1	Johanna Danois	France	Q	23.29
4	6	Chisato Fukushima	Japan		23.40
5	3	Darlenis Obregón	Colombia		23.42
6	7	Andreea Ograzeanu	Romania		23.42
7	5	Nomvula Dlamini	Swaziland		25.70
	4	Munira Saleh	Syria		DNF

Heat 2   19 August 2009

Position	Lane	Athlete	Country		Time
1	7	Muna Lee	United States	Q	22.76
2	5	Kelly-Ann Baptiste	Trinidad & Tobago	Q	23.00
3	8	Yulia Gushchina	Russia	Q	23.07
4	1	Virgil Hodge	St Kitts & Nevis	q	23.34
5	3	Carol Rodríguez	Puerto Rico		23.54
6	6	Sabina Veit	Slovenia		23.77
7	4	Sunayna Wahi	Suriname		24.74
8	2	Saria Traboulsi	Lebanon		26.90

Women's 200m (continued)

Heat 3   19 August 2009

Position	Lane	Athlete	Country		Time
1	6	Allyson Felix	United States	Q	22.88
2	5	Monique Williams	New Zealand	Q	22.96
3	8	Tameka Williams	St Kitts & Nevis	Q	23.27
4	4	Olga Zaytseva	Russia	q	23.28
5	2	Rakia Al-Gassra	Brunei	q	23.34
6	3	Adrienne Power	Canada		23.38
7	7	Momoko Takahashi	Japan		23.61
8	1	Selloane Tsoaeli	Lesotho		28.34

Heat 4   19 August 2009

Position	Lane	Athlete	Country		Time
1	8	Marshevet Hooker	United States	Q	22.51
2	5	Debbie Ferguson-McKenzie	Bahamas	Q	22.71
3	2	Eleni Artymata	Cyprus	Q	22.83
4	4	Yelena Bolsun	Russia	q	23.06
5	6	Alena Kievich	Belarus		23.59
6	3	Ivet Lalova	Bulgaria		23.60
7	7	Meritzer Williams	St Kitts & Nevis		23.72

Heat 5   19 August 2009

Position	Lane	Athlete	Country		Time
1	7	Cydonie Mothersille	Cayman Islands	Q	22.69
2	6	Anneisha McLaughlin	Jamaica	Q	22.91
3	4	LaVerne Jones-Ferrette	US Virgin Islands	Q	22.97
4	5	Vida Amin	Ghana	q	23.33
5	3	Isabel Le Roux	South Africa		23.61
6	8	Makelesi Batimala	Fiji		24.13
7	2	Oludamola Osayomi	Nigeria		24.24

Heat 6   19 August 2009

Position	Lane	Athlete	Country		Time
1	3	Veronica Campbell-Brown	Jamaica	Q	23.01
2	7	Emily Freeman	Great Britain	Q	23.10
3	8	Olivia Borlee	Belgium	Q	23.25
4	5	Sheniqua Ferguson	Bahamas	q	23.35
5	6	Guzel Khubbieva	Uzbekistan		23.61
6	2	Jade Bailey	Barbados		23.84
	4	Elizaveta Bryzhina	Ukraine		DNS

Qualification for Final: first two in each quarter-final plus the next two fastest finishers.

Semi-Final 1   20 August 2009

Position	Lane	Athlete	Country		Time
1	6	Debbie Ferguson-McKenzie	Bahamas	Q	22.24
2	5	Veronica Campbell-Brown	Jamaica	Q	22.29
3	3	Emily Freeman	Great Britain	q	22.64
4	8	Eleni Artymata	Cyprus	q	22.64
5	7	Johanna Danois	France		23.03
6	2	Rakia Al-Gassra	Brunei		23.26
7	1	Yelena Bolsun	Russia		23.27
	4	Marshevet Hooker	United States		DNF

Women's 200m (continued)

Semi-Final 2   20 August 2009

Position	Lane	Athlete	Country		Time
1	5	Allyson Felix	United States	Q	22.44
2	6	Anneisha McLaughlin	Jamaica	Q	22.55
3	8	LaVerne Jones-Ferrette	US Virgin Islands		22.74
4	4	Cydonie Mothersille	Cayman Islands		22.80
5	3	ChaRonda Williams	United States		22.81
6	2	Olga Zaytseva	Russia		23.19
7	1	Sheniqua Ferguson	Bahamas		23.40
8	7	Tameka Williams	St Kitts & Nevis		23.47

Semi-Final 3   20 August 2009

Position	Lane	Athlete	Country		Time
1	4	Muna Lee	United States	Q	22.44
2	5	Simone Facey	Jamaica	Q	22.55
3	6	Monique Williams	New Zealand		22.74
4	3	Kelly-Ann Baptiste	Trinidad & Tobago		22.80
5	1	Virgil Hodge	St Kitts & Nevis		22.81
6	7	Yulia Gushchina	Russia		23.19
7	2	Vida Anim	Ghana		23.40
8	8	Olivia Borlee	Belgium		23.47

FINAL   21 August 2009

Position	Lane	Athlete	Country	Time
GOLD	6	Allyson Felix	United States	22.02
SILVER	5	Veronica Campbell-Brown	Jamaica	22.35
BRONZE	4	Debbie Ferguson-McKenzie	Bahamas	22.41
4	3	Muna Lee	United States	22.48
5	8	Anneisha McLaughlin	Jamaica	22.62
6	7	Simone Facey	Jamaica	22.80
7	2	Emily Freeman	Great Britain	22.98
8	1	Eleni Artymata	Cyprus	23.05

Men's 400m

Qualification for semi-finals: first three in each heat plus the next three fastest finishers.

Heat 1 — 18 August 2009

Position	Lane	Athlete	Country		Time
1	5	Robert Tobin	Great Britain	Q	45.50
2	7	David Gillick	Ireland	Q	45.54
3	4	Rabah Yousif	Sudan	Q	45.55
4	3	Lionel Larry	United States	q	45.64
5	8	Young Talkmore Nyongani	Zimbabwe		45.92
6	2	Cedric van Branteghem	Belgium		45.94
7	6	Hideyuki Hirose	Japan		46.80

Heat 2 — 18 August 2009

Position	Lane	Athlete	Country		Time
1	4	Renny Quow	Trinidad & Tobago	Q	45.21
2	1	William Collazo	Cuba	Q	45.52
3	8	Kévin Borlée	Belgium	Q	45.61
4	3	Marcin Marciniszyn	Poland		45.77
5	2	Arismendy Peguero	Dominican Republic		46.13
6	6	Mathieu Gnanligo	Benin		47.00
7	5	Nelson Stone	Papua New Guinea		47.13
	7	Michael Mathieu	Bahamas		DQ

Heat 3 — 18 August 2009

Position	Lane	Athlete	Country		Time
1	2	Chris Brown	Bahamas	Q	45.53
2	5	Michael Bingham	Great Britain	Q	45.54
3	8	Joel Milburn	Australia	Q	45.56
4	4	Eric Milazar	Mauritius		46.39
5	3	Isaac Makwala	Botswana		46.45
6	1	Nagmeldin Ali Abubakr	Sudan		46.48
7	7	Andrés Silva	Uruguay		46.86
8	6	Zaw Win Thet	Myanmar		51.41

Heat 4 — 18 August 2009

Position	Lane	Athlete	Country		Time
1	4	LaShawn Merritt	United States	Q	45.23
2	3	John Steffensen	Australia	Q	45.37
3	6	Matteo Galvan	Italy	Q	45.86
4	7	Héctor Carrasquillo	Puerto Rico		46.11
5	8	Alvin Harrison	Dominican Republic		46.67
	5	Gary Kikaya	Democratic Republic of Congo		DQ
	2	Yannick Fonsat	France		DNS

Heat 5 — 18 August 2009

Position	Lane	Athlete	Country		Time
1	4	Ramon Miller	Bahamas	Q	45.00
2	7	Leslie Djhone	France	Q	45.20
3	2	Johan Wissman	Sweden	Q	45.83
4	6	Maksim Dyldin	Russia		45.91
5	5	Gil Roberts	United States		46.41
6	8	Mark Kiprotich Muttai	Kenya		47.04
7	3	Naiel d'Almeida	São Tomé & Príncipe		49.47
	1	James Godday	Nigeria		DNS

Men's 400m (continued)

Heat 6   18 August 2009

Position	Lane	Athlete	Country		Time
1	4	Jeremy Wariner	United States	Q	45.54
2	5	Ricardo Chambers	Jamaica	Q	45.57
3	2	Teddy Venel	France	Q	46.16
4	7	Yuzo Kanemaru	Japan		46.83
5	3	Yousef Ahmed Masrahi	Saudi Arabia		47.03
6	8	Pieter Smith	South Africa		48.14
	6	Nery Brenes	Costa Rica		DNS

Heat 7   18 August 2009

Position	Lane	Athlete	Country		Time
1	5	Tabarie Henry	US Virgin Islands	Q	45.14
2	8	Sean Wroe	Australia	Q	45.31
3	1	Martyn Rooney	Great Britain	Q	45.45
4	6	Erison Hurtault	Dominica	q	45.55
5	3	Mohamed Ashour Khouaja	Libya	q	45.56
6	7	Saul Welgopwa	Nigeria		46.42
7	4	Rondell Bartholomew	Grenada		46.85
8	2	Moumouni Kimba	Niger		50.93

Qualification for Final: first two in each semi-final plus the next two fastest finishers.

Semi-Final 1   19 August 2009

Position	Lane	Athlete	Country		Time
1	4	Jeremy Wariner	United States	Q	44.69
2	8	Michael Bingham	Great Britain	Q	44.74
3	3	Leslie Djhone	France	q	44.80
4	6	David Gillick	Ireland	q	44.88
5	5	Ramon Miller	Bahamas		44.99
6	7	Joel Milburn	Australia		46.06
7	2	Mohamed Ashour Khouaja	Libya		46.43
	1	Johan Wissman	Sweden		DNS

Semi-Final 2   19 August 2009

Position	Lane	Athlete	Country		Time
1	3	LaShawn Merritt	United States	Q	44.37
2	4	Renny Quow	Trinidad & Tobago	Q	44.53
3	5	William Collazo	Cuba		44.93
4	6	Sean Wroe	Australia		45.32
5	2	Erison Hurtault	Dominica		45.59
6	7	Rabah Yousif	Sudan		45.63
7	8	Martyn Rooney	Great Britain		45.98
8	1	Teddy Venel	France		46.30

Semi-Final 3   19 August 2009

Position	Lane	Athlete	Country		Time
1	3	Chris Brown	Bahamas	Q	44.95
2	4	Tabarie Henry	US Virgin Islands	Q	44.97
3	7	Ricardo Chambers	Jamaica		45.13
4	8	Kévin Borlée	Belgium		45.28
5	5	John Steffensen	Australia		45.50
6	1	Lionel Larry	United States		45.85
7	6	Robert Tobin	Great Britain		45.90
8	2	Matteo Galvan	Italy		46.87

Men's 400m (continued)

FINAL 21 August 2009

Position	Lane	Athlete	Country		Time
GOLD	4	LaShawn Merritt	United States		44.06
SILVER	6	Jeremy Wariner	United States		44.60
BRONZE	3	Renny Quow	Trinidad & Tobago		45.02
4	7	Tabarie Henry	US Virgin Islands		45.42
5	5	Chris Brown	Bahamas		45.47
6	2	David Gillick	Ireland		45.53
7	8	Michael Bingham	Great Britain		45.56
8	1	Leslie Djhone	France		45.90

Women's 400m

Qualification for semi-finals: first three in each heat plus the next six fastest finishers.

Heat 1 15 August 2009

Position	Lane	Athlete	Country		Time
1	4	Lyudmila Litvinova	Russia	Q	51.31
2	5	Libania Grenot	Italy	Q	51.45
3	2	Indira Terrero	Cuba	Q	51.98
4	7	Tiandra Ponteen	St Kitts & Nevis	q	52.54
5	8	Christine Day	Jamaica	q	53.13
6	6	Marina Maslenko	Kazakhstan		54.38
7	3	Phyo Thet Khin	Myanmar		1:00.35

Heat 2 15 August 2009

Position	Lane	Athlete	Country		Time
1	4	Novlene Williams-Mills	Jamaica	Q	51.55
2	7	Jessica Beard	United States	Q	51.72
3	6	Sorina Nwachukwu	Germany	Q	51.74
4	5	Kineke Alexander	St Vincent & the Grenadines	q	52.44
5	2	Joy Nakhumicha Sakari	Kenya	q	52.88
6	8	Kia Davis	Liberia		56.85
	3	Khoury Keita	Mauritania		DQ

Heat 3 15 August 2009

Position	Lane	Athlete	Country		Time
1	8	Amantle Montsho	Botswana	Q	50.65
2	3	Shericka Williams	Jamaica	Q	51.23
3	6	Solene Désert-Mariller	France	Q	51.63
4	5	Folasade Abugan	Nigeria	q	51.70
5	2	Racheal Nachula	Zambia		53.21
	7	Nawal El Jack	Sudan		DNF
	4	Evodie Lydie Saramandji	Central African Republic		DNS

Women's 400m (continued)

Heat 4   15 August 2009

Position	Lane	Athlete	Country		Time
1	5	Debbie Dunn	United States	Q	51.13
2	6	Anastasiya Kapachinskaya	Russia	Q	51.17
3	4	Chandrika Rasnayake	Sri Lanka		53.68
4	8	Fatou Bintou Fall	Senegal		54.46
5	2	Rozina Shafqat	Pakistan		1.00.72
	7	Christine Amertil	Bahamas		DQ
	3	Amaka Ogoegbunam *	Nigeria		DQ

* results subsequently removed due to failed drugs test.

Heat 5   15 August 2009

Position	Lane	Athlete	Country		Time
1	7	Sanya Richards	United States	Q	51.06
2	4	Christine Ohuruogu	Great Britain	Q	51.30
3	6	Aliann Pompey	Guyana	Q	51.38
4	3	Norma González	Colombia	q	51.86
5	8	Makelesi Batimala	Fiji		54.65
6	2	Trish Bartholomew	Grenada		54.89
7	5	Claudine Yemalin	Benin		58.82

Heat 6   15 August 2009

Position	Lane	Athlete	Country		Time
1	4	Antonina Krivoshapka	Russia	Q	51.03
2	3	Nicola Sanders	Great Britain	Q	51.64
3	6	Amy Mbacke Thiam	Senegal	Q	52.79
4	5	Esther Akinsulie	Canada		53.21
5	2	Asami Tanno	Japan		53.30
6	7	Sharolyn Scott	Costa Rica		55.63
7	8	Rania Alqebali	Jordan		1:00.90

Qualification for Final: first two in each semi-final plus the next two fastest finishers.

Semi-Final 1   16 August 2009

Position	Lane	Athlete	Country		Time
1	5	Novlene Williams-Mills	Jamaica	Q	49.88
2	4	Amantle Montsho	Botswana	Q	49.89
3	6	Anastasiya Kapachinskaya	Russia	q	50.30
4	8	Aliann Pompey	Guyana		50.71
5	3	Jessica Beard	United States		51.20
6	1	Norma González	Colombia		51.91
7	2	Kineke Alexander	St Vincent & the Grenadines		53.43
	7	Amaka Ogoegbunam	Nigeria		DQ

Semi-Final 2   16 August 2009

Position	Lane	Athlete	Country		Time
1	4	Shericka Williams	Jamaica	Q	49.51
2	5	Antonina Krivoshapka	Russia	Q	49.67
3	3	Debbie Dunn	United States	q	49.95
4	6	Nicola Sanders	Great Britain		50.45
5	8	Amy Mbacke Thiam	Senegal		51.70
6	1	Folasade Abugan	Nigeria		51.75
7	2	Joy Nakhumicha Sakari	Kenya		52.69
8	7	Solene Désert-Mariller	France		53.26

Women's 400m (continued)

Semi-Final 3 16 August 2009

Position	Lane	Athlete	Country		Time
1	3	Sanya Richards	United States	Q	50.21
2	4	Christine Ohuruogu	Great Britain	Q	50.35
3	6	Lyudmila Litvinova	Russia		50.52
4	5	Libania Grenot	Italy		50.85
5	7	Indira Terrero	Cuba		51.87
6	8	Sorina Nwachukwu	Germany		51.98
7	1	Tiandra Ponteen	St Kitts & Nevis		43.22
8	2	Christine Day	Jamaica		53.46

FINAL 18 August 2009

Position	Lane	Athlete	Country	Time
GOLD	3	Sanya Richards	United States	49.00
SILVER	4	Shericka Williams	Jamaica	49.32
BRONZE	5	Antonina Krivoshapka	Russia	49.71
4	6	Novlene Williams-Mills	Jamaica	49.77
5	7	Christine Ohuruogu	Great Britain	50.21
6	1	Debbie Dunn	United States	50.35
7	2	Anastasiya Kapachinskaya	Russia	50.53
8	8	Amantle Montsho	Botswana	50.65

Men's 800m

Qualification for semi-finals: first three in each heat plus the next three fastest finishers.

Heat 1   20 August 2009

Position	Lane	Athlete	Country		Time
1	2	Mbulaeni Mulaudzi	South Africa	Q	1:46.40
2	6	Abubaker Kaki	Sudan	Q	1:46.41
3	8	Fabiano Peçanha	Brazil	Q	1:46.68
4	5	Sajad Moradi	Iran		1:47.68
5	7	Abraham Chepkirwok	Uganda		1:48.57
6	4	Eduard Villanueva	Venezuela		1:48.61
	3	Manuel Olmedo	Spain		DNF

Heat 2   20 August 2009

Position	Lane	Athlete	Country		Time
1	1	Nick Symmonds	United States	Q	1:47.12
2	6	Belal Mansoor Ali	Brunei	Q	1:47.16
3	8	Ismail Ahmed Ismail	Sudan	Q	1:47.20
4	3	Mattias Claesson	Sweden		1:48.02
5	4	Thomas Chamney	Ireland		1:48.09
6	7	Prince Mumba	Zambia		1:48.13
7	5	Ilija Ranitovic	Montenegro		1:53.17
8	2	Iulio Lafai	Samoa		2:03.51

Heat 3   20 August 2009

Position	Lane	Athlete	Country		Time
1	6	Gary Reed	Canada	Q	1:45.76
2	4	Yuriy Borzakovskiy	Russia	Q	1:45.86
3	2	Jeff Lastennet	France	Q	1:46.30
4	8	Samson Ngoepe	South Africa	q	1:46.54
5	5	Ryan Brown	United States		1:46.92
6	3	Mike Schumacher	Luxembourg		1:48.18
7	7	Robin Schembera	Germany		1:54.47

Heat 4   20 August 2009

Position	Lane	Athlete	Country		Time
1	6	Yusuf Saad Kamel	Brunei	Q	1:46.43
2	3	Asbel Kiprop	Kenya	Q	1:46.52
3	5	Khadevis Robinson	United States	Q	1:46.79
4	4	Lukas Rifesser	Italy		1:47.07
5	7	Kleberson Davide	Brazil		1:47.51
6	8	Mahamoud Farah	Djibouti		1:48.23
	2	Ali Al-Deraan	Saudi Arabia		DNS

Heat 5   20 August 2009

Position	Lane	Athlete	Country		Time
1	8	Alfred Kirwa Yego	Kenya	Q	1:48.32
2	1	Tamás Kazi	Hungary	Q	1:48.40
3	4	Marcin Lewandowski	Poland	Q	1:48.41
4	3	Mohammed Al-Salhi	Saudi Arabia		1:48.43
5	2	Luis Alberto Marco	Spain		1:48.47
6	5	Jozef Repcìk	Slovakia		1:48.73
7	6	Evans Pinto	Bolivia		1:52.23
8	7	Arnold Sorina	Vanuatu		2:00.13

Men's 800m (continued)

Heat 6 20 August 2009

Position	Lane	Athlete	Country		Time
1	6	David Lekuta Rudisha	Kenya	Q	1:47.83
2	2	Yeimer López	Cuba	Q	1:48.04
3	5	Michael Rimmer	Great Britain	Q	1:48.20
4	4	Abdoulaye Wagne	Senegal		1:48.22
5	3	Dmitrijs Milkevics	Latvia		1:48.43
6	8	Mohammad Al-Azemi	Kuwait		1:51.73
	7	Nadjim Manseur	Algeria		DNS

Heat 7 20 August 2009

Position	Lane	Athlete	Country		Time
1	2	Jackson Mumbwa Kivuva	Kenya	Q	1:46.17
2	6	Bram Som	Netherlands	Q	1:46.33
3	3	Amine Laalou	Morocco	Q	1:46.38
4	7	Moise Joseph	Haiti	q	1:46.68
5	5	Adam Kszczot	Poland	q	1:46.70
6	4	Dmitrijs Jurkevics	Latvia		1:46.90
7	8	Pablo Solares	Mexico		1:47.96

Qualification for Final: first two in each quarter-final plus the next two fastest finishers.

Semi-Final 1 21 August 2009

Position	Lane	Athlete	Country		Time
1	5	Nick Symmonds	United States	Q	1:45.96
2	7	Jackson Mumbwa Kivuva	Kenya	Q	1:46.32
3	8	Belal Mansoor Ali	Brunei		1:46.57
4	2	Tamás Kazi	Hungary		1:47.01
5	1	Jeff Lastennet	France		1:57.43
6	6	Marcin Lewandowski	Poland		2:01.62
	4	Bram Som	Netherlands		DNF
	3	Abubaker Kaki	Sudan		DNF

Semi-Final 2 21 August 2009

Position	Lane	Athlete	Country		Time
1	1	Yusuf Saad Kamel	Brunei	Q	1:45.01
2	6	Yuriy Borzakovskiy	Russia	Q	1:45.16
3	8	Alfred Kirwa Yego	Kenya	q	1:45.22
4	7	Mbulaeni Mulaudzi	South Africa	q	1:45.26
5	4	Khadevis Robinson	United States		1:45.91
6	2	Adam Kszczot	Poland		1:46.33
7	3	Asbel Kiprop	Kenya		1:52.05
	5	Ismail Ahmed Ismail	Sudan		DNF

Semi-Final 3 21 August 2009

Position	Lane	Athlete	Country		Time
1	3	Amine Laalou	Morocco	Q	1:45.27
2	4	Yeimer López	Cuba	Q	1:45.33
3	5	David Lekuta Rudisha	Kenya		1:45.40
4	6	Gary Reed	Canada		1:45.60
5	2	Moise Joseph	Haiti		1:45.87
6	7	Fabiano Peçanha	Brazil		1:45.94
7	1	Michael Rimmer	Great Britain		1:46.77
8	8	Samson Ngoepe	South Africa		1:49.03

Men's 800m (continued)

FINAL 23 August 2009

Position	Lane	Athlete	Country	Time
GOLD	8	Mbulaeni Mulaudzi	South Africa	1:45.29
SILVER	1	Alfred Kirwa Yego	Kenya	1:45.35
BRONZE	2	Yusuf Saad Kamel	Brunei	1:45.35
4	4	Yuriy Borzakovskiy	Russia	1:45.57
5	5	Amine Laalou	Morocco	1:45.66
6	6	Nick Symmonds	United States	1:45.71
7	1	Bram Som	Netherlands	1:45.86
8	8	Marcin Lewandowski	Poland	1:46.17
9	7	Jackson Mumbwa Kivuva	Kenya	1:46.39
10	3	Yeimer López	Cuba	1:47.80

Women's 800m

Qualification for semi-finals: first three in each heat plus the next six fastest finishers.

Heat 1 16 August 2009

Position	Lane	Athlete	Country		Time
1	8	Caster Semenya	South Africa	Q	2:02.51
2	2	Geena Gall	United States	Q	2:02.63
3	7	Tetiana Petlyuk	Ukraine	Q	2:02.87
4	5	Olga Cristea	Moldova		2:03.99
5	4	Neisha Bernard-Thomas	Grenada		2:04.55
6	3	Madeleine Pape	Australia		2:05.85
7	6	Janeth Jepkosgei Busienei	Kenya		2:12.81

Heat 2 16 August 2009

Position	Lane	Athlete	Country		Time
1	5	Mariya Savinova	Russia	Q	2:03.27
2	2	Jemma Simpson	Great Britain	Q	2:03.33
3	8	Mayte Martínez	Spain	Q	2:03.39
4	7	Élodie Guégan	France	q	2:03.87
5	6	Irina Krakoviak	Lithuania		2:04.26
6	3	Elena Mirela Lavric	Romania		2:04.49
7	4	Leonor Piuza	Mozambique		2:08.08

Heat 3 16 August 2009

Position	Lane	Athlete	Country		Time
1	6	Yuliya Krevsun	Ukraine	Q	2:02.20
2	2	Jennifer Meadows	Great Britain	Q	2:02.47
3	1	Hazel Clark	United States	Q	2:02.67
4	5	Lucia Klocová	Slovakia	q	2:02.98
5	7	Marian Burnett	Guyana	q	2:03.89
6	3	Yeliz Kurt	Turkey		2:13.42
7	4	Aishath Reesha	Maldives		2:28.00
	8	Sanaa Abubkheet	Palestine		DQ

Women's 800m (continued)

Heat 4   16 August 2009

Position	Lane	Athlete	Country		Time
1	7	Elisa Cusma Piccione	Italy	Q	2:02.33
2	3	Anna Rostkowska	Poland	Q	2:02.37
3	5	Halima Hachlaf	Morocco	Q	2:02.46
4	6	Elena Kofanova	Russia	q	2:02.49
5	2	Lenka Masná	Czech Republic	q	2:03.32
6	4	Eléni Filándra	Greece		2:06.39
7	8	Natalia Gallego	Andorra		2:18.75

Heat 5   16 August 2009

Position	Lane	Athlete	Country		Time
1	8	Pamela Jelimo	Kenya	Q	2:03.50
2	6	Maggie Vessey	United States	Q	2:04.07
3	4	Kenia Sinclair	Jamaica	Q	2:04.52
4	2	Rosibel García	Colombia		2:04.73
5	5	Jana Hartmann	Germany		2:04.99
6	3	Nataliia Lupu	Ukraine		2:06.74
7	7	Salome Dell	Papua New Guinea		2:08.22

Heat 6   16 August 2009

Position	Lane	Athlete	Country		Time
1	8	Zulia Calatayud	Cuba	Q	2:02:33
2	7	Hasna Benhassi	Morocco	Q	2:02.83
3	2	Marilyn Okoro	Great Britain	Q	2:03.07
4	5	Svetlana Klyuka	Russia	q	2:03.40
5	3	Daniela Reina	Italy		2:06.30
6	4	Anabelle Lascar	Mauritius		2:06.53
7	6	Nikki Hamblin	New Zealand		2:31.94

Qualification for Final: first two in each quarter-final plus the next two fastest finishers.

Semi-Final 1   17 August 2009

Position	Lane	Athlete	Country		Time
1	3	Mariya Savinova	Russia	Q	1:59.30
2	6	Yuliya Krevsun	Ukraine	Q	1:59.38
3	1	Mayte Martínez	Spain	q	1:59.72
4	5	Hasna Benhassi	Morocco		2:00.06
5	4	Jemma Simpson	Great Britain		2:00.57
6	7	Geena Gall	United States		2:01.30
7	2	Zulia Calatayud	Cuba		2:01.53
8	8	Élodie Guégan	France		2:04.38

Semi-Final 2   17 August 2009

Position	Lane	Athlete	Country		Time
1	4	Caster Semenya	South Africa	Q	1:58.66
2	6	Jennifer Meadows	Great Britain	Q	1:59.45
3	7	Janeth Jepkosgei Busienei	Kenya	q	1:59.47
4	7	Hazel Clark	United States		1:59.96
5	5	Svetlana Klyuka	Russia		2:00.48
6	3	Tetiana Petlyuk	Ukraine		2:00.90
7	8	Lucia Klocová	Slovakia		2:01.56
8	1	Marian Burnett	Guyana		2:02.75
	2	Halima Hachlaf	Morocco		DNF

Women's 800m (continued)

Semi-Final 3   17 August 2009

Position	Lane	Athlete	Country		Time
1	6	Elisa Cusma Piccione	Italy	Q	2:00.62
2	1	Marilyn Okoro	Great Britain	Q	2:01.01
3	8	Anna Rostkowska	Poland		2:01.40
4	5	Elena Kofanova	Russia		2:02.02
5	3	Kenia Sinclair	Jamaica		2:02.31
6	2	Lenka Masná	Czech Republic		2:02.55
7	4	Maggie Vessey	United States		2:03.55
8	7	Pamela Jelimo	Kenya		DNF

FINAL   19 August 2009

Position	Lane	Athlete	Country	Time
GOLD	4	Caster Semenya	South Africa	1:55.45
SILVER	7	Janeth Jepkosgei Busienei	Kenya	1:57.90
BRONZE	5	Jennifer Meadows	Great Britain	1:57.93
4	3	Yuliya Krevsun	Ukraine	1:58.00
5	6	Mariya Savinova	Russia	1:58.68
6	8	Elisa Cusma Piccione	Italy	1:58.81
7	2	Mayte Martínez	Spain	1:58.81
8	1	Marilyn Okoro	Great Britain	2:00.32

Men's 1500m

Qualification for semi-finals: first five in each heat plus the next four fastest finishers.

Heat 1   15 August 2009

Position	Athlete	Country		Time
1	Mehdi Baala	France	Q	3:42.77
2	Leonel Manzano	United States	Q	3:42.87
3	Abdalaati Iguider	Morocco	Q	3:42.88
4	Jeffrey Riseley	Australia	Q	3:43.03
5	Belal Mansoor Ali	Brunei	Q	3:43.06
6	Arturo Casado	Spain		3:43.21
7	Mekonnen Gebremedhin	Ethiopia		3:43.22
8	Christian Obrist	Italy		3:43.41
9	Hais Welday	Eritrea		3:43.84
10	Goran Nava	Serbia		3:44.13
11	Mohammed Shaween	Saudi Arabia		3:49.03
12	Chauncy Master	Malawi		3:50.73
13	Abdallahi Nanou	Mauritania		4:09.77
	Boampouguini Djigban	Togo		DNF

Heat 2   15 August 2009

Position	Athlete	Country		Time
1	Asbel Kiprop	Kenya	Q	3:41.42
2	Bernard Lagat	United States	Q	3:41.60
3	Juan Carlos Higuero	Spain	Q	3:41.77
4	Rui Silva	Portugal	Q	3:41.98
5	Peter van der Westhuizen	South Africa	Q	3:42.33
6	Anter Zerguelaine	Algeria		3:42.37
7	Thomas Chamney	Ireland		3:42.54
8	Thomas Lancashire	Great Britain		3:42.68
9	Carsten Schlangen	Germany		3:44.00
10	Ryan Gregson	Australia		3:44.79
11	Abdalla Abdelgadir	Sudan		3:47.78
12	Bayron Piedra	Ecuador		3:49.60
13	Bunting Hem	Cambodia		4:08.64
14	Benjamín Enzema	Equatorial Guinea		4:13.17

Heat 3   15 August 2009

Position	Athlete	Country		Time
1	Augustine Kiprono Choge	Kenya	Q	3:44.73
2	Amine Laalou	Morocco	Q	3:44.75
3	Lopez Lomong	United States	Q	3:44.89
4	Andrew Baddeley	Great Britain	Q	3:45.23
5	Henok Legesse	Ethiopia	Q	3:45.63
6	Tarek Boukensa	Algeria		3:45.65
7	Kristof van Malderen	Belgium		3:46.03
8	Yoann Kowal	France		3:46.42
9	Johan Cronje	South Africa		3:46.45
10	Jeremy Roff	Australia		3:47.08
11	Mohamad Al-Garni	Qatar		3:50.55
12	Álvaro Vásquez	Nicaragua		3:55.06
13	Antoine Berlin	Monaco		4:27.52

Men's 1500m (continued)

Heat 4 15 August 2009

Position	Athlete	Country		Time
1	Deresse Mekonnen	Ethiopia	Q	3:37.04
2	Haron Keitany	Kenya	Q	3:37.13
3	James Brewer	Great Britain	Q	3:37.17
4	Mohamed Moustaoui	Morocco	Q	3:37.34
5	Yusuf Saad Kamel	Brunei	Q	3:37.59
6	Reyes Estévez	Spain	q	3:38.23
7	Nathan Brannen	Canada	q	3:38.35
8	Dorian Ulrey	United States	q	3:38.86
9	Taoufik Makhloufi	Algeria	q	3:40.04
10	Stefan Eberhardt	Germany		3:40.05
11	Mounir Yemmouni	France		3:42.06
12	Tiidrek Nurme	Estonia		3:43.73
13	Víctor Martínez	Andorra		4:02.10

Qualification for Final: first five in each quarter-final plus the next two fastest finishers.

Semi-Final 1 17 August 2009

Position	Athlete	Country		Time
1	Amine Laalou	Morocco	Q	3:36.68
2	Lopez Lomong	United States	Q	3:36.75
3	Bernard Lagat	United States	Q	3:36.86
4	Yusuf Saad Kamel	Brunei	Q	3:36.87
5	Mehdi Baala	France	Q	3:37.07
6	James Brewer	Great Britain		3:37.27
7	Juan Carlos Higuero	Spain		3:37.33
8	Henok Legesse	Ethiopia		3:37.79
9	Nathan Brannen	Canada		3:38.97
10	Peter van der Westhuizen	South Africa		3:40.00
11	Rui Silva	Portugal		3:41.30
	Haron Keitany	Kenya		DNS

Semi-Final 2 17 August 2009

Position	Athlete	Country		Time
1Q	Asbel Kiprop	Kenya	Q	3:36.24
2Q	Leonel Manzano	United States	Q	3:36.29
3q	Augustine Kiprono Choge	Kenya	Q	3:36.43
4q	Deresse Mekonnen	Ethiopia	Q	3:36.86
5	Belal Mansoor Ali	Brunei	Q	3:36.87
6	Mohamed Moustaoui	Morocco	q	3:36.94
7	Abdalaati Iguider	Morocco	q	3:37.19
8	Reyes Estévez	Spain		3:37.55
9	Taoufik Makhloufi	Algeria		3:37.87
10	Jeffrey Riseley	Australia		3:38.00
11	Andrew Baddeley	Great Britain		3:38.23
12	Dorian Ulrey	United States		3:39.33

Men's 1500m (continued)

FINAL 19 August 2009

Position	Athlete	Country	Time
GOLD	Yusuf Saad Kamel	Brunei	3:35.93
SILVER	Deresse Mekonnen	Ethiopia	3:36.01
BRONZE	Bernard Lagat	United States	3:36.20
4	Asbel Kiprop	Kenya	3:36.47
5	Augustine Kiprono Choge	Kenya	3:36.53
6	Mohamed Moustaoui	Morocco	3:36.57
7	Mehdi Baala	France	3:36.99
8	Lopez Lomong	United States	3:37.62
9	Belal Mansoor Ali	Brunei	3:37.72
10	Amine Laalou	Morocco	3:37.83
11	Abdalaati Iguider	Morocco	3:38.35
12	Leonel Manzano	United States	3:40.05

Women's 1500m

Qualification for semi-finals: first six in each heat plus the next six fastest finishers.

Heat 1 18 August 2009

Position	Athlete	Country		Time
1	Maryam Yusuf Jamal	Brunei	Q	4:08.76
2	Nuria Fernández	Spain	Q	4:08.79
3	Meskerem Assefa	Ethiopia	Q	4:08.86
4	Iryna Lishchynska	Ukraine	Q	4:08.95
5	Irina Krakoviak	Lithuania	Q	4:08.96
6	Viola Jelagat Kibiwot	Kenya	q	4:09.18
7	Lidia Chojecka	Poland	q	4:09.38
8	Oksana Zbrozhek	Russia		4:09.84
9	Charlene Thomas	Great Britain		4:09.91
10	Shannon Rowbury	United States	q	4:10.30
11	Marina Muncan	Serbia		4:15.18
12	Eliane Saholinirina	Madagascar		4:16.63
13	Eva Pereira	Cape Verde		5:04.95
	Mariem Alaoui Selsouli*	Morocco		DQ

* results subsequently removed due to failed drugs test.

Heat 2 18 August 2009

Position	Athlete	Country		Time
1	Gelete Burka	Ethiopia	Q	4:07.75
2	Natalia Rodríguez	Spain	Q	4:07.84
3	Lisa Dobriskey	Great Britain	Q	4:07.90
4	Natalya Evdokimova	Russia	Q	4:08.06
5	Anna Pierce	United States	Q	4:08.13
6	Btissam Lakhouad	Morocco	Q	4:08.21
7	Mimi Belete	Brunei	q	4:08.36
8	Nikki Hamblin	New Zealand	q	4:09.60
9	Hind Déhiba Chahyd	France	q	4:11.41
10	Tamara Tverdostup	Ukraine		4:13.36
11	Alemitu Bekele	Turkey		4:13.69
12	Susan Kuijken	Netherlands		4:18.10
13	Irene Jelagat	Kenya		4:27.36
14	Aldy Villalobos	Nicaragua		4:50.55

Women's 1500m (continued)

Heat 3 18 August 2009

Position	Athlete	Country		Time
1	Anna Alminova	Russia	Q	4:08.13
2	Nancy Jebet Langat	Kenya	Q	4:08.16
3	Kalkidan Gezahegne	Ethiopia	Q	4:08.23
4	Christin Wurth-Thomas	United States	Q	4:08.23
5	Sylwia Ejdys	Poland	Q	4:08.59
6	Sonja Roman	Slovenia	Q	4:08.65
7	Anna Mishchenko	Ukraine	q	4:09.26
8	Iris Fuentes-Pila	Spain	q	4:09.71
9	Adrienne Herzog	Netherlands		4:10.10
10	Siham Hilali	Morocco		4:10.57
11	Deirdre Byrne	Ireland		4:12.19
12	Stephanie Twell	Great Britain		4:18.23
12	Sladjana Pejovic	Montenegro		4:28.67
13	Francine Nzilampa	Democratic Republic of Congo		4:30.56

Qualification for Final: first five in each quarter-final plus the next two fastest finishers.

Semi-Final 1 21 August 2009

Position	Athlete	Country		Time
1	Maryam Yusuf Jamal	Brunei	Q	4:03.64
2	Natalia Rodríguez	Spain	Q	4:03.73
3	Lisa Dobriskey	Great Britain	Q	4:03.84
4	Christin Wurth-Thomas	United States	Q	4:04.16
5	Kalkidan Gezahegne	Ethiopia	Q	4:0475
6	Natalya Evdokimova	Russia	q	4:04.93
7	Lidia Chojecka	Poland	q	4:06.53
8	Viola Jelagat Kibiwot	Kenya		4:06.88
9	Iris Fuentes-Pila	Spain		4:07.10
10	Sonja Roman	Slovenia		4:07.20
11	Btissam Lakhouad	Morocco		4:08.72
12	Anna Mishchenko	Ukraine		4:11.02
13	Irina Krakoviak	Lithuania		4:12.54

Semi-Final 2 21 August 2009

Position	Athlete	Country		Time
1	Gelete Burka	Ethiopia	Q	4:10.19
2	Anna Pierce	United States	Q	4:10.47
3	Shannon Rowbury	United States	Q	4:10.51
4	Nuria Fernández	Spain	Q	4:10.64
5	Nikki Hamblin	New Zealand		4:10.96
6	Nancy Jebet Langat	Kenya		4:11.10
7	Hind Déhiba Chahyd	France		4:11.22
8	Sylwia Ejdys	Poland		4:11.33
9	Anna Alminova	Russia		4:12.55
10	Mimi Belete	Brunei		4:13.30
	Mariem Alaoui Selsouli	Morocco		DQ
	Iryna Lishchynska	Ukraine		DNF
	Meskerem Assefa	Ethiopia		DNS

Women's 1500m (continued)

FINAL 23 August 2009

Position	Athlete	Country	Time
GOLD	Maryam Yusuf Jamal	Brunei	4:03.74
SILVER	Lisa Dobriskey	Great Britain	4:03.75
BRONZE	Shannon Rowbury	United States	4:04.18
4	Nuria Fernández	Spain	4:04.91
5	Christin Wurth-Thomas	United States	4:05.21
6	Anna Pierce	United States	4:06.19
7	Lidia Chojecka	Poland	4:07.17
8	Natalya Evdokimova	Russia	4:07.71
9	Kalkidan Gezahegne	Ethiopia	4:08.81
10	Gelete Burka	Ethiopia	4:11.21
	Natalia Rodríguez	Spain	DQ
	Mariem Alaoui Selsouli	Morocco	DQ

Men's 5000m

Qualification for final: first five in each heat plus the next five fastest finishers.

Heat 1   20 August 2009

Position	Athlete	Country		Time
1	Kenenisa Bekele	Ethiopia	Q	13:19.77
2	Matthew Tegenkamp	United States	Q	13:19.87
3	Mohammed Farah	Great Britain	Q	13:19.94
4	Vincent Kiprop Chepkok	Kenya	Q	13:20.24
5	Jesús España	Spain	Q	13:20.40
6	Chris Solinsky	United States	q	13:20.64
7	Joseph Ebuya	Kenya	q	13:22.41
8	Anis Selmouni	Morocco	q	13:22.95
9	Teklemariam Medhin	Eritrea	q	13:23.48
10	Collis Birmingham	Australia	q	13:23.48
11	Saif Saaeed Shaheen	Qatar		13:26.35
12	Geofrey Kusuro	Uganda		13:28.48
13	Ali Abdosh	Ethiopia	q	13.36.52
14	Daniele Meucci	Italy		13:37.79
15	Etienne Bizimana	Burundi		14:06.02
16	Yuichiro Ueno	Japan		14:30.76
	Bayron Piedra	Ecuador		DNF
	Juan Luis Barrios	Mexico		DNS
	Fabiano Joseph Naasi	Tanzania		DNS

Heat 2   20 August 2009

Position	Athlete	Country		Time
1	Moses Ndiema Kipsiro	Uganda	Q	13:22.98
2	Eliud Kipchoge	Kenya	Q	13:23.34
3	James Kwalia C'Kurui	Qatar	Q	13:23.57
4	Bernard Lagat	United States	Q	13:23.73
5	Chakir Boujattaoui	Morocco	Q	13:23.83
6	Bekana Daba	Ethiopia		13:23.86
7	Samuel Tsegay	Eritrea		13:26.78
8	Morhad Amdouni	France		13:29.64
9	Kidane Tadasse	Eritrea		13:30.85
10	Alemayehu Bezabeh	Spain		13:33.52
11	Evan Jager	United States		13:39.80
12	Hussain Jamaan Alhamdah	Saudi Arabia		13:44.59
13	Alistair Ian Cragg	Ireland		13:46.34
14	Arne Gabius	Germany		13:49.13
15	Moses Kibet	Uganda		13:52.38
16	Sergio Sánchez	Spain		13:53.51
17	Marco Joseph	Tanzania		13:53.67
18	Tonny Wamulwa	Zambia		14:01.67
19	Mohamed Ali Mohamed	Somalia		14:34.62
20	Omar Abusaid	Palestine		15:14:88

Men's 5000m (continued)

FINAL 23 August 2009

Position	Athlete	Country	Time
GOLD	Kenenisa Bekele	Ethiopia	13:17.09
SILVER	Bernard Lagat	United States	13:17.33
BRONZE	James Kwalia C'Kurui	Qatar	13:17.78
4	Moses Ndiema Kipsiro	Uganda	13:18.11
5	Eliud Kipchoge	Kenya	13:18.95
6	Ali Abdosh	Ethiopia	13:19.11
7	Mohammed Farah	Great Britain	13:19.69
8	Matthew Tegenkamp	United States	13:20.23
9	Vincent Kiprop Chepkok	Kenya	13:21.31
10	Jesús España	Spain	13:22.07
11	Chakir Boujattaoui	Morocco	13:23.05
12	Chris Solinsky	United States	13:25.87
13	Joseph Ebuya	Kenya	13:39.59
14	Anis Selmouni	Morocco	13:44.59
15	Teklemariam Medhin	Eritrea	13:44.65
16	Collis Birmingham	Australia	13:55.58

Women's 5000m

Qualification for final: first five in each heat plus the next five fastest finishers.

Heat 1 19 August 2009

Position	Athlete	Country		Time
1	Sentayehu Ejigu	Ethiopia	Q	15:17.64
2	Sylvia Jebiwott Kibet	Kenya	Q	15:17.77
3	Meselech Melkamu	Ethiopia	Q	15:18.39
4	Krisztina Papp	Hungary	Q	15:19.90
5	Sara Moreira	Portugal	Q	15:19.93
6	Yurika Nakamura	Japan	q	15:21.01
7	Julie Culley	United States		15:32.33
8	Natalya Popkova	Russia		15:32.62
9	Inés Melchor	Peru		16:00.83
10	Marriam Thole	Malawi		17:12.21
	Elvan Abeylegesse	Turkey		DNS

Heat 2 19 August 2009

Position	Athlete	Country		Time
1	Meseret Defar	Ethiopia	Q	15:16.46
2	Vivian Cheruiyot	Kenya	Q	15:16.59
3	Iness Chepkesis Chenonge	Kenya	Q	15:18.40
4	Genzebe Dibaba	Ethiopia	Q	15:19.66
5	Alemitu Bekele	Turkey	Q	15:19.88
6	Jennifer Rhines	United States	q	15:20.20
7	Silvia Weissteiner	Italy	q	15:20.88
8	Yuriko Kobayashi	Japan	q	15:23.96
9	Zakia Mrisho Mohamed	Tanzania	q	15:25.09
10	Elizaveta Grechishnikova	Russia		15:53.41
11	Judith Plá	Spain		15:54.32
12	Pauline Niyongere	Burundi		16:33.77

FINAL 23 August 2009

Position	Athlete	Country	Time
GOLD	Vivian Cheruiyot	Kenya	14:57.97
SILVER	Sylvia Jebiwott Kibet	Kenya	14:58.33
BRONZE	Meseret Defar	Ethiopia	14:58.41
4	Sentayehu Ejigu	Ethiopia	15:03.38
5	Meselech Melkamu	Ethiopia	15:03.72
6	Iness Chepkesis Chenonge	Kenya	15:06.06
7	Silvia Weissteiner	Italy	15:09.74
8	Genzebe Dibaba	Ethiopia	15:11.12
9	Jennifer Rhines	United States	15:11.63
10	Sara Moreira	Portugal	15:12.22
11	Yuriko Kobayashi	Japan	15:12.44
12	Yurika Nakamura	Japan	15:13.01
13	Alemitu Bekele	Turkey	15:18.18
14	Krisztina Papp	Hungary	15:20.36
15	Zakia Mrisho Mohamed	Tanzania	15:31.73

Men's 10000m

FINAL 17 August 2009

Position	Athlete	Country		Time
GOLD	Kenenisa Bekele	Ethiopia	CR	26:26.31
SILVER	Zersenay Tadese	Eritrea		26:50.12
BRONZE	Moses Ndiema Masai	Kenya		26:57.39
4	Imane Merga	Ethiopia		27:15.94
5	Bernard Kiprop Kipyego	Kenya		27:18.47
6	Dathan Ritzenhein	United States		27:22.28
7	Micah Kipkemboi Kogo	Kenya		27:26.33
8	Galen Rupp	United States		27:37.99
9	Kidane Tadasse	Eritrea		27:41.50
10	Gebre-egziabher Gebremariam	Ethiopia		27:44.04
11	Ahmad Hassan Abdullah	Qatar		27:45.03
12	Teklemariam Medhin	Eritrea		27:58.89
13	Fabiano Joseph Naasi	Tanzania		28:04.32
14	Juan Carlos Romero	Mexico		28:09.78
15	Carles Castillejo	Spain		28:09.89
16	Dickson Marwa Mkami	Tanzania		28:18.00
17	Tim Nelson	United States		28:18.04
18	Juan Luis Barrios	Mexico		28:31.40
19	Surendra Kumar Singh	India		28:35.51
20	Anatoliy Rybakov	Russia		28:42.28
21	Ezekiel Jafari	Tanzania		28:45.34
22	Martin Toroitich	Uganda		28:49.49
23	Rui Pedro Silva	Portugal		28:51.40
24	David McNeill	Australia		29:18.59
25	Yuki Iwai	Japan		29:24.12
	Collis Birmingham	Australia		DNF
	Ayad Lamdassem	Spain		DNF
	Manuel Ángel Penas	Spain		DNF
	Abebe Dinkesa	Ethiopia		DNF
	Nicholas Kemboi	Qatar		DNF
	Martin Fagan	Ireland		DNS

Women's 10000m

FINAL 15 August 2009

Position	Athlete	Country	Time
GOLD	Linet Chepkwemoi Masai	Kenya	30:51.24
SILVER	Meselech Melkamu	Ethiopia	30:51.34
BRONZE	Wude Ayalew	Ethiopia	30:51.95
4	Grace Kwamboka Momanyi	Kenya	30:52.25
5	Meseret Defar	Ethiopia	30:52.37
6	Amy Yoder Begley	United States	31:13.78
7	Yurika Nakamura	Japan	31:14.39
8	Kimberley Smith	New Zealand	31:21.42
9	Kayoko Fukushi	Japan	31:23.49
10	Inês Monteiro	Portugal	31:25.67
11	Mariya Konovalova	Russia	31:26.94
12	Florence Jebet Kiplagat	Kenya	31:30.85
13	Ana Dulce Félix	Portugal	31:30.90
14	Shalane Flanagan	United States	31:32.19
15	Kseniya Agafonova	Russia	31:43.14
16	Ana Dias	Portugal	31:49.91
17	Katie McGregor	United States	32:18.49
18	Yingying Zhang	China	32:33.63
19	Liliya Shobukhova	Russia	32:42.36
20	Yukari Sahaku	Japan	33:41.17
	Elvan Abeylegesse	Turkey	DNF
	Olivera Jevtic	Serbia	DNS

Men's Marathon

FINAL 22 August 2009

Position	Athlete	Country		Time
GOLD	Abel Kirui	Kenya	CR	2:06.54
SILVER	Emmanuel Kipchirchir Mutai	Kenya		2:07.48
BRONZE	Tsegay Kebede	Ethiopia		2:08.35
4	Yemane Tsegay	Ethiopia		2:08.42
5	Robert Kipkoech Cheruiyot	Kenya		2:10.46
6	Atsushi Sato	Japan		2:12.05
7	Adil Ennani	Morocco		2:12.12
8	José Manuel Martínez	Spain		2:14.04
9	José Moreira	Portugal		2:14.05
10	Luís Feiteira	Portugal		2:14.06
11	Masaya Shimizu	Japan		2:14.06
12	Norman Dlomo	South Africa		2:14.39
13	Fernando Silva	Portugal		2:14.48
14	Satoshi Irifune	Japan		2:14.54
15	Dejene Yirdaw	Ethiopia		2:15.09
16	Marilson dos Santos	Brazil		2:15.13
17	Johannes Kekana	South Africa		2:15.28
18	André Pollmächer	Germany		2:15.36
19	Adriano Bastos	Brazil		2:15.39
20	Oleg Kulkov	Russia		2:15.40
21	Martin Dent	Australia		2:16.05
22	Coolboy Ngamole	South Africa		2:16.20
23	José de Souza	Brazil		2:16.40
24	Daniel Browne	United States		2:16.49
25	Reid Coolsaet	Canada		2:16.53
26	Rachid Kisri	Morocco		2:17.01
27	Yuriy Abramov	Russia		2:17.04
28	Phaustin Baha Sulle	Tanzania		2:17.11
29	Ser-Od Bat-Ochir	Mongolia		2:17.22
30	Andrew Letherby	Australia		2:17.29
31	Daniel Kipkorir Chepyegon	Uganda		2:17.47
32	Simon Munyutu	France		2:17.53
33	Dylan Wykes	Canada		2:18.00
34	Martin Beckmann	Germany		2:18.08
35	George Majaji	Zimbabwe		2:18.37
36	Matt Gabrielson	United States		2:18.41
37	Alejandro Suárez	Mexico		2:18.55
38	Chia-Che Chang	Chinese Taipei		2:19.32
39	Kazuhiro Maeda	Japan		2:19.59
40	Khalid Kamal Yaseen	Brunei		2:20.11
41	James Kibocha Theuri	France		2:20.24
42	Roman Kejžar	Slovenia		2:20.25
43	Song-Chol Pak	North Korea		2:21.12
44	Driss El Himer	France		2:21.19
45	Mikhail Lemaev	Russia		2:21.47
46	Myongseung Lee	South Korea		2:21.54
47	Mark Tucker	Australia		2:21.57
48	José Amado García	Guatemala		2:22.00
49	Carlos Cordero	Mexico		2:22.16
50	Falk Cierpinski	Germany		2:22.36
51	Hyon U Ri	North Korea		2:22.48
52	Constantino León	Peru		2:23.34
53	Andrew Smith	Canada		2:24.48
54	Samir Baala	France		2:25.12
55	Juan Gualberto Vargas	Mexico		2:25.26
56	Giitah Macharia	Canada		2:25.40
57	Getuli Bayo	Tanzania		2:25.52

Men's Marathon (continued)

Position	Athlete	Country	Time
58	Scott Westcott	Australia	2:26.02
59	Nelson Cruz	Cape Verde	2:27.16
60	Andrea Silvini	Tanzania	2:28.48
61	Arata Fujiwara	Japan	2:31.06
62	Valery Pisarev	Kyrgyzstan	2:31.32
63	Nate Jenkins	United States	2:32.16
64	Wodage Zvadya	Israel	2:34.58
65	Myong-Ki Lee	South Korea	2:35.12
66	Tobias Sauter	Germany	2:35.43
67	Pedro Nimo	Spain	2:36.39
68	Tesfayohannes Mesfin	Eritrea	2:39.51
69	Geuntae Yook	South Korea	2:40.47
70	Sangay Wangchuk	Bhutan	2:47.55
	Stephen Loruo Kamar	Brunei	DNF
	Franklin Tenorio	Ecuador	DNF
	Yared Asmerom	Eritrea	DNF
	Yonas Kifle	Eritrea	DNF
	Rafael Iglesias	Spain	DNF
	Deressa Chimsa	Ethiopia	DNF
	Deriba Merga	Ethiopia	DNF
	Loïc Letellier	France	DNF
	Benjamin Kolum Kiptoo	Kenya	DNF
	Youngjun Ji	South Korea	DNF
	Sechaba Bohosi	Lesotho	DNF
	Abderrahim Goumri	Morocco	DNF
	Reinhold Ndalikokule Iita	Namibia	DNF
	Michael Aish	New Zealand	DNF
	Mubarak Hassan Shami	Qatar	DNF
	Dieudonné Disi	Rwanda	DNF
	Lucian Disdery Hombo	Tanzania	DNF
	Christopher Isengwe	Tanzania	DNF
	Nicholas Kiprono	Uganda	DNF
	Amos Masai	Uganda	DNF
	Justin Young	United States	DNF
	Ruggero Pertile	Italy	DNS
	Kensuke Takahashi	Japan	DNS
	Daniel Rono	Kenya	DNS
	Junhyeon Hwang	South Korea	DNS
	Ali Mabrouk El Zaidi	Libya	DNS
	Jaouad Gharib	Morocco	DNS
	Edwardo Torres	United States	DNS

Women's Marathon

FINAL 23 August 2009

Position	Athlete	Country	Time
GOLD	Xue Bai	China	2:25.15
SILVER	Yoshimi Ozaki	Japan	2:25.25
BRONZE	Aselefech Mergia	Ethiopia	2:25.32
4	Chunxiu Zhou	China	2:25.39
5	Xiaolin Zhu	China	2:26.08
6	Marisa Barros	Portugal	2:26.50
7	Yuri Kano	Japan	2:26.57
8	Nailiya Yulamanova	Russia	2:27.08
9	Alevtina Biktimirova	Russia	2:27.39
10	Kara Goucher	United States	2:27.48
11	Desireé Davila	United States	2:27.53
12	Julia Mumbi Muraga	Kenya	2:28.59
13	Weiwei Sun	China	2:29.39
14	Yoshiko Fujinaga	Japan	2:29.53
15	Svetlana Zakharova	Russia	2:29.55
16	Bezunesh Bekele	Ethiopia	2:30.03
17	Sabrina Mockenhaupt	Germany	2:30.07
18	Lisa Jane Weightman	Australia	2:30.42
19	Zivilé Balciūnaité	Lithuania	2:31.06
20	Kum-Ok Kim	North Korea	2:31.24
21	Irene Limika	Kenya	2:31.29
22	Lidia Simon	Romania	2:32.03
23	Dire Tune	Ethiopia	2:32.42
24	Beata Naigambo	Namibia	2:33.05
25	Alessandra Aguilar	Spain	2:33.38
26	Epiphanie Nyirabarame	Rwanda	2:33.59
27	Atsede Baysa	Ethiopia	2:36.04
28	Tera Moody	United States	2:36.39
29	Olga Glok	Russia	2:36.57
30	Paige Higgins	United States	2:37.11
31	Yukiko Akaba	Japan	2:37.43
32	Lyubov Morgunova	Russia	2:38.23
33	Yong-Ok Jong	North Korea	2:38.29
34	Susanne Hahn	Germany	2:38.39
35	Mary Davies	New Zealand	2:38.48
36	Tara Quinn-Smith	Canada	2:39.19
37	Risper Jemeli Kimaiyo	Kenya	2:39.23
38	Patrizia Morceli	Switzerland	2:39.37
39	Sun Suk Yun	South Korea	2:39.56
40	Judith Ramírez	Mexico	2:40.18
41	Fiona Docherty	New Zealand	2:40.18
42	Un Suk Phyo	North Korea	2:40.39
43	Adriana Aparecida da Silva	Brazil	2:40.54
44	Shireen Crumpton	New Zealand	2:41.31
45	Tanith Maxwell	South Africa	2:41.48
46	Annemette Aagaard	Denmark	2:42.03
47	Martha Komu	Kenya	2:42.14
48	Chol Sun Kim	North Korea	2:42.18
49	Patricia Lossouarn	France	2:42.40
50	Laurence Klein	France	2:42.47
51	Zoila Gómez	United States	2:42.49
52	Renalda Kergyte	Lithuania	2:45.28
53	Ho-sun Park	South Korea	2:47.16
54	Stephanie Briand	France	2:48.16
55	Yamna Oubouhou	France	2:50.02
56	Helalia Johannes	Namibia	2:50.19
57	Sandra Ruales	Ecuador	2:50.36

Women's Marathon (continued)

Position	Athlete	Country	Time
58	Jane Suuto	Uganda	2:52.44
59	Cecile Moynot	France	2:54.21
60	Nuta Olaru	Romania	3:00.59
	Magdaliní Gazéa	Greece	DQ
	Maria Zeferina Baldaia	Brazil	DNF
	Robe Guta	Ethiopia	DNF
	Ulrike Maisch	Germany	DNF
	Luminita Zaituc	Germany	DNF
	Yeoryía Abatzídou	Greece	DNF
	Helena Loshanyang Kirop	Kenya	DNF
	Victoria Poludina	Kyrgyzstan	DNF
	Sun-young Lee	South Korea	DNF
	Dulce María Rodríguez	Mexico	DNF
	Luvsanlkhundeg Otgonbayar	Mongolia	DNF
	Clara Morales	Chile	DNS
	Luminita Talpos	Romania	DNS

Men's 3000m Steeplechase

Qualification for Final: first four in each heat plus the next three fastest finishers.

Heat 1   16 August 2009

Position	Athlete	Country		Time
1	Richard Kipkemboi Mateelong	Kenya	Q	8:17.99
2	Tareq Mubarak Taher	Brunei	Q	8:18.13
3	Paul Kipsiele Koech	Kenya	Q	8:18.16
4	Roba Gary	Ethiopia	Q	8:18.22
5	Abubaker Ali Kamal	Qatar	q	8:18.95
6	Abdelatif Chemlal	Morocco		8:25.68
7	Tomasz Szymkowiak	Poland		8:27.93
8	Mario Bazán	Peru		8:28.67
9	Pieter Desmet	Belgium		8:31.81
10	Vincent Zouaoui-Dandrieaux	France		8:41.85
11	Per Jacobsen	Sweden		8:44.80
12	Ángel Mullera	Spain		8:47.40
	Kyle Alcorn	United States		DNF

Heat 2   16 August 2009

Position	Athlete	Country		Time
1	Brimin Kiprop Kipruto	Kenya	Q	8:18.07
2	Bouabdellah Tahri	France	Q	8:18.23
3	Ruben Ramolefi	South Africa	Q	8:18.24
4	Benjamin Kiplagat	Uganda	Q	8:18.55
5	Jukka Keskisalo	Finland	q	8:22.00
6	Mustafa Mohamed	Sweden	q	8:22.92
7	José Luis Blanco	Spain		8:24.07
8	Krijn van Koolwijk	Belgium		8:24.22
9	Ildar Minshin	Russia		8:33.89
10	Rob Watson	Canada		8:44.73
11	Youcef Abdi	Australia		8:49.88
12	Legese Lamiso	Ethiopia		8:51.63
13	Joshua McAdams	United States		9:02.19

Heat 3   16 August 2009

Position	Athlete	Country		Time
1	Ezekiel Kemboi	Kenya	Q	8:19.36
2	Yacob Jarso	Ethiopia	Q	8:20.91
3	Eliseo Martín	Spain	Q	8:24.29
4	Ion Luchianov	Moldova		8:27.41
5	Bjørnar Ustad Kristensen	Norway		8:28.49
6	Steffen Uliczka	Germany		8:37.83
7	Simon Ayeko	Uganda		8:37.86
8	Yoshitaka Iwamizu	Japan		8:39.03
9	Boštjan Buc	Slovenia		8:40.56
10	Alberto Paulo	Portugal		8:43.13
11	Daniel Huling	United States		8:46.79
12	Jamel Chatbi*	Morocco		DQ
13	Mahiedine Mekhissi-Benabbad	France		DNF

* results subsequently removed due to failed drugs test.

Men's 3000m Steeplechase (continued)

FINAL 18 August 2009

Position	Athlete	Country		Time
GOLD	Ezekiel Kemboi	Kenya	CR	8:00.43
SILVER	Richard Kipkemboi Mateelong	Kenya		8:00.89
BRONZE	Bouabdellah Tahri	France		8:01.18
4	Paul Kipsiele Koech	Kenya		8:01.26
5	Yacob Jarso	Ethiopia		8:12.13
6	Roba Gary	Ethiopia		8:12.40
7	Brimin Kiprop Kipruto	Kenya		8:12.61
8	Jukka Keskisalo	Finland		8:14.47
9	Eliseo Martín	Spain		8:16.51
10	Tareq Mubarak Taher	Brunei		8:17.08
11	Benjamin Kiplagat	Uganda		8:17.82
12	Abubaker Ali Kamal	Qatar		8:19.72
13	Ruben Ramolefi	South Africa		8:32.54
14	Mustafa Mohamed	Sweden		8:35.77
	Jamel Chatbi	Morocco		DQ

Women's 3000m Steeplechase

Qualification for final: first four in each heat plus the next three fastest finishers.

Heat 1 15 August 2009

Position	Athlete	Country		Time
1	Gulnara Galkina	Russia	Q	9:17.67
2	Antje Möldner	Germany	Q	9:21.73
3	Sofia Assefa	Ethiopia	Q	9:22.63
4	Milcah Chemos Cheywa	Kenya	Q	9:23.87
5	Eva Arias	Spain	q	9:25.14
6	Jessica Augusto	Portugal	q	9:26.64
7	Ancuta Bobocel	Romania		9:34.39
8	Iríni Kokkinaríou	Greece		9:35.61
9	Yelena Sidorchenkova	Russia		9:37.16
10	Minori Hayakari	Japan		9:39.28
11	Lindsey Anderson	United States		9:46.03
12	Donna MacFarlane	Australia		9:52.46
13	Durka Mana	Sudan		9:52.90
14	Elena Romagnolo	Italy		9:56.61

Heat 2 15 August 2009

Position	Athlete	Country		Time
1	Habiba Ghribi	Tunisia	Q	9:26.40
2	Yuliya Zarudneva	Russia	Q	9:26.64
3	Jennifer Barringer	United States	Q	9:26.81
4	Katarzyna Kowalska	Poland	Q	9:26.93
5	Ruth Bisibori Nyangau	Kenya	q	9:27.04
6	Sara Moreira	Portugal		9:28.64
7	Korahubsh Itaa	Ethiopia		9:33.67
8	Ulrika Johansson	Sweden		9:38.88
9	Helen Clitheroe	Great Britain		9:41.71
10	Diana Martín	Spain		9:42.39
11	Élodie Olivarès	France		9:43.83
12	Sabine Heitling	Brazil		9:50.96
13	Roisin McGettigan	Ireland		9:59.10
14	Silje Fjørtoft	Norway		10:01.04

Women's 3000m Steeplechase (continued)

Heat 3 15 August 2009

Position	Athlete	Country		Time
1	Zemzem Ahmed	Ethiopia	Q	9:29.36
2	Gladys Jerotich Kipkemoi	Kenya	Q	9:29.36
3	Sophie Duarte	France	Q	9:34.08
4	Marta Domínguez	Spain	Q	9:34.78
5	Hanane Ouhaddou	Morocco		9:35.78
6	Oxana Juravel	Moldova		9:36.63
7	Ekaterina Volkova	Russia		9:43.52
8	Lívia Tóth	Hungary		9:45.14
9	Sandra Eriksson	Finland		9:46.62
10	Karoline Bjerkeli Grøvdal	Norway		9:48.47
11	Cristina Casandra	Romania		9:49.88
12	Bridget Franek	United States		9:50.02
13	Asli Cakir	Turkey		10:06.64

FINAL 17 August 2009

Position	Athlete	Country	Time
GOLD	Marta Domínguez	Spain	9:07.32
SILVER	Yuliya Zarudneva	Russia	9:08.39
BRONZE	Milcah Chemos Cheywa	Kenya	9:08.57
4	Gulnara Galkina	Russia	9:11.09
5	Jennifer Barringer	United States	9:12.50
6	Habiba Ghribi	Tunisia	9:12.52
7	Ruth Bisibori Nyangau	Kenya	9:13.16
8	Gladys Jerotich Kipkemoi	Kenya	9:14.62
9	Antje Möldner	Germany	9:18.54
10	Zemzem Ahmed	Ethiopia	9:22.64
11	Jessica Augusto	Portugal	9:25.25
12	Katarzyna Kowalska	Poland	9:30.37
13	Sofia Assefa	Ethiopia	9:31.29
14	Eva Arias	Spain	9:33.34
15	Sophie Duarte	France	9:33.85

Men's 110m Hurdles

Qualification for semi-finals: first four in each heat plus the next four fastest finishers.

Heat 1   19 August 2009

Position	Lane	Athlete	Country		Time
1	2	Dongpeng Shi	China	Q	13.56
2	7	Dwight Thomas	Jamaica	Q	13.57
3	8	Jackson Quiñónez	Spain	Q	13.63
4	3	Lehann Fourie	South Africa		13.67
5	4	Andrew Turner	Great Britain		13.73
6	6	Jung-joon Lee	South Korea		13.83
7	5	Tasuku Tanonaka	Japan		13.84
	1	Joseph-Berlioz Randriamihaja	Madagascar		DNF

Heat 2   19 August 2009

Position	Lane	Athlete	Country		Time
1	3	Maurice Wignall	Jamaica	Q	13.62
2	7	Helge Schwarzer	Germany	Q	13.66
3	2	Dayron Robles	Cuba	Q	13.67
4	4	Cédric Lavanne	France		13.72
5	6	Felipe Vivancos	Spain		13.72
6	8	Damien Broothaerts	Belgium		14.15
	5	Jing Yin	China		DNS

Heat 3   19 August 2009

Position	Lane	Athlete	Country		Time
1	6	Petr Svoboda	Czech Republic	Q	13.56
2	2	Garfield Darien	France	Q	13.56
3	3	Artur Noga	Poland	Q	13.56
4	7	Aries Merritt	United States		13.70
5	8	Serhiy Demydyuk	Ukraine		13.71
6	1	Adrien Deghelt	Belgium		13.78
7	4	Gianni Frankis	Great Britain		13.83
8	5	Toriki Urarii	French Polynesia		15.01

Heat 4   19 August 2009

Position	Lane	Athlete	Country		Time
1	2	Ryan Brathwaite	Barbados	Q	13.35
2	5	Alexander John	Germany	Q	13.41
3	1	William Sharman	Great Britain	Q	13.52
4	8	Stanislavs Olijars	Latvia	q	13.59
5	3	Maksim Lynsha	Belarus	q	13.61
6	7	Evgeniy Borisov	Russia	q	13.63
7	6	Tae-kyong Park	South Korea		13.93
8	4	Ahmad Hazer	Lebanon		14.74

Heat 5   19 August 2009

Position	Lane	Athlete	Country		Time
1	2	Wei Ji	China	Q	13.51
2	8	Terrence Trammell	United States	Q	13.51
3	7	Gregory Sedoc	Netherlands	Q	13.54
4	6	Dimitri Bascou	France	q	13.55
5	4	Shamar Sands	Bahamas	q	13.57
6	3	Selim Nurudeen	Nigeria		13.68
7	5	Héctor Cotto	Puerto Rico		13.81
8	1	Rayzam Shah Wan Sofian	Malaysia		14.06

Men's 110m Hurdles (continued)

Heat 6   19 August 2009

Position	Lane	Athlete	Country		Time
1	7	Dániel Kiss	Hungary	Q	13.34
2	2	Paulo Villar	Colombia	Q	13.52
3	6	David Payne	United States	Q	13.54
4	4	Dayron Capetillo	Cuba	q	13.61
5	3	Richard Phillips	Jamaica		13.70
6	8	Matthias Bühler	Germany		13.75
7	1	David Ilariani	Georgia		13.86
8	5	Abdul Hakeem Abdul Halim	Singapore		14.63

Qualification for the Final: first two in each semi-final, plus the next two fastest finishers.

Semi-Final 1   20 August 2009

Position	Lane	Athlete	Country		Time
1	6	Terrence Trammell	United States	Q	13.24
2	3	Petr Svoboda	Czech Republic	Q	13.33
3	4	Wei Ji	China	q	13.41
4	7	Artur Noga	Poland		13.43
5	5	Paulo Villar	Colombia		13.44
6	1	Stanislavs Olijars	Latvia		13.5
7	8	Jackson Quiñónez	Spain		13.54
8	2	Dayron Capetillo	Cuba		13.55

Semi-Final 2   20 August 2009

Position	Lane	Athlete	Country		Time
1	4	Ryan Brathwaite	Barbados	Q	13.18
2	7	David Payne	United States	Q	13.24
3	5	Dwight Thomas	Jamaica	q	13.37
4	3	Dongpeng Shi	China		13.42
5	8	Gregory Sedoc	Netherlands		13.45
6	1	Maksim Lynsha	Belarus		13.46
7	2	Dimitri Bascou	France		13.49
8	6	Alexander John	Germany		13.64

Semi-Final 3   20 August 2009

Position	Lane	Athlete	Country		Time
1	8	William Sharman	Great Britain	Q	13.38
2	4	Maurice Wignall	Jamaica	Q	13.43
3	3	Dániel Kiss	Hungary		13.45
4	1	Shamar Sands	Bahamas		13.47
5	5	Garfield Darien	France		13.57
6	2	Evgeniy Borisov	Russia		13.63
7	6	Helge Schwarzer	Germany		13.72
8	7	Dayron Robles	Cuba		DNF

FINAL   20 August 2009

Position	Lane	Athlete	Country	Time
GOLD	4	Ryan Brathwaite	Barbados	13.14
SILVER	5	Terrence Trammell	United States	13.15
BRONZE	3	David Payne	United States	13.15
4	6	William Sharman	Great Britain	13.30
5	8	Maurice Wignall	Jamaica	13.31
6	7	Petr Svoboda	Czech Republic	13.38
7	2	Dwight Thomas	Jamaica	13.56
8	1	Wei Ji	China	13.57

Women's 100m Hurdles

Qualification for semi-finals: first four in each heat plus the next four fastest finishers.

Heat 1   18 August 2009

Position	Lane	Athlete	Country		Time
1	1	Dawn Harper	United States	Q	12.70
2	3	Delloreen Ennis-London	Jamaica	Q	12.73
3	6	Cindy Billaud	France	Q	13.12
4	2	Tatyana Dektyareva	Russia		13.51
5	8	Andrea Miller	New Zealand		13.83
6	4	Jeimy Bernárdez	Honduras		14.53
	7	Olutoyin Augustus*	Nigeria		DQ
	5	Jessica Ennis	Great Britain		DNS

* results subsequently removed due to failed drugs test.

Heat 2   18 August 2009

Position	Lane	Athlete	Country		Time
1	4	Damu Cherry	United States	Q	12.71
2	6	Lacena Golding-Clarke	Jamaica	Q	12.9
3	5	Carolin Nytra	Germany	Q	13.03
4	3	Irina Lenskiy	Israel	Q	13.18
5	2	Angela Whyte	Canada		13.27
6	1	Seun Adigun	Nigeria		13.33
7	7	Sonata Tamošaityte	Lithuania		13.44
8	8	Ekaterina Shtepa	Russia		13.50

Heat 3   18 August 2009

Position	Lane	Athlete	Country		Time
1	2	Sally McLellan	Australia	Q	12.82
2	4	Derval O'Rourke	Ireland	Q	12.86
3	3	Yuliya Kondakova	Russia	Q	12.88
4	8	Lucie Škrobáková	Czech Republic	Q	13.04
5	7	Brigitte Merlano	Colombia	q	13.19
6	5	Asuka Terada	Japan		13.41
7	6	Michelle Perry	United States		13.68
8	1	Tamla Pietersen	Zimbabwe		14.50

Heat 4   18 August 2009

Position	Lane	Athlete	Country		Time
1	3	Priscilla Lopes-Schliep	Canada	Q	12.56
2	6	Ginnie Powell	United States	Q	12.77
3	7	Nevin Yanit	Turkey	Q	12.92
4	1	Christina Vukicevic	Norway	Q	12.95
5	5	Eline Berings	Belgium	q	13.04
6	8	Aleesha Barber	Trinidad & Tobago	q	13.19
7	4	Lisa Urech	Switzerland		13.36
	2	Jessica Ohanaja	Nigeria		DNS

Heat 5   18 August 2009

Position	Lane	Athlete	Country		Time
1	5	Brigitte Foster-Hylton	Jamaica	Q	12.67
2	3	Perdita Felicien	Canada	Q	12.77
3	2	Anay Tejeda	Cuba	Q	12.82
4	6	Sarah Claxton	Great Britain	Q	12.86
5	7	Joanna Kocielnik	Poland	q	13.16
6	1	Sandra Gomis	France		13.23
7	8	Natalya Ivoninskaya	Kazakhstan		13.41
	4	Elisabeth Davin	Belgium		DNF

Women's 100m Hurdles (continued)

Qualification for the Final: first two in each semi-final, plus the next two fastest finishers.

Semi-Final 1 19 August 2009

Position	Lane	Athlete	Country		Time
1	3	Priscilla Lopes-Schliep	Canada	Q	12.60
2	4	Delloreen Ennis-London	Jamaica	Q	12.64
3	6	Ginnie Powell	United States	q	12.73
4	7	Lucie Škrobáková	Czech Republic		12.92
5	8	Nevin Yanit	Turkey		12.99
6	5	Yuliya Kondakova	Russia		13.00
7	1	Aleesha Barber	Trinidad & Tobago		13.06
8	2	Cindy Billaud	France		13.20

Semi-Final 2 19 August 2009

Position	Lane	Athlete	Country		Time
1	5	Brigitte Foster-Hylton	Jamaica	Q	12.54
2	4	Perdita Felicien	Canada	Q	12.58
3	3	Damu Cherry	United States		12.76
4	6	Anay Tejeda	Cuba		12.82
5	7	Christina Vukicevic	Norway		13.00
6	1	Brigitte Merlano	Colombia		13.23
7	2	Irina Lenskiy	Israel		13.29
8	8	Olutoyin Augustus	Nigeria		DQ

Semi-Final 3 19 August 2009

Position	Lane	Athlete	Country		Time
1	4	Dawn Harper	United States	Q	12.48
2	6	Sally McLellan	Australia	Q	12.66
3	5	Derval O'Rourke	Ireland	q	12.73
4	3	Lacena Golding-Clarke	Jamaica		12.76
5	8	Carolin Nytra	Germany		12.94
6	1	Eline Berings	Belgium		12.94
7	2	Joanna Kocielnik	Poland		13.21
8	7	Sarah Claxton	Great Britain		13.21

FINAL 19 August 2009

Position	Lane	Athlete	Country	Time
GOLD	4	Brigitte Foster-Hylton	Jamaica	12.51
SILVER	6	Priscilla Lopes-Schliep	Canada	12.54
BRONZE	8	Delloreen Ennis-London	Jamaica	12.55
4	1	Derval O'Rourke	Ireland	12.67
5	7	Sally McLellan	Australia	12.70
6	2	Ginnie Powell	United States	12.78
7	5	Dawn Harper	United States	12.81
8	3	Perdita Felicien	Canada	15.53

Men's 400m Hurdles

Qualification for semi-finals: first three in each heat plus the next four fastest finishers.

Heat 1   15 August 2009

Position	Lane	Athlete	Country		Time
1	8	Isa Phillips	Jamaica	Q	48.99
2	4	Periklís Iakovákis	Greece	Q	49.12
3	6	Johnny Dutch	United States	Q	49.38
4	3	Andrés Silva	Uruguay	q	49.51
5	7	Kenji Narisako	Japan		49.60
6	1	Stanislav Melnykov	Ukraine		50.41
7	2	Mahau Sugimachi	Brazil		51.05
	5	Jussi Heikkilä	Finland		51.42

Heat 2   15 August 2009

Position	Lane	Athlete	Country		Time
1	1	Javier Culson	Puerto Rico	Q	49.27
2	2	Bershawn Jackson	United States	Q	49.34
3	4	Kazuaki Yoshida	Japan	Q	49.45
4	6	Tristan Thomas	Australia	q	49.53
5	8	Rhys Williams	Great Britain		49.88
6	3	Ibrahim Maïga	Mali		51.70
	7	Héni Kechi	France		DQ
	5	Josef Robertson	Jamaica		DQ

Heat 3   15 August 2009

Position	Lane	Athlete	Country		Time
1	5	Kerron Clement	United States	Q	48.39
2	6	Danny McFarlane	Jamaica	Q	48.65
3	8	Jehue Gordon	Trinidad & Tobago	Q	48.66
4	7	Felix Sánchez	Dominican Republic	q	48.76
5	1	Omar Cisneros	Cuba	q	49.27
6	2	Michaël Bultheel	Belgium		49.67
7	4	Jonathan Williams	Belize		52.41
	3	Joseph G Abraham	India		DQ

Heat 4   15 August 2009

Position	Lane	Athlete	Country		Time
1	7	David Greene	Great Britain	Q	48.76
2	3	Louis van Zyl	South Africa	Q	49.48
3	8	Brendan Cole	Australia	Q	49.63
4	5	Angelo Taylor	United States		49.64
5	2	Fadil Bellaabouss	France		49.73
6	6	Aleksandr Derevyagin	Russia		49.83
	4	Kurt Couto	Mozambique		DQ
	1	Ali Obaid Shirook	United Arab Emirates		DNF

Men's 400m Hurdles (continued)

Qualification for Final: first three in each semi-final plus the next two fastest finishers.

Semi-Final 1   16 August 2009

Position	Lane	Athlete	Country		Time
1	3	Kerron Clement	United States	Q	48.00
2	1	Felix Sánchez	Dominican Republic	Q	48.34
3	5	Javier Culson	Puerto Rico	Q	48.43
4	4	Danny McFarlane	Jamaica	q	48.49
5	7	Jehue Gordon	Trinidad & Tobago	q	48.77
6	6	Louis van Zyl	South Africa		48.80
7	2	Andrés Silva	Uruguay		49.34
8	8	Brendan Cole	Australia		49.92

Semi-Final 2   16 August 2009

Position	Lane	Athlete	Country		Time
1	5	Bershawn Jackson	United States	Q	48.23
2	4	David Greene	Great Britain	Q	48.27
3	3	Periklís Iakovákis	Greece	Q	48.73
4	6	Isa Phillips	Jamaica		48.93
5	1	Omar Cisneros	Cuba		49.21
6	8	Johnny Dutch	United States		49.28
7	2	Tristan Thomas	Australia		49.76
8	7	Kazuaki Yoshida	Japan		50.34

FINAL   18 August 2009

Position	Lane	Athlete	Country	Time
GOLD	5	Kerron Clement	United States	47.91
SILVER	4	Javier Culson	Puerto Rico	48.09
BRONZE	3	Bershawn Jackson	United States	48.23
4	6	Jehue Gordon	Trinidad & Tobago	48.26
5	1	Periklís Iakovákis	Greece	48.42
6	8	Danny McFarlane	Jamaica	48.65
7	2	David Greene	Great Britain	48.68
8	7	Felix Sánchez	Dominican Republic	50.11

Women's 400m Hurdles

Qualification for semi-finals: first four in each heat plus the next four fastest finishers.

Heat 1   17 August 2009

Position	Lane	Athlete	Country		Time
1	3	Kaliese Spencer	Jamaica	Q	55.12
2	8	Josanne Lucas	Trinidad & Tobago	Q	55.41
3	5	Xiaoxiao Huang	China	Q	55.52
4	2	Vania Stambolova	Bulgaria	Q	56.01
5	1	Satomi Kubokura	Japan		56.91
6	7	Tatyana Azarova	Kazakhstan		57.90
7	6	Hanna Titimets	Ukraine		58.22
8	4	Déborah Rodríguez	Uruguay		59.21

Women's 400m Hurdles (continued)

Heat 2 — 17 August 2009

Position	Lane	Athlete	Country		Time
1	2	Nickiesha Wilson	Jamaica	Q	55.37
2	8	Anna Jesien	Poland	Q	55.57
3	7	Eilidh Child	Great Britain	Q	55.96
4	5	Sheena Tosta	United States	Q	56.00
5	3	Ieva Zunda	Latvia	q	56.05
6	1	Aurore Kassambara	France		57.25
7	4	Sayaka Aoki	Japan		1:03.56
	6	Tsvetelina Kirilova	Bulgaria		DQ

Heat 3 — 17 August 2009

Position	Lane	Athlete	Country		Time
1	6	Melaine Walker	Jamaica	Q	55.17
2	3	Natalya Antyukh	Russia	Q	55.40
3	7	Perri Shakes-Drayton	Great Britain	Q	56.49
4	5	Sara Petersen	Denmark	Q	56.51
5	4	Michelle Carey	Ireland		56.91
6	1	Kou Luogon	Liberia		57.70
7	2	Laia Forcadell	Spain		58.57
8	8	Merjen Ishangulyyeva	Turkmenistan		1:00.75

Heat 4 — 17 August 2009

Position	Lane	Athlete	Country		Time
1	3	Angela Morosanu	Romania	Q	54.70
2	7	Tiffany Williams	United States	Q	55.25
3	2	Zuzana Hejnová	Czech Republic	Q	55.68
4	5	Elena Churakova	Russia	q	56.13
5	4	Elodie Ouédraogo	Belgium	q	56.60
	6	Yolanda Osana	Dominican Republic		59.18
	8	Aïssata Soulama	Burkina Faso		59.20
	1	Amaka Ogoegbunam*	Nigeria		DQ

* results subsequently removed due to failed drugs test.

Heat 5 — 17 August 2009

Position	Lane	Athlete	Country		Time
1	5	Lashinda Demus	United States	Q	54.66
2	6	Anastasiya Rabchenyuk	Ukraine	Q	55.63
3	3	Natalya Ivanova	Russia	Q	56.11
4	2	Muizat Ajoke Odumosu	Nigeria	Q	56.62
5	4	Jonna Tilgner	Germany	q	56.73
6	8	Carole Kaboud Mebam	Cameroon		58.10
	7	Muna Jabir Adam	Sudan		DNS

Women's 400m Hurdles (continued)

Qualification for Final: first two in each quarter-final plus the next two fastest finishers.

Semi-Final 1   18 August 2009

Position	Lane	Athlete	Country		Time
1	6	Melaine Walker	Jamaica	Q	53.26
2	3	Josanne Lucas	Trinidad & Tobago	Q	53.98
3	5	Angela Morosanu	Romania	q	54.15
4	4	Xiaoxiao Huang	China		55.40
5	7	Natalya Ivanova	Russia		56.08
6	8	Sheena Tosta	United States		56.31
7	2	Muizat Ajoke Odumosu	Nigeria		56.80
8	1	Elodie Ouédraogo	Belgium		57.58

Semi-Final 2   18 August 2009

Position	Lane	Athlete	Country		Time
1	3	Kaliese Spencer	Jamaica	Q	54.37
2	6	Anastasiya Rabchenyuk	Ukraine	Q	54.49
3	5	Tiffany Williams	United States	q	54.79
4	4	Anna Jesien	Poland		54.82
5	2	Elena Churakova	Russia		56.11
6	1	Ieva Zunda	Latvia		56.66
7	8	Perri Shakes-Drayton	Great Britain		57.57
8	7	Amaka Ogoegbunam	Nigeria		DQ

Semi-Final 3   18 August 2009

Position	Lane	Athlete	Country		Time
1	6	Lashinda Demus	United States	Q	54.25
2	5	Natalya Antyukh	Russia	Q	54.86
3	3	Nickiesha Wilson	Jamaica		54.89
4	4	Zuzana Hejnová	Czech Republic		54.99
5	8	Vania Stambolova	Bulgaria		56.12
6	7	Eilidh Child	Great Britain		56.21
7	1	Sara Petersen	Denmark		56.99
8	2	Jonna Tilgner	Germany		57.11

FINAL   20 August 2009

Position	Lane	Athlete	Country		Time
GOLD	4	Melaine Walker	Jamaica	CR	52.42
SILVER	5	Lashinda Demus	United States		52.96
BRONZE	3	Josanne Lucas	Trinidad & Tobago		53.20
4	6	Kaliese Spencer	Jamaica		53.56
5	2	Tiffany Williams	United States		53.83
6	7	Natalya Antyukh	Russia		54.11
7	8	Anastasiya Rabchenyuk	Ukraine		54.78
8	1	Angela Morosanu	Romania		55.04

Men's High Jump

Qualification for the Final: Minimum achieved height 2.30m or 12 best qualifiers.

Group A   19 August 2009

Position	Athlete	Country		Height
1	Kyriakos Ioannou	Cyprus	Q	2.30
2	Kabelo Kgosiemang	Botswana	Q	2.30
3	Yaroslav Rybakov	Russia	Q	2.30
4	Giulio Ciotti	Italy	q	2.27
5	Martijn Nuyens	Netherlands	q	2.27
6	Keith Moffatt	United States	q	2.27
7	Jaroslav Bába	Czech Republic	q	2.27
8	Konstadínos Baniótis	Greece		2.24
9	Trevor Barry	Bahamas		2.24
10	Andrey Tereshin	Russia		2.24
11	Tora Harris	United States		2.24
12	Andriy Protsenko	Ukraine		2.20
13	Grzegorz Sposób	Poland		2.20
14	Dragutin Topic	Serbia		2.15
	Sergey Zassimovich	Kazakhstan		DNS

Athlete	2.10	2.15	2.20	2.24	2.27	2.30
Kyriakos Ioannou	-	O	O	O	O	O
Kabelo Kgosiemang	-	O	O	O	XO	XO
Yaroslav Rybakov	-	-	O	O	O	XXO
Giulio Ciotti	-	O	O	O	O	XXX
Martijn Nuyens	O	O	O	O	O	XXX
Keith Moffatt	-	O	O	O	O	XXX
Jaroslav Bába	-	-	O	XO	O	XXX
Konstadínos Baniótis	-	O	O	O	XXX	
Trevor Barry	-	XO	O	O	XXX	
Andrey Tereshin	-	O	O	XO	XXX	
Tora Harris	-	O	XXO	XXO	X-	XX
Andriy Protsenko	O	XO	O	XXX		
Grzegorz Sposób	O	O	XO	XXX		
Dragutin Topic	-	XXO	XXX			
Sergey Zassimovich						

Group B   19 August 2009

Position	Athlete	Country		Height
1	Linus Thörnblad	Sweden	Q	2.30
2	Raul Spank	Germany	Q	2.30
3	Andra Manson	United States	Q	2.30
4	Ivan Ukhov	Russia	Q	2.30
5	Mickael Hanany	France	Q	2.30
6	Sylwester Bednarek	Poland	q	2.27
7	Jessé de Lima	Brazil		2.27
8	Donald Thomas	Bahamas		2.27
9	Yuriy Krymarenko	Ukraine		2.24
10	Oskari Frösén	Finland		2.24
11	Javier Bermejo	Spain		2.20
12	Naoyuki Daigo	Japan		2.20
13	Viktor Shapoval	Ukraine		2.20
14	Peter Horák	Slovakia		2.20
15	Artsiom Zaitsau	Belarus		2.15
15	Majed Aldin Gazal	Syria		2.15

Men's High Jump (continued)

Athlete	2.10	2.15	2.20	2.24	2.27	2.30
Linus Thörnblad	-	O	O	O	O	XO
Raul Spank	-	-	O	XO	XXO	XO
Andra Manson	-	O	O	XXO	XXO	XO
Ivan Ukhov	-	O	O	O	O	XXO
Mickael Hanany	-	O	O	XXO	O	XXO
Sylwester Bednarek	O	XO	O	O	O	XXX
Jessé de Lima	-	O	O	XXO	O	XXX
Donald Thomas	O	O	O	O	XO	XXX
Yuriy Krymarenko	O	O	O	XO	XXX	
Oskari Frösén	-	O	-	XXO	XX-	X
Javier Bermejo	O	O	O	X-	XX	
Naoyuki Daigo	-	O	O	XXX		
Viktor Shapoval	O	O	O	XXX		
Peter Horák	O	O	XXO	XXX		
Artsiom Zaitsau	-	O	XX			
Majed Aldin Gazal	O	O	XXX			

FINAL   21 August 2009

Position	Athlete	Country	Height
GOLD	Yaroslav Rybakov	Russia	2.32
SILVER	Kyriakos Ioannou	Cyprus	2.32
=BRONZE	Raul Spank	Germany	2.32
=BRONZE	Sylwester Bednarek	Poland	2.32
5	Jaroslav Bába	Czech Republic	2.23
6	Mickael Hanany	France	2.23
7	Martijn Nuyens	Netherlands	2.23
8	Linus Thörnblad	Sweden	2.23
9	Andra Manson	United States	2.23
10	Ivan Ukhov	Russia	2.23
11	Giulio Ciotti	Italy	2.23
12	Keith Moffatt	United States	2.23
13	Kabelo Kgosiemang	Botswana	2.18

Athlete	2.18	2.23	2.28	2.32	2.35
Yaroslav Rybakov	O	O	XO	O	XXX
Kyriakos Ioannou	O	O	XXO	O	XXX
Raul Spank	O	O	XXO	XO	XXX
Sylwester Bednarek	XO	O	XO	XO	XXX
Jaroslav Bába	O	O	XXX		
Mickael Hanany	O	O	XXX		
Martijn Nuyens	O	O	XXX		
Linus Thörnblad	O	O	XXX		
Andra Manson	XO	O	XXX		
Ivan Ukhov	O	XO	XXX		
Giulio Ciotti	XO	XXO	XXX		
Keith Moffatt	XO	XXO	XXX		
Kabelo Kgosiemang	XXO	XXX	XXX		

Women's High Jump

Qualification for the Final: Minimum achieved height 1.95m or 12 best qualifiers.

Group A 18 August 2009

Position	Athlete	Country		Height
1	Blanka Vlašic	Croatia	Q	1.95
2	Ruth Beitia	Spain	Q	1.95
3	Chaunté Howard Lowe	United States	Q	1.95
4	Meike Kröger	Germany	q	1.92
5	Melanie Melfort	France	q	1.92
6	Svetlana Shkolina	Russia	q	1.92
7	Marina Aitova	Kazakhstan		1.92
8	Anna Iljuštšenko	Estonia		1.89
9	Vita Palamar	Ukraine		1.89
10	Sharon Day	United States		1.89
11	Iva Straková	Czech Republic		1.89
12	Svetlana Radzivil	Uzbekistan		1.89
13	Levern Spencer	St Lucia		1.89
14	Noengrothai Chaipetch	Thailand		1.89
15	Caterine Ibargüen	Colombia		1.85
16	Deirdre Ryan	Ireland		1.85
17	Romary Rifka	Mexico		1.80

Athlete	1.80	1.85	1.89	1.92	1.95
Blanka Vlašic	-	O	O	O	O
Ruth Beitia	-	O	O	XO	O
Chaunté Howard Lowe	O	O	XO	O	O
Meike Kröger	O	O	O	O	XXX
Melanie Melfort	O	O	O	XO	XXX
Svetlana Shkolina	O	O	O	XO	XXX
Marina Aitova	O	O	XO	XO	XXX
Anna Iljuštšenko	O	O	O	XXX	
Vita Palamar	-	O	O	XXX	
Sharon Day	O	O	O	XXX	
Iva Straková	O	O	XO	XXX	
Svetlana Radzivil	O	O	XO	XXX	
Levern Spencer	-	O	XXO	XXX	
Noengrothai Chaipetch	XXO	O	XXO	XXX	
Caterine Ibargüen	O	XO	XXX		
Deirdre Ryan	O	XXO	XXX		
Romary Rifka	O	XXX			

Group B 18 August 2009

Position	Athlete	Country		Height
1	Ariane Friedrich	Germany	Q	1.95
2	Emma Green	Sweden	Q	1.95
3	Antonietta Di Martino	Italy	Q	1.95
4	Anna Chicherova	Russia	Q	1.95
5	Amy Acuff	United States	Q	1.95
6	Elena Slesarenko	Russia	Q	1.95
7	Adonía Steryíou	Greece		1.92
8	Venelina Veneva-Mateeva	Bulgaria		1.92
9	Kamila Stepaniuk	Poland		1.92
10	Petrina Price	Australia		1.89
11	Hanna Grobler	Finland		1.89
12	Nadiya Dusanova	Uzbekistan		1.89
13	Doreen Amata	Nigeria		1.85
14	Stine Kufaas	Norway		1.85
15	Yekaterina Yevseyeva	Kazakhstan		1.85
	Nhung Bui Thi	Vietnam		-

Women's High Jump (continued)

Athlete	1.80	1.85	1.89	1.92	1.95
Ariane Friedrich	-	-	-	-	O
Emma Green	-	O	-	O	O
Antonietta Di Martino	O	O	XO	O	O
Anna Chicherova	-	O	O	XO	O
Amy Acuff	O	O	O	XXO	XO
Elena Slesarenko	-	O	O	XXO	XXO
Adonía Steryíou	XO	O	O	XO	XXX
Venelina Veneva-Mateeva	O	XO	O	XXO	XXX
Kamila Stepaniuk	O	O	XXO	XXO	XXX
Petrina Price	O	O	O	XXX	
Hanna Grobler	O	O	XO	XXX	
Nadiya Dusanova	O	O	XXO	XXX	
Doreen Amata	O	O	XXX		
Stine Kufaas	O	XO	XXX		
Yekaterina Yevseyeva	XO	XO	XXX		
Nhung Bui Thi	XXX				

FINAL 20 August 2009

Position	Athlete	Country	Height
GOLD	Blanka Vlašic	Croatia	2.04
SILVER	Anna Chicherova	Russia	2.02
BRONZE	Ariane Friedrich	Germany	2.02
4	Antonietta Di Martino	Italy	1.99
5	Ruth Beitia	Spain	1.99
6	Svetlana Shkolina	Russia	1.96
7	Emma Green	Sweden	1.96
8	Chaunté Howard Lowe	United States	1.96
9	Melanie Melfort	France	1.92
10	Elena Slesarenko	Russia	1.92
11	Meike Kröger	Germany	1.87
12	Amy Acuff	United States	1.87

Athlete	1.87	1.92	1.96	1.99	2.02	2.04	2.06	2.10
Blanka Vlašic	O	O	O	O	XO	XO	-	XXX
Anna Chicherova	O	O	XO	O	O	XXX		
Ariane Friedrich	-	O	-	O	XXO	XX-	x	
Antonietta Di Martino	O	O	XO	XO	XXX			
Ruth Beitia	O	O	O	XXO	XXX			
Svetlana Shkolina	O	O	O	XXX				
Emma Green	O	O	XO	XXX				
Chaunté Howard Lowe	O	O	XO	XXX				
Melanie Melfort	XO	O	XXX					
Elena Slesarenko	O	XXO	XXX					
Meike Kröger	O	XXX						
Amy Acuff	XXO	XXX						

Men's Pole Vault

Qualification for the Final: Minimum achieved height 5.75m or 12 best qualifiers.

Group A   20 August 2009

Position	Athlete	Country		Height
1	Steven Hooker	Australia	q	5.65
2	Romain Mesnil	France	q	5.65
3	Maksym Mazuryk	Ukraine	q	5.65
4	Damiel Dossévi	France	q	5.65
5	Giuseppe Gibilisco	Italy	q	5.65
6	Malte Mohr	Germany	q	5.65
7	Aleksandr Gripich	Russia	q	5.65
8	Derek Miles	United States	q	5.55
9	Jeremy Scott	United States		5.55
10	Konstadínos Filippídis	Greece		5.55
11	Yoo Suk Kim	South Korea		5.55
12	Igor Pavlov	Russia		5.55
13	Spas Bukhalov	Bulgaria		5.40
14	Jan Kudlicka	Czech Republic		5.40
15	Luke Cutts	Great Britain		5.40
16	Yavgeniy Olhovsky	Israel		5.40
17	Takafumi Suzuki	Japan		5.25
	Jesper Fritz	Sweden		-

Athlete	5.25	5.40	5.55	5.65
Steven Hooker	-	-	-	O
Romain Mesnil	-	-	XO	O
Maksym Mazuryk	-	O	XO	O
Damiel Dossévi	-	O	O	XO
Giuseppe Gibilisco	-	O	O	XXO
Malte Mohr	-	-	XO	XXO
Aleksandr Gripich	O	O	XO	XXO
Derek Miles	-	-	O	XXX
Jeremy Scott	-	O	XO	XXX
Konstadínos Filippídis	O	O	XXO	XXX
Yoo Suk Kim	XO	O	XXO	XXX
Igor Pavlov	-	XO	XXO	XXX
Spas Bukhalov	-	XO	-	XXX
Jan Kudlicka	-	XO	XXX	
Luke Cutts	-	XO	XXX	
Yavgeniy Olhovsky	XO	XO	XXX	
Takafumi Suzuki	XO	XXX		
Jesper Fritz	-	x		

Men's Pole Vault (continued)

Group B   20 August 2009

Position	Athlete	Country		Height
1	Renaud Lavillenie	France	q	5.65
2	Alexander Straub	Germany	q	5.65
3	Steven Lewis	Great Britain	q	5.65
4	Alhaji Jeng	Sweden	q	5.65
5	Kevin Rans	Belgium	q	5.55
6	Daichi Sawano	Japan	q	5.55
7	Viktor Chistiakov	Russia	q	5.55
8	Björn Otto	Germany		5.55
9	Leonid Andreev	Uzbekistan		5.55
10	Eemeli Salomäki	Finland		5.40
11	Lukasz Michalski	Poland		5.40
12	Toby Stevenson	United States		5.40
13	Jurij Rovan	Slovenia		5.40
14	Denys Fedas	Ukraine		5.25
	Fábio Gomes da Silva	Brazil		-
	Oleksandr Korchmid	Ukraine		-
	Brad Walker	United States		DNS

Athlete	5.25	5.40	5.55	5.65
Renaud Lavillenie	-	O	O	O
Alexander Straub	-	-	O	O
Steven Lewis	-	O	XO	XXO
Alhaji Jeng	-	XO	XXO	XXO
Kevin Rans	-	O	O	XXX
Daichi Sawano	-	-	O	XXX
Viktor Chistiakov	-	-	O	XXX
Björn Otto	-	XO	XXO	XXX
Leonid Andreev	XXO	O	XXO	XXX
Eemeli Salomäki	O	O	XXX	
Lukász Michalski	-	O	XXX	
Toby Stevenson	-	XO	XXX	
Jurij Rovan	XO	XO	XXX	
Denys Fedas	O	XXX		
Fábio Gomes da Silva	-	XXX		
Oleksandr Korchmid	-	XXX		
Brad Walker				

Men's Pole Vault (continued)

FINAL 22 August 2009

Position	Athlete	Country	Height
GOLD	Steven Hooker	Australia	5.90
SILVER	Romain Mesnil	France	5.85
BRONZE	Renaud Lavillenie	France	5.80
4	Maksym Mazuryk	Ukraine	5.75
5	Aleksandr Gripich	Russia	5.75
6	Damiel Dossévi	France	5.75
7	Steven Lewis	Great Britain	5.65
8	Alexander Straub	Germany	5.65
9	Giuseppe Gibilisco	Italy	5.65
10	Daichi Sawano	Japan	5.50
11	Viktor Chistiakov	Russia	5.50
12	Kevin Rans	Belgium	5.50
13	Alhaji Jeng	Sweden	5.50
14	Malte Mohr	Germany	5.50
	Derek Miles	United States	-

Athlete	5.50	5.65	5.75	5.80	5.85	5.90	5.95
Steven Hooker	-	-	-	-	X-	O	-
Romain Mesnil	O	O	X-	O	O	X-	XX
Renaud Lavillenie	O	O	XXO	O	X-	X-	X
Maksym Mazuryk	O	XO	O	X-	XX		
Aleksandr Gripich	O	XXO	O	XXX			
Damiel Dossévi	O	O	XO	XXX			
Steven Lewis	XO	XO	XXX				
Alexander Straub	XO	XO	XXX				
Giuseppe Gibilisco	XO	XO	XX-	X			
Daichi Sawano	O	XXX					
Viktor Chistiakov	O	XXX					
Kevin Rans	XO	XXX					
Alhaji Jeng	XO	XXX					
Malte Mohr	XXO	XXX					
Derek Miles	XXX						

Women's Pole Vault

Qualification for the Final: Minimum achieved height 4.60m or 12 best qualifiers.

Group A 15 August 2009

Position	Athlete	Country		Height
1	Fabiana Murer	Brazil	q	4.55
2	Anna Rogowska	Poland	q	4.55
3	Yuliya Golubchikova	Russia	q	4.55
4	Kate Dennison	Great Britain	q	4.55
5	Anna Battke	Germany	q	4.55
6	Tatyana Polnova	Russia	q	4.55
7	Anna Giordano Bruno	Italy		4.50
8	Nicole Büchler	Switzerland		4.50
9	Joanna Piwowarska	Poland		4.25
10	Stacy Dragila	United States		4.25
11	Mariánna Zaharíadi	Cyprus		4.25
12	Sandra-Helena Tavares	Portugal		4.25
13	Télie Mathiot	France		4.10
14	Romana Malácová	Czech Republic		4.10
	Shuying Gao	China		-

Athlete	4.10	4.25	4.40	4.50	4.55
Fabiana Murer	-	-	O	O	O
Anna Rogowska	-	-	O	-	O
Yuliya Golubchikova	-	-	O	-	O
Kate Dennison	O	O	O	XO	O
Anna Battke	-	O	O	XO	O
Tatyana Polnova	O	XO	XO	XO	O
Anna Giordano Bruno	O	XO	XO	O	XXX
Nicole Büchler	O	O	O	XO	XXX
Joanna Piwowarska	O	O	XXX		
Stacy Dragila	-	O	XXX		
Mariánna Zaharíadi	XO	XO	XXX		
Sandra-Helena Tavares	XO	XXO	XXX		
Télie Mathiot	O	XXX			
Romana Malácová	XO	XXX			
Shuying Gao	-	XXX			

Women's Pole Vault (continued)

Group B 15 August 2009

Position	Athlete	Country		Height
1	Silke Spiegelburg	Germany	q	4.55
2	Elena Isinbaeva	Russia	q	4.55
3	Chelsea Johnson	United States	q	4.55
4	Monika Pyrek	Poland	q	4.55
5	Aleksandra Kiryashova	Russia	q	4.55
6	Kristina Gadschiew	Germany	q	4.50
7	Jillian Schwartz	United States		4.50
8	Kelsie Hendry	Canada		4.40
9	Jirina Ptácniková	Czech Republic		4.40
10	Ling Li	China		4.40
11	Nikoléta Kiriakopoúlou	Greece		4.40
12	Minna Nikkanen	Finland		4.40
13	Naroa Agirre	Spain		4.40
14	Roslinda Samsu	Malaysia		4.25
15	Takayo Kondo	Japan		4.10
16	Eun-ji Lim	South Korea		4.10

Athlete	4.10	4.25	4.40	4.50	4.55
Silke Spiegelburg	-	-	O	O	O
Elena Isinbaeva	-	-	-	-	O
Chelsea Johnson	-	XXO	O	O	O
Monika Pyrek	-	-	O	XO	XO
Aleksandra Kiryashova	-	O	O	XO	XXO
Kristina Gadschiew	-	O	O	O	XXX
Jillian Schwartz	-	O	XO	XO	XXX
Kelsie Hendry	-	O	O	XXX	
Jirina Ptácniková	-	O	O	XXX	
Ling Li	O	O	XO	XXX	
Nikoléta Kiriakopoúlou	O	XO	XO	XXX	
Minna Nikkanen	O	O	XXO	XXX	
Naroa Agirre	O	XO	XXO	XXX	
Roslinda Samsu	XO	XO	XXX		
Takayo Kondo	O	XXX			
Eun-ji Lim	XO	XXX			

Women's Pole Vault (continued)

FINAL 17 August 2009

Position	Athlete	Country	Height
GOLD	Anna Rogowska	Poland	4.75
=SILVER	Monika Pyrek	Poland	4.65
=SILVER	Chelsea Johnson	United States	4.65
4	Silke Spiegelburg	Germany	4.65
5	Fabiana Murer	Brazil	4.55
6	Kate Dennison	Great Britain	4.55
7	Anna Battke	Germany	4.40
8	Tatyana Polnova	Russia	4.40
9	Aleksandra Kiryashova	Russia	4.40
10	Kristina Gadschiew	Germany	4.40
	Elena Isinbaeva	Russia	-
	Yuliya Golubchikova	Russia	DNS

Athlete	4.25	4.40	4.55	4.65	4.75	4.80
Anna Rogowska	-	O	O	XO	O	XXX
Monika Pyrek	-	O	O	O	XX-	X
Chelsea Johnson	-	O	O	O	XXX	
Silke Spiegelburg	-	O	XO	XO	XXX	
Fabiana Murer	-	O	O	XXX		
Kate Dennison	O	O	XO	XXX		
Anna Battke	-	O	XXX			
Tatyana Polnova	O	O	XXX			
Aleksandra Kiryashova	XO	XO	XXX			
Kristina Gadschiew	O	XXO	XXX			
Elena Isinbaeva	-	-	-	-	X-	XX
Yuliya Golubchikova						

Men's Long Jump

Qualification for the Final: Minimum achieved distance 8.15m or 12 best qualifiers.

Group A   20 August 2009

Position	Athlete	Country	Wind		Distance
1	Dwight Phillips	United States	0.50	Q	8.44
2	Mitchell Watt	Australia	0.30	q	8.14
3	Christopher Tomlinson	Great Britain	0.30	q	8.06
4	Loúis Tsátoumas	Greece	1.00	q	8.01
5	Jinzhe Li	China	0.80		8.01
6	Tommi Evilä	Finland	1.10		8.01
7	Deokhyeon Kim	South Korea	-0.70		7.99
8	Viktor Kuznyetsov	Ukraine	1.70		7.98
9	Sebastian Bayer	Germany	0.90		7.98
10	Kafétien Gomis	France	0.20		7.90
11	Alain Bailey	Jamaica	0.10		7.88
12	Andriy Makarchev	Ukraine	-0.40		7.87
13	Luis Felipe Méliz	Spain	-0.70		7.87
14	Stephan Louw	Namibia	-0.40		7.74
15	Aleksandr Menkov	Russia	0.60		7.72
16	Ibrahin Camejo	Cuba	1.40		7.71
17	Štepán Wagner	Czech Republic	0.30		7.68
18	Mohamed Salman Al Khuwalidi	Saudi Arabia	-0.30		7.66
19	Nikolay Atanasov	Bulgaria	0.60		7.63
20	Hugo Chila	Ecuador	1.00		7.54
21	Konstantin Safronov	Kazakhstan	2.60		7.54
22	Daisuke Arakawa	Japan	0.30		7.53
	Henry Dagmil	Philippines			-

Athlete	Jump 1	Jump 2	Jump 3
Dwight Phillips	8.44	-	-
Mitchell Watt	8.14	X	-
Christopher Tomlinson	8.06	8.02	8.00
Loúis Tsátoumas	8.01	7.98	7.86
Jinzhe Li	8.01	7.92	7.90
Tommi Evilä	X	7.84	8.01
Deokhyeon Kim	7.62	7.89	7.99
Viktor Kuznyetsov	7.98	7.87	7.95
Sebastian Bayer	7.98	X	X
Kafétien Gomis	7.82	7.90	7.68
Alain Bailey	7.63	7.70	7.88
Andriy Makarchev	X	7.68	7.87
Luis Felipe Méliz	7.87	X	X
Stephan Louw	X	7.74	7.69
Aleksandr Menkov	7.72	X	X
Ibrahin Camejo	7.69	7.71	7.57
Štepán Wagner	7.52	7.68	7.49
Mohamed Salman Al Khuwalidi	X	7.37	7.66
Nikolay Atanasov	7.63	X	X
Hugo Chila	7.29	7.54	-
Konstantin Safronov	X	7.54	7.29
Daisuke Arakawa	7.39	7.50	7.53
Henry Dagmil	X	X	X

Men's Long Jump (continued)

Group B   20 August 2009

Position	Athlete	Country	Wind		Distance
1	Greg Rutherford	Great Britain	-0.50	Q	8.30
2	Godfrey Khotso Mokoena	South Africa	0.70	Q	8.29
3	Irving Saladino	Panama	0.50	Q	8.16
4	Fabrice Lapierre	Australia	-0.20	q	8.14
5	Brian Johnson	United States	0.80	q	8.09
6	Yahya Berrabah	Morocco	1.50	q	8.08
7	Salim Sdiri	France	0.40	q	8.04
8	Gable Garenamotse	Botswana	-0.40	q	8.03
9	Hussein Taher Al-Sabee	Saudi Arabia	0.40		7.99
10	Ndiss Kaba Badji	Senegal	0.10		7.98
11	Nicholas Gordon	Jamaica	0.10		7.92
12	Olexiy Lukashevych	Ukraine	1.00		7.87
13	Roman Novotný	Czech Republic	0.50		7.86
14	Stanley Gbagbeke	Nigeria	-0.30		7.82
15	Michel Tornéus	Sweden	0.80		7.78
16	Morten Jensen	Denmark	0.50		7.75
17	Tyrone Smith	Bermuda	-0.10		7.72
18	Nils Winter	Germany	0.00		7.69
19	Miguel Pate	United States	-0.10		7.61
20	Yochai Halevi	Israel	0.70		7.42
	Carlos Jorge	Dominican Republic			-
	Clayton Latham	St Vincent & the Grenadines			-

Athlete	Jump 1	Jump 2	Jump 3
Greg Rutherford	8.3	-	-
Godfrey Khotso Mokoena	X	8.29	-
Irving Saladino	8	8.16	-
Fabrice Lapierre	8.14	-	-
Brian Johnson	X	7.94	8.09
Yahya Berrabah	8.08	X	X
Salim Sdiri	7.88	X	8.04
Gable Garenamotse	7.81	8.03	8.01
Hussein Taher Al-Sabee	7.89	7.99	X
Ndiss Kaba Badji	7.95	7.98	7.61
Nicholas Gordon	X	7.72	7.92
Olexiy Lukashevych	X	7.87	6.18
Roman Novotný	X	7.86	X
Stanley Gbagbeke	7.82	X	X
Michel Tornéus	7.78	7.63	7.78
Morten Jensen	7.69	7.75	7.71
Tyrone Smith	7.62	7.72	7.71
Nils Winter	X	X	7.69
Miguel Pate	X	X	7.61
Yochai Halevi	7.42	7.39	X
Carlos Jorge	X	X	X
Clayton Latham	X	X	X

Men's Long Jump (continued)

FINAL 22 August 2009

Position	Athlete	Country	Wind	Distance
GOLD	Dwight Phillips	United States	0.10	8.54
SILVER	Godfrey Khotso Mokoena	South Africa	0.10	8.47
BRONZE	Mitchell Watt	Australia	-0.40	8.37
4	Fabrice Lapierre	Australia	-0.20	8.21
5	Greg Rutherford	Great Britain	0.70	8.17
6	Salim Sdiri	France	0.20	8.07
7	Gable Garenamotse	Botswana	-0.20	8.06
8	Christopher Tomlinson	Great Britain	-0.20	8.06
9	Brian Johnson	United States	0.10	7.86
10	Yahya Berrabah	Morocco	0.40	7.83
11	Loúis Tsátoumas	Greece	0.40	7.59
	Irving Saladino	Panama		-

Athlete	Jump 1	Jump 2	Jump 3	Jump 4	Jump 5
Dwight Phillips	8.40	8.54	8.37	8.25	-
Godfrey Khotso Mokoena	X	8.47	8.31	8.19	X
Mitchell Watt	8.28	X	X	X	8.37
Fabrice Lapierre	8.21	7.77	8.19	X	8.21
Greg Rutherford	7.83	7.96	X	8.05	8.15
Salim Sdiri	7.78	X	7.99	8.07	7.92
Gable Garenamotse	8.06	8.04	X	7.77	7.83
Christopher Tomlinson	8.02	7.93	7.93	7.66	8.06
Brian Johnson	6.30	X	7.86		
Yahya Berrabah	5.91	X	7.83		
Loúis Tsátoumas	X	7.59	X		
Irving Saladino	X	X	X		

Women's Long Jump

Qualification for the Final: Minimum achieved distance 6.75m or 12 best qualifiers.

Group A   21 August 2009

Position	Athlete	Country	Wind		Distance
1	Naide Gomes	Portugal	0.20	Q	6.86
2	Maurren Higa Maggi	Brazil	0.30	q	6.68
3	Nastassia Mironchyk	Belarus	-1.10	q	6.55
4	Teresa Dobija	Poland	-0.10	q	6.55
5	Brianna Glenn	United States	-0.90	q	6.53
6	Shara Proctor	Anguilla	-0.30	q	6.52
7	Elena Sokolova	Russia	-1.20		6.51
8	Soon-ok Jung	South Korea	0.00		6.49
9	Ruky Abdulai	Canada	-1.70		6.45
10	Irina Meleshina	Russia	0.10		6.39
11	Funmi Jimoh	United States	-0.80		6.34
12	Bianca Kappler	Germany	0.20		6.29
13	Viktoriya Molchanova	Ukraine	0.10		6.29
14	Ola Sesay	Sierra Leone	-0.90		6.23
15	Sachiko Masumi	Japan	0.50		6.23
16	Jana Veldáková	Slovakia	-0.90		6.16
17	Sirkka-Liisa Kivine	Estonia	-1.00		6.10
18	Nina Kolaric	Slovenia	-0.50		6.00

Athlete	Jump 1	Jump 2	Jump 3
Naide Gomes	6.60	6.86	-
Maurren Higa Maggi	6.68	6.58	6.30
Nastassia Mironchyk	6.08	6.55	6.42
Teresa Dobija	6.55	X	X
Brianna Glenn	X	X	6.53
Shara Proctor	6.43	6.52	6.47
Elena Sokolova	6.44	6.51	6.46
Soon-ok Jung	6.45	6.31	6.49
Ruky Abdulai	6.37	6.45	X
Irina Meleshina	6.39	6.14	X
Funmi Jimoh	X	X	6.34
Bianca Kappler	6.26	6.21	6.29
Viktoriya Molchanova	6.29	6.20	X
Ola Sesay	5.92	6.23	6.19
Sachiko Masumi	6.23	6.06	6.13
Jana Veldáková	X	6.16	X
Sirkka-Liisa Kivine	X	5.92	6.10
Nina Kolaric	X	X	6.00

Women's Long Jump (continued)

Group B   21 August 2009

Position	Athlete	Country	Wind		Distance
1	Brittney Reese	United States	0.00	Q	6.78
2	Tatyana Lebedeva	Russia	0.10	Q	6.76
3	Olga Kucherenko	Russia	0.00	q	6.68
4	Karin Mey Melis	Turkey	-0.50	q	6.67
5	Keila Costa	Brazil	-0.50	q	6.66
6	Ksenija Balta	Estonia	0.50	q	6.59
7	Jovanee Jarrett	Jamaica	1.30		6.43
8	Viktoriya Rybalko	Ukraine	-0.60		6.40
9	Éloyse Lesueur	France	0.40		6.40
10	Natallia Dobrynska	Ukraine	-0.70		6.38
11	Yarianny Argüelles	Cuba	-0.80		6.32
12	Melanie Bauschke	Germany	-0.70		6.32
13	Margrethe Renstrøm	Norway	-0.10		6.31
14	Marestella Torres	Philippines	-0.70		6.22
15	Janice Josephs	South Africa	-0.10		6.22
16	Beatrice Marscheck	Germany	-0.70		6.19
17	Alice Falaiye	Canada	-0.90		6.09
18	Patricia Sylvester	Grenada	0.30		5.92
	Blessing Okagbare	Nigeria			DNS

Athlete	Jump 1	Jump 2	Jump 3
Brittney Reese	6.78	-	-
Tatyana Lebedeva	6.76	-	-
Olga Kucherenko	6.68	6.65	-
Karin Mey Melis	6.57	6.61	6.67
Keila Costa	6.66	X	6.55
Ksenija Balta	X	6.23	6.59
Jovanee Jarrett	6.29	6.42	6.43
Viktoriya Rybalko	6.40	6.18	X
Éloyse Lesueur	6.40	6.09	6.11
Natallia Dobrynska	6.32	6.38	6.36
Yarianny Argüelles	6.31	5.97	6.32
Melanie Bauschke	6.32	6.13	6.14
Margrethe Renstrøm	6.31	X	6.10
Marestella Torres	6.21	6.03	6.22
Janice Josephs	6.22	5.75	X
Beatrice Marscheck	6.07	X	6.19
Alice Falaiye	6.07	6.09	X
Patricia Sylvester	5.92	5.80	X
Blessing Okagbare			

Women's Long Jump (continued)

FINAL 23 August 2009

Position	Athlete	Country	Wind	Distance
GOLD	Brittney Reese	United States	1.00	7.10
SILVER	Tatyana Lebedeva	Russia	1.00	6.97
BRONZE	Karin Mey Melis	Turkey	0.40	6.80
4	Naide Gomes	Portugal	0.50	6.77
5	Olga Kucherenko	Russia	1.10	6.77
6	Shara Proctor	Anguilla	1.20	6.71
7	Maurren Higa Maggi	Brazil	0.70	6.68
8	Ksenija Balta	Estonia	0.30	6.62
9	Brianna Glenn	United States	-0.10	6.59
10	Teresa Dobija	Poland	0.70	6.58
11	Nastassia Mironchyk	Belarus	0.00	6.29
	Keila Costa	Brazil		-

Athlete	Jump 1	Jump 2	Jump 3	Jump 4	Jump 5
Brittney Reese	6.92	6.85	7.10	X	X
Tatyana Lebedeva	6.78	6.97	X	X	X
Karin Mey Melis	6.76	X	6.80	X	X
Naide Gomes	6.77	X	6.52	6.68	6.69
Olga Kucherenko	X	X	6.77	6.63	X
Shara Proctor	X	6.56	6.71	X	X
Maurren Higa Maggi	6.68	X	X	6.64	-
Ksenija Balta	6.62	6.52	X	6.15	6.60
Brianna Glenn	X	6.59	X		
Teresa Dobija	X	6.58	6.51		
Nastassia Mironchyk	X	6.24	6.29		
Keila Costa	X	X	X		

Men's Triple Jump

Qualification for the Final: Minimum achieved distance 17.15m or 12 best qualifiers.

Group A   16 August 2009

Position	Athlete	Country	Wind		Distance
1	Phillips Idowu	Great Britain	0.3	Q	17.32
2	Leevan Sands	Bahamas	-0.4	Q	17.20
3	Arnie David Girat	Cuba	-0.2	Q	17.15
4	Momchil Karailiev	Bulgaria	0.0	q	17.07
5	Igor Spasovkhodskiy	Russia	0.1	q	17.02
6	Nathan Douglas	Great Britain	0.0	q	17.00
7	Dmitrij Valukevic	Slovakia	-0.8	q	16.96
8	Onochie Achike	Great Britain	0.3		16.94
9	Fabrizio Schembri	Italy	-0.4		16.88
10	Yoandris Betanzos	Cuba	0.0		16.77
11	Dzmitry Dziatsuk	Belarus	0.5		16.58
12	Deokhyeon Kim	South Korea	-0.2		16.58
13	Yevgen Semenenko	Ukraine	0.2		16.54
14	Julian Reid	Jamaica	0.7		16.49
15	Jefferson Sabino	Brazil	-0.6		16.34
16	Samyr Laine	Haiti	0.0		16.34
17	Kenta Bell	United States	0.0		16.32
18	Mohamed Yusuf Salman	Brunei	0.2		16.05
19	Vladimir Letnicov	Moldova	0.0		15.88
20	Fabrizio Donato	Italy	0.0		15.81
21	Andrés Capellán	Spain	-0.5		15.80
22	Charles Michael Friedek	Germany			-
23	Yochai Halevi	Israel			DNS

Athlete	Jump 1	Jump 2	Jump 3
Phillips Idowu	17.10	17.32	-
Leevan Sands	17.02	16.84	17.20
Arnie David Girat	16.92	X	17.15
Momchil Karailiev	X	16.87	17.07
Igor Spasovkhodskiy	16.87	16.84	17.02
Nathan Douglas	17.00	X	16.90
Dmitrij Valukevic	16.96	16.69	16.85
Onochie Achike	16.88	16.94	X
Fabrizio Schembri	16.88	16.88	X
Yoandris Betanzos	X	X	16.77
Dzmitry Dziatsuk	16.58	16.15	X
Deokhyeon Kim	X	16.02	16.58
Yevgen Semenenko	16.29	16.52	16.54
Julian Reid	16.41	16.49	16.16
Jefferson Sabino	X	16.24	16.34
Samyr Laine	X	16.06	16.34
Kenta Bell	X	16.32	16.18
Mohamed Yusuf Salman	X	16.05	15.71
Vladimir Letnicov	15.28	15.77	15.88
Fabrizio Donato	15.81	X	X
Andrés Capellán	15.35	15.80	15.67
Charles Michael Friedek	X	X	X
Yochai Halevi			

Men's Triple Jump (continued)

Group B   16 August 2009

Position	Athlete	Country	Wind		Distance
1	Nelson Évora	Portugal	0.6	Q	17.44
2	Yanxi Li	China	0.9	Q	17.27
3	Teddy Tamgho	France	0.2	q	17.11
4	Jadel Gregório	Brazil	0.8	q	17.06
5	Alexis Copello	Cuba	0.2	q	16.99
6	Brandon Roulhac	United States	0.5		16.94
7	Tosin Oke	Nigeria	0.5		16.87
8	Randy Lewis	Grenada	0.2		16.73
9	Mykola Savolaynen	Ukraine	0.2		16.72
10	Hugo Chila	Ecuador	0.2		16.70
11	Hugo Mamba-Schlick	Cameroon	-0.2		16.63
12	Walter Davis	United States	0.4		16.62
13	Alwyn Jones	Australia	0.3		16.57
14	Viktor Yastrebov	Ukraine	-0.7		16.31
15	Evgeniy Plotnir	Russia	-0.5		16.29
16	Dimítrios Tsiámis	Greece	0.2		16.23
17	Daniele Greco	Italy	0.1		16.18
18	Yevgeniy Ektov	Kazakhstan	0.0		16.13
19	Mantas Dilys	Lithuania	0.7		16.09
20	Lauri Leis	Estonia	0.4		15.98
21	Leonardo Elisiario dos Santos	Brazil	0.7		15.95
22	Hung Nguyen Van	Vietnam	-0.3		15.56
23	Kuan Wong Si	Macau	0.0		14.78

Athlete	Jump 1	Jump 2	Jump 3
Nelson Évora	17.44	-	-
Yanxi Li	16.78	17.27	-
Teddy Tamgho	X	17.11	X
Jadel Gregório	17.06	X	15.48
Alexis Copello	16.99	16.78	16.98
Brandon Roulhac	16.78	16.56	16.94
Tosin Oke	16.87	16.82	X
Randy Lewis	16.73	13.38	16.52
Mykola Savolaynen	16.68	16.64	16.72
Hugo Chila	16.34	16.70	16.52
Hugo Mamba-Schlick	16.21	16.06	16.63
Walter Davis	16.27	16.62	15.87
Alwyn Jones	16.20	16.57	16.50
Viktor Yastrebov	X	16.31	16.15
Evgeniy Plotnir	16.13	16.29	15.96
Dimítrios Tsiámis	15.68	16.23	X
Daniele Greco	16.18	X	X
Yevgeniy Ektov	16.13	X	16.01
Mantas Dilys	16.09	16.02	15.70
Lauri Leis	15.28	15.98	15.84
Leonardo Elisiario dos Santos	15.95	X	15.85
Hung Nguyen Van	X	15.03	15.56
Kuan Wong Si	X	14.78	14.71

Men's Triple Jump (continued)

FINAL 18 August 2009

Position	Athlete	Country	Wind	Distance
GOLD	Phillips Idowu	Great Britain	0.0	17.73
SILVER	Nelson Évora	Portugal	0.1	17.55
BRONZE	Alexis Copello	Cuba	0.1	17.36
4	Leevan Sands	Bahamas	-0.5	17.32
5	Arnie David Girat	Cuba	0.0	17.26
6	Yanxi Li	China	1.1	17.23
7	Igor Spasovkhodskiy	Russia	-0.3	16.91
8	Jadel Gregório	Brazil	-0.1	16.89
9	Momchil Karailiev	Bulgaria	0.3	16.82
10	Nathan Douglas	Great Britain	-0.1	16.79
11	Teddy Tamgho	France	-0.6	16.79
12	Dmitrij Valukevic	Slovakia	0.3	16.54

Athlete	Jump 1	Jump 2	Jump 3	Jump 4	Jump 5	Jump 6
Phillips Idowu	17.51	17.44	17.73	X	X	X
Nelson Évora	17.54	X	17.38	X	17.33	17.55
Alexis Copello	17.06	17.19	14.82	X	17.04	17.36
Leevan Sands	17.20	17.08	16.96	17.05	17.32	16.99
Arnie David Girat	17.26	17.18	X	17.19	17.01	17.06
Yanxi Li	16.95	16.92	14.23	17.23	X	16.75
Igor Spasovkhodskiy	16.73	16.91	14.66	14.75	16.37	X
Jadel Gregório	X	16.89	16.84	16.70	X	X
Momchil Karailiev	16.82	16.78	16.81			
Nathan Douglas	16.78	15.44	16.79			
Teddy Tamgho	X	16.79	X			
Dmitrij Valukevic	X	X	16.54			

Women's Triple Jump

Qualification for the Final: Minimum achieved distance 14.45m or 12 best qualifiers.

Group A 1508/2009

Position	Athlete	Country	Wind		Distance
1	Yargeris Savigne	Cuba	-1.5	Q	14.53
2	Tatyana Lebedeva	Russia	-1.2	Q	14.45
3	Teresa Nzola Meso	France	0.9	q	14.32
4	Anna Pyatykh	Russia	0.2	q	14.27
5	Dana Veldáková	Slovakia	-1.0	q	14.25
6	Yamilé Aldama	Sudan	0.1		14.11
7	Petia Dacheva	Bulgaria	0.6		14.11
8	Kimberly Williams	Jamaica	0.9		14.08
9	Snežana Rodic	Slovenia	0.0		13.92
10	Svetlana Bolshakova	Belgium	0.3		13.89
11	Magdelín Martínez	Italy	-0.4		13.87
12	Martina Šestáková	Czech Republic	-0.9		13.84
13	Irina Litvinenko	Kazakhstan	0.1		13.82
14	Shani Marks	United States	0.3		13.67
15	Paraskeví Papahrístou	Greece	0.8		13.58
16	Liliya Kulyk	Ukraine	-1.8		13.41
17	Erica McLain	United States	-0.3		13.39
18	Patricia Sylvester	Grenada	0.9		13.22

Athlete	Jump 1	Jump 2	Jump 3
Yargeris Savigne	X	14.53	-
Tatyana Lebedeva	14.45	-	-
Teresa Nzola Meso	X	13.87	14.32
Anna Pyatykh	X	14.01	14.27
Dana Veldáková	X	14.25	14.20
Yamilé Aldama	13.96	13.83	14.11
Petia Dacheva	13.63	13.56	14.11
Kimberly Williams	X	14.08	X
Snežana Rodic	13.92	X	X
Svetlana Bolshakova	13.89	X	13.73
Magdelín Martínez	13.80	13.72	13.87
Martina Šestáková	X	13.69	13.84
Irina Litvinenko	13.63	13.77	13.82
Shani Marks	X	X	13.67
Paraskeví Papahrístou	13.58	X	13.58
Liliya Kulyk	13.37	13.41	13.41
Erica McLain	13.34	X	13.39
Patricia Sylvester	13.22	13.05	12.98

Women's Triple Jump (continued)

Group B 15 August 2009

Position	Athlete	Country	Wind		Distance
1	Limei Xie	China	0.5	Q	14.62
2	Mabel Gay	Cuba	-1.2	Q	14.53
3	Biljana Topic	Serbia	0.3	q	14.37
4	Cristina Bujin	Romania	0.3	q	14.29
5	Trecia Smith	Jamaica	0.1	q	14.21
6	Gisele de Oliveira	Brazil	0.6	q	14.14
7	Olga Rypakova	Kazakhstan	-0.7	q	14.13
8	Malgorzata Trybanska	Poland	1.2		14.06
9	Shakeema Walker-Welsch	United States	3.2		14.01
10	Svitlana Mamyeyeva	Ukraine	0.7		13.92
11	Natalia Iastrebova	Ukraine	-0.8		13.74
12	Athanasía Pérra	Greece	0.2		13.69
13	Marija Šestak	Slovenia	-0.8		13.69
14	Nadezhda Alekhina	Russia	-0.7		13.60
15	Vanessa Gladone	France	0.8		13.51
16	Katja Demut	Germany	-1.3		11.38
	Françoise Mbango Etone	Cameroon			DNS

Athlete	Jump 1	Jump 2	Jump 3
Limei Xie	14.62	-	-
Mabel Gay	X	14.53	-
Biljana Topic	14.37	13.80	-
Cristina Bujin	14.22	12.82	14.29
Trecia Smith	X	X	14.21
Gisele de Oliveira	13.70	13.79	14.14
Olga Rypakova	14.02	X	14.13
Malgorzata Trybanska	X	14.06	13.80
Shakeema Walker-Welsch	X	X	14.01
Svitlana Mamyeyeva	13.92	13.35	13.70
Natalia Iastrebova	X	13.58	13.74
Athanasía Pérra	13.69	X	X
Marija Šestak	X	X	13.69
Nadezhda Alekhina	X	X	13.60
Vanessa Gladone	13.51	13.42	13.40
Katja Demut	X	11.38	X
Françoise Mbango Etone			

Women's Triple Jump (continued)

FINAL 17 August 2009

Position	Athlete	Country	Wind	Distance
GOLD	Yargeris Savigne	Cuba	1.3	14.95
SILVER	Mabel Gay	Cuba	-0.2	14.61
BRONZE	Anna Pyatykh	Russia	-0.4	14.58
4	Biljana Topic	Serbia	-0.1	14.52
5	Trecia Smith	Jamaica	-0.2	14.48
6	Tatyana Lebedeva	Russia	0.0	14.37
7	Cristina Bujin	Romania	-0.2	14.26
8	Dana Veldáková	Slovakia	-0.2	14.25
9	Limei Xie	China	-0.1	14.16
10	Olga Rypakova	Kazakhstan	-0.2	13.91
11	Teresa Nzola Meso	France	0.0	13.79
12	Gisele de Oliveira	Brazil	-0.2	13.19

Athlete	Jump 1	Jump 2	Jump 3	Jump 4	Jump 5	Jump 6
Yargeris Savigne	14.45	14.14	14.89	14.85	14.95	0.36
Mabel Gay	13.87	14.50	X	14.61	14.48	14.04
Anna Pyatykh	13.72	14.23	13.66	14.58	14.46	14.53
Biljana Topic	14.21	14.38	14.27	14.52	14.43	14.10
Trecia Smith	14.31	X	X	14.41	14.48	X
Tatyana Lebedeva	X	14.37	14.23	14.22	14.26	14.28
Cristina Bujin	14.26	14.00	14.03	14.20	14.16	14.15
Dana Veldáková	14.25	X	12.86	14.14	14.19	14.13
Limei Xie	14.16	11.46	14.06			
Olga Rypakova	X	13.91	13.71			
Teresa Nzola Meso	13.77	13.79	X			
Gisele de Oliveira	X	13.19	-			

Men's Shot Put

Qualification for the Final: Minimum achieved distance 20.30m or 12 best qualifiers.

Group A   15 August 2009

Position	Athlete	Country		Distance
1	Tomasz Majewski	Poland	Q	21.19
2	Pavel Lyzhyn	Belarus	Q	20.72
3	Christian Cantwell	United States	Q	20.63
4	Adam Nelson	United States	Q	20.50
5	Miroslav Vodovnik	Slovenia	q	20.22
6	Peter Sack	Germany	q	20.2
7	Pavel Sofin	Russia	q	20.16
8	Hamza Alic	Bosnia & Herzegovina	q	20.10
9	Sultan Abdulmajeed Alhabashi	Saudi Arabia		20.04
10	Justin Anlezark	Australia		19.94
11	Maris Urtans	Latvia		19.89
12	Dylan Armstrong	Canada		19.86
13	Carlos Véliz	Cuba		19.62
14	Nedžad Mulabegovic	Croatia		19.15
15	Valeriy Kokoyev	Russia		19.13
16	Yasser Ibrahim Farag	Egypt		18.69
17	Borja Vivas	Spain		18.38
18	Adriatik Hoxha	Albania		15.89

Athlete	Throw 1	Throw 2	Throw 3
Tomasz Majewski	21.19	-	-
Pavel Lyzhyn	X	20.72	-
Christian Cantwell	20.20	20.63	-
Adam Nelson	20.50	-	-
Miroslav Vodovnik	19.80	20.22	20.05
Peter Sack	20.09	20.20	19.98
Pavel Sofin	X	X	20.16
Hamza Alic	X	20.01	20.10
Sultan Abdulmajeed Alhabashi	19.91	X	20.04
Justin Anlezark	19.94	19.41	19.33
Maris Urtans	19.89	X	X
Dylan Armstrong	19.46	19.86	X
Carlos Véliz	18.82	19.62	19.48
Nedžad Mulabegovic	19.15	X	X
Valeriy Kokoyev	18.02	19.13	18.90
Yasser Ibrahim Farag	18.40	18.69	18.54
Borja Vivas	17.70	18.38	X
Adriatik Hoxha	15.78	15.89	X

Men's Shot Put (continued)

Group B   15 August 2009

Position	Athlete	Country		Distance
1	Andrei Mikhnevich	Belarus	Q	20.65
2	Ralf Bartels	Germany	Q	20.41
3	Reese Hoffa	United States	q	20.23
4	Carl Myerscough	Great Britain	q	20.17
5	Taavi Peetre	Estonia		19.91
6	Marco Fortes	Portugal		19.81
7	Manuel Martínez	Spain		19.80
8	Antonín Žalský	Czech Republic		19.77
9	Yury Bialou	Belarus		19.75
10	Asmir Kolašinac	Serbia		19.67
11	Lajos Kürthy	Hungary		19.64
12	Scott Martin	Australia		19.52
13	Daniel Taylor	United States		19.39
14	Yves Niaré	France		19.37
15	David Storl	Germany		19.19
16	Maksim Sidorov	Russia		18.92
17	Georgi Ivanov	Bulgaria		18.11
	Germán Lauro	Argentina		-

Athlete	Throw 1	Throw 2	Throw 3
Andrei Mikhnevich	20.65	-	-
Ralf Bartels	20.16	X	20.41
Reese Hoffa	20.23	19.90	X
Carl Myerscough	20.17	X	19.79
Taavi Peetre	19.91	19.79	19.69
Marco Fortes	18.70	X	19.81
Manuel Martínez	19.74	19.80	19.73
Antonín Žalský	19.63	19.46	19.77
Yury Bialou	19.38	19.75	19.35
Asmir Kolašinac	19.62	19.67	X
Lajos Kürthy	19.16	19.64	X
Scott Martin	19.16	19.52	19.45
Daniel Taylor	X	X	19.39
Yves Niaré	X	X	19.37
David Storl	19.19	X	19.18
Maksim Sidorov	18.92	18.77	X
Georgi Ivanov	18.11	X	X
Germán Lauro	X	X	X

Men's Shot Put (continued)

FINAL   15 August 2009

Position	Athlete	Country	Distance
GOLD	Christian Cantwell	United States	22.03
SILVER	Tomasz Majewski	Poland	21.91
BRONZE	Ralf Bartels	Germany	21.37
4	Reese Hoffa	United States	21.28
5	Adam Nelson	United States	21.11
6	Pavel Lyzhyn	Belarus	20.98
7	Andrei Mikhnevich	Belarus	20.74
8	Miroslav Vodovnik	Slovenia	20.50
9	Hamza Alic	Bosnia & Herzegovina	20.00
10	Pavel Sofin	Russia	19.89
11	Carl Myerscough	Great Britain	18.42
	Peter Sack	Germany	-

Athlete	Throw 1	Throw 2	Throw 3	Throw 4	Throw 5	Throw 6
Christian Cantwell	21.54	20.72	21.03	21.21	22.03	-
Tomasz Majewski	21.36	21.19	20.80	21.68	21.91	21.18
Ralf Bartels	20.35	20.18	21.37	20.80	20.94	21.2
Reese Hoffa	21.02	X	20.95	21.14	20.97	21.28
Adam Nelson	21.11	20.93	X	X	X	X
Pavel Lyzhyn	X	20.98	X	X	X	X
Andrei Mikhnevich	20.34	20.31	20.62	20.74	20.54	X
Miroslav Vodovnik	19.60	19.50	20.50	X	19.82	20.14
Hamza Alic	20.00	X	19.80			
Pavel Sofin	19.89	19.69	19.85			
Carl Myerscough	18.42	X	X			
Peter Sack	X	X	X			

Women's Shot Put

Qualification for the Final: Minimum achieved distance 18.50m or 12 best qualifiers.

Group A   16 August 2009

Position	Athlete	Country		Distance
1	Natallia Mikhnevich	Belarus	Q	19.12
2	Anna Avdeeva	Russia	Q	18.92
3	Denise Hinrichs	Germany	Q	18.69
4	Meiju Li	China	Q	18.53
5	Christina Schwanitz	Germany	q	18.25
6	Mailín Vargas	Cuba	q	18.14
7	Anca Heltne	Romania		17.92
8	Chiara Rosa	Italy		17.89
9	Austra Skujyte	Lithuania		17.86
10	Laurence Manfredi	France		17.25
11	Helena Engman	Sweden		17.19
12	Jillian Camarena	United States		16.92
13	Annie Alexander	Trinidad & Tobago		16.01
14	Kristin Heaston	United States		14.98

Athlete	Throw 1	Throw 2	Throw 3
Natallia Mikhnevich	19.12	-	-
Anna Avdeeva	18.45	18.31	18.92
Denise Hinrichs	18.69	-	-
Meiju Li	18.53	-	-
Christina Schwanitz	18.25	X	18.11
Mailín Vargas	18.14	17.95	17.98
Anca Heltne	17.92	17.82	17.69
Chiara Rosa	17.89	X	X
Austra Skujyte	X	17.52	17.86
Laurence Manfredi	17.04	X	17.25
Helena Engman	17.19	X	X
Jillian Camarena	16.92	X	X
Annie Alexander	16.01	15.82	X
Kristin Heaston	X	X	14.98

Women's Shot Put (continued)

Group B 16 August 2009

Position	Athlete	Country		Distance
1	Valerie Vili	New Zealand	Q	19.70
2	Nadine Kleinert	Germany	Q	19.36
3	Lijiao Gong	China	Q	19.08
4	Misleydis González	Cuba	Q	18.62
5	Michelle Carter	United States	q	18.44
6	Xiangrong Liu	China	q	18.10
7	Cleopatra Borel-Brown	Trinidad & Tobago		17.99
8	Mariam Kevkhishvili	Georgia		17.95
9	Yaniuvis López	Cuba		17.71
10	Natalia Ducó	Chile		17.61
11	Jessica Cérival	France		17.30
12	Anita Márton	Hungary		16.80
13	Leyla Rajabi	Iran		16.60
14	Ana Pouhila	Tonga		16.09

Athlete	Throw 1	Throw 2	Throw 3
Valerie Vili	19.70	-	-
Nadine Kleinert	18.38	X	19.36
Lijiao Gong	19.08	-	-
Misleydis González	18.62	-	-
Michelle Carter	17.43	18.07	18.44
Xiangrong Liu	X	17.97	18.10
Cleopatra Borel-Brown	17.19	17.31	17.99
Mariam Kevkhishvili	17.95	17.68	17.75
Yaniuvis López	17.71	17.65	X
Natalia Ducó	17.61	17.45	17.43
Jessica Cérival	17.06	16.90	17.30
Anita Márton	15.99	16.80	16.76
Leyla Rajabi	16.12	16.60	X
Ana Pouhila	15.50	X	16.09

Women's Shot Put (continued)

FINAL 16 August 2009

Position	Athlete	Country	Distance
GOLD	Valerie Vili	New Zealand	20.44
SILVER	Nadine Kleinert	Germany	20.20
BRONZE	Lijiao Gong	China	19.89
4	Natallia Mikhnevich	Belarus	19.66
5	Anna Avdeeva	Russia	19.66
6	Michelle Carter	United States	18.96
7	Meiju Li	China	18.76
8	Misleydis González	Cuba	18.74
9	Mailín Vargas	Cuba	18.67
10	Xiangrong Liu	China	18.52
11	Denise Hinrichs	Germany	18.39
12	Christina Schwanitz	Germany	17.84

Athlete	Throw 1	Throw 2	Throw 3	Throw 4	Throw 5	Throw 6
Valerie Vili	19.40	X	20.25	20.16	20.44	20.25
Nadine Kleinert	20.06	19.52	20.20	19.61	X	X
Lijiao Gong	19.69	19.89	19.68	19.75	X	X
Natallia Mikhnevich	19.66	X	19.27	19.51	X	X
Anna Avdeeva	18.66	18.78	19.48	19.66	X	X
Michelle Carter	X	18.93	18.96	X	18.30	X
Meiju Li	18.76	18.35	18.66	X	X	X
Misleydis González	18.73	18.57	X	18.60	18.74	18.43
Mailín Vargas	18.67	18.10	18.11			
Xiangrong Liu	18.52	X	16.79			
Denise Hinrichs	18.30	18.39	X			
Christina Schwanitz	17.84	X	X			

Men's Discus

Qualification for the Final: Minimum achieved distance 64.50m or 12 best qualifiers.

Group A   18 August 2009

Position	Athlete	Country		Distance
1	Robert Harting	Germany	Q	66.81
2	Gerd Kanter	Estonia	Q	66.73
3	Casey Malone	United States	Q	65.13
4	Mario Pestano	Spain	Q	65.03
5	Bogdan Pishchalnikov	Russia	q	62.93
6	Omar Ahmed El Ghazaly	Egypt	q	62.84
7	Aleksander Tammert	Estonia		62.24
8	Ian Waltz	United States		62.04
9	Benn Harradine	Australia		61.74
10	Gaute Myklebust	Norway		60.80
11	Bertrand Vili	France		60.68
12	Jorge Balliengo	Argentina		59.19
13	Oleksiy Semenov	Ukraine		58.78
14	Daniel Schärer	Switzerland		58.50
	Haider Naser Abdulshaheed	Iraq		-

Athlete	Throw 1	Throw 2	Throw 3
Robert Harting	66.81	-	-
Gerd Kanter	66.73	-	-
Casey Malone	65.13	-	-
Mario Pestano	65.03	-	-
Bogdan Pishchalnikov	62.93	61.09	60.08
Omar Ahmed El Ghazaly	62.84	62.09	X
Aleksander Tammert	62.24	61.93	59.44
Ian Waltz	X	60.27	62.04
Benn Harradine	60.73	61.74	60.79
Gaute Myklebust	X	60.80	X
Bertrand Vili	60.68	X	X
Jorge Balliengo	56.69	55.32	59.19
Oleksiy Semenov	58.78	57.31	X
Daniel Schärer	58.50	58.23	57.22
Haider Naser Abdulshaheed	X	X	X

Men's Discus (continued)

Group B   18 August 2009

Position	Athlete	Country		Distance
1	Zoltán Kövágó	Hungary	Q	65.82
2	Jarred Rome	United States	Q	65.51
3	Virgilijus Alekna	Lithuania	Q	65.04
4	Piotr Malachowski	Poland	q	64.48
5	Gerhard Mayer	Austria	q	62.53
6	Frantz Kruger	Finland	q	62.29
7	Yennifer Frank Casañas	Spain		61.10
8	Erik Cadee	Netherlands		60.64
9	Markus Münch	Germany		60.55
10	Ivan Hryshyn	Ukraine		59.93
11	Märt Israel	Estonia		59.58
12	Ahmed Mohamed Dheeb	Qatar		59.16
13	Nikolay Sedyuk	Russia		59.03
14	Germán Lauro	Argentina		57.88
15	Ercüment Olgundeniz	Turkey		57.52

Athlete	Throw 1	Throw 2	Throw 3
Zoltán Kövágó	X	65.82	-
Jarred Rome	60.92	65.51	-
Virgilijus Alekna	65.04	-	-
Piotr Malachowski	64.20	64.48	62.65
Gerhard Mayer	62.53	59.33	62.19
Frantz Kruger	62.29	X	60.45
Yennifer Frank Casañas	X	X	61.10
Erik Cadee	X	60.64	X
Markus Münch	60.55	X	59.12
Ivan Hryshyn	59.93	57.28	X
Märt Israel	59.58	X	-
Ahmed Mohamed Dheeb	55.33	59.16	X
Nikolay Sedyuk	X	59.03	58.62
Germán Lauro	57.88	X	X
Ercüment Olgundeniz	56.54	X	57.52

Men's Discus (continued)

FINAL 19 August 2009

Position	Athlete	Country	Distance
GOLD	Robert Harting	Germany	69.43
SILVER	Piotr Malachowski	Poland	69.15
BRONZE	Gerd Kanter	Estonia	66.88
4	Virgilijus Alekna	Lithuania	66.36
5	Casey Malone	United States	66.06
6	Zoltán Kövágó	Hungary	65.17
7	Bogdan Pishchalnikov	Russia	65.02
8	Gerhard Mayer	Austria	63.17
9	Omar Ahmed El Ghazaly	Egypt	62.83
10	Mario Pestano	Spain	62.76
11	Jarred Rome	United States	62.47
12	Frantz Kruger	Finland	59.77

Athlete	Throw 1	Throw 2	Throw 3	Throw 4	Throw 5	Throw 6
Robert Harting	68.25	67.04	67.80	X	67.80	69.43
Piotr Malachowski	68.77	68.05	67.00	X	69.15	67.33
Gerd Kanter	65.91	65.65	X	66.88	66.24	65.45
Virgilijus Alekna	66.36	66.32	65.68	64.53	66.24	X
Casey Malone	63.61	61.59	65.64	64.84	65.98	66.06
Zoltán Kövágó	X	63.09	62.47	X	65.17	61.69
Bogdan Pishchalnikov	62.03	63.29	63.18	64.26	65.02	X
Gerhard Mayer	62.16	60.49	63.17	X	60.83	X
Omar Ahmed El Ghazaly	62.13	62.83	62.76			
Mario Pestano	62.76	X	62.27			
Jarred Rome	58.48	62.47	X			
Frantz Kruger	X	59.77	X			

Women's Discus

Qualification for the Final: Minimum achieved distance 61.50m or 12 best qualifiers.

Group A   19 August 2009

Position	Athlete	Country		Distance
1	Xuejun Ma	China	Q	63.38
2	Yarelis Barrios	Cuba	Q	62.19
3	Sandra Perkovic	Croatia	Q	62.16
4	Nicoleta Grasu	Romania	Q	61.78
5	Nadine Müller	Germany	Q	61.63
6	Stephanie Brown Trafton	United States	q	61.23
7	Elizna Naude	South Africa		59.67
8	Wioletta Potepa	Poland		59.54
9	Dragana Tomaševic	Serbia		59.38
10	Svetlana Ivanova-Saykina	Russia		59.31
11	Becky Breisch	United States		58.50
12	Yania Ferrales	Cuba		58.24
13	Kateryna Karsak	Ukraine		56.79
14	Krishna Poonia	India		56.75
15	Elisângela Adriano	Brazil		55.75
16	Sofia Larsson	Sweden		54.28
17	Olena Antonova	Ukraine		54.28
18	Venera Getova	Bulgaria		53.33
	Ellina Zvereva	Belarus		-

Athlete	Throw 1	Throw 2	Throw 3
Xuejun Ma	63.38	-	-
Yarelis Barrios	X	X	62.19
Sandra Perkovic	61.02	X	62.16
Nicoleta Grasu	60.25	61.78	-
Nadine Müller	61.63	-	-
Stephanie Brown Trafton	60.15	57.44	61.23
Elizna Naude	59.46	59.46	59.67
Wioletta Potepa	X	59.54	X
Dragana Tomaševic	58.32	59.30	59.38
Svetlana Ivanova-Saykina	59.31	X	58.45
Becky Breisch	58.50	X	58.08
Yania Ferrales	57.71	55.84	58.24
Kateryna Karsak	56.79	X	X
Krishna Poonia	X	X	56.75
Elisângela Adriano	54.99	52.00	55.75
Sofia Larsson	51.87	X	54.28
Olena Antonova	X	54.28	X
Venera Getova	53.33	X	X
Ellina Zvereva	X	X	X

Women's Discus (continued)

Group B 19 August 2009

Position	Athlete	Country		Distance
1	Aimin Song	China	Q	62.80
2	Dani Samuels	Australia	Q	62.67
3	Zaneta Glanc	Poland	Q	62.43
4	Natalya Sadova	Russia	Q	61.94
5	Mélina Robert-Michon	France	Q	61.53
6	Aretha Thurmond	United States	q	61.08
7	Shaoyang Xu	China		61.02
8	Yarisley Collado	Cuba		60.37
9	Seema Antil	India		59.85
10	Vera Pospíšilová-Cechlová	Czech Republic		59.52
11	Joanna Wisniewska	Poland		58.85
12	Franka Dietzsch	Germany		58.44
13	Vera Begic	Croatia		58.25
14	Anna Söderberg	Sweden		57.92
15	Rocío Comba	Argentina		54.69
16	Zinaida Sendriute	Lithuania		54.55
17	Wen-Hua Li	Taipei		53.88
18	Kazai Suzanne Kragbé	Ivory Coast		53.84
19	Tereapii Tapoki	Cook Islands		45.29
	Iryna Yatchenko	Belarus		-
	Natalya Fokina-Semenova	Ukraine		DNS

Athlete	Throw 1	Throw 2	Throw 3
Aimin Song	X	62.80	-
Dani Samuels	62.67	-	-
Zaneta Glanc	49.79	62.43	-
Natalya Sadova	61.94	-	-
Mélina Robert-Michon	58.36	61.53	-
Aretha Thurmond	60.09	59.09	61.08
Shaoyang Xu	59.67	61.02	57.96
Yarisley Collado	59.56	59.23	60.37
Seema Antil	59.85	X	X
Vera Pospíšilová-Cechlová	57.87	58.37	59.52
Joanna Wisniewska	X	58.85	X
Franka Dietzsch	X	X	58.44
Vera Begic	54.63	X	58.25
Anna Söderberg	56.38	57.92	X
Rocío Comba	52.62	54.69	X
Zinaida Sendriute	52.85	54.55	X
Wen-Hua Li	53.88	49.91	52.49
Kazai Suzanne Kragbé	52.24	53.84	52.79
Tereapii Tapoki	X	45.29	X
Iryna Yatchenko	X	X	X

Women's Discus (continued)

FINAL 21 August 2009

Position	Athlete	Country	Distance
GOLD	Dani Samuels	Australia	65.44
SILVER	Yarelis Barrios	Cuba	65.31
BRONZE	Nicoleta Grasu	Romania	65.20
4	Zaneta Glanc	Poland	62.66
5	Aimin Song	China	62.42
6	Nadine Müller	Germany	62.04
7	Natalya Sadova	Russia	61.78
8	Mélina Robert-Michon	France	60.92
9	Sandra Perkovic	Croatia	60.77
10	Aretha Thurmond	United States	59.89
11	Xuejun Ma	China	58.79
12	Stephanie Brown Trafton	United States	58.53

Athlete	Throw 1	Throw 2	Throw 3	Throw 4	Throw 5	Throw 6
Dani Samuels	X	59.05	62.71	64.76	65.44	X
Yarelis Barrios	64.44	63.87	61.17	X	X	65.31
Nicoleta Grasu	X	65.20	62.38	60.68	63.41	X
Zaneta Glanc	58.69	59.83	62.66	X	57.71	X
Aimin Song	51.69	60.50	61.78	X	61.39	62.42
Nadine Müller	57.53	57.62	62.04	60.40	X	X
Natalya Sadova	60.70	61.78	59.31	60.44	58.26	61.44
Mélina Robert-Michon	59.80	60.92	60.89	X	59.90	59.69
Sandra Perkovic	X	60.77	X			
Aretha Thurmond	X	59.89	59.88			
Xuejun Ma	58.79	X	58.58			
Stephanie Brown Trafton	58.53	X	57.94			

Men's Hammer

Qualification for the Final: Minimum achieved distance 77.50m or 12 best qualifiers.

Group A   15 August 2009

Position	Athlete	Country		Distance
1	Szymon Ziólkowski	Poland	Q	77.89
2	Sergej Litvinov	Germany	Q	77.68
3	Primož Kozmus	Slovenia	Q	77.55
4	Igor Vinichenko	Russia	Q	77.54
5	Nicola Vizzoni	Italy	q	76.95
6	András Haklits	Croatia	q	76.39
7	Dilshod Nazarov	Tajikistan	q	75.83
8	Ali Mohamed Al-Zinkawi	Kuwait		75.10
9	Olli-Pekka Karjalainen	Finland		74.09
10	Mohsen El Anany	Egypt		72.68
11	Michael Mai	United States		72.58
12	Yury Shayunou	Belarus		71.37
13	Alfred Kruger	United States		70.19
14	Artem Rubanko	Ukraine		69.81
15	Ainars Vaiculens	Latvia		66.89
16	Amanmurad Hommadov	Turkmenistan		57.39
	Chris Harmse	South Africa		-

Athlete	Throw 1	Throw 2	Throw 3
Szymon Ziólkowski	77.89	-	-
Sergej Litvinov	77.68	-	-
Primož Kozmus	77.55	-	-
Igor Vinichenko	77.54	-	-
Nicola Vizzoni	76.71	X	76.95
András Haklits	75.50	76.39	75.73
Dilshod Nazarov	73.84	74.73	75.83
Ali Mohamed Al-Zinkawi	X	73.82	75.10
Olli-Pekka Karjalainen	X	73.25	74.09
Mohsen El Anany	71.42	72.68	72.05
Michael Mai	72.58	X	67.47
Yury Shayunou	71.37	X	X
Alfred Kruger	67.40	X	70.19
Artem Rubanko	X	69.81	X
Ainars Vaiculens	65.70	66.89	X
Amanmurad Hommadov	57.39	56.46	X
Chris Harmse	X	X	X

Men's Hammer (continued)

Group B 15 August 2009

Position	Athlete	Country		Distance
1	Krisztián Pars	Hungary	Q	76.68
2	Pavel Kryvitski	Belarus	Q	77.85
3	Markus Esser	Germany	q	76.81
4	Libor Charfreitag	Slovakia	q	76.29
5	Aleksey Zagornyi	Russia	q	75.38
6	Lukáš Melich	Czech Republic		74.47
7	Thomas Freeman	United States		74.19
8	Igors Sokolovs	Latvia		73.97
9	David Söderberg	Finland		73.69
10	Jérôme Bortoluzzi	France		73.09
11	Olexiy Sokyrskiyy	Ukraine		72.56
12	Aléxandros Papadimitríou	Greece		72.02
13	Javier Cienfuegos	Spain		72.01
14	Dzmitry Shako	Belarus		71.80
15	Esref Apak	Turkey		70.70
16	Juan Ignacio Cerra	Argentina		69.37
17	Bergur Ingi Pétursson	Iceland		68.62

Athlete	Throw 1	Throw 2	Throw 3
Krisztián Pars	72.94	78.68	-
Pavel Kryvitski	70.70	72.14	77.85
Markus Esser	76.81	76.67	X
Libor Charfreitag	69.71	75.39	76.29
Aleksey Zagornyi	75.38	74.93	73.75
Lukáš Melich	74.40	72.98	74.47
Thomas Freeman	71.38	74.19	72.58
Igors Sokolovs	73.96	73.97	73.12
David Söderberg	73.69	73.14	73.56
Jérôme Bortoluzzi	X	73.09	70.69
Olexiy Sokyrskiyy	70.67	X	72.56
Aléxandros Papadimitríou	X	X	72.02
Javier Cienfuegos	69.60	71.63	72.01
Dzmitry Shako	71.80	70.57	X
Esref Apak	X	70.70	X
Juan Ignacio Cerra	66.77	67.98	69.37
Bergur Ingi Pétursson	67.32	68.62	X

Men's Hammer (continued)

FINAL 17 August 2009

Position	Athlete	Country	Distance
GOLD	Primož Kozmus	Slovenia	80.84
SILVER	Szymon Ziółkowski	Poland	79.30
BRONZE	Aleksey Zagornyi	Russia	78.09
4	Krisztián Pars	Hungary	77.45
5	Sergej Litvinov	Germany	76.58
6	Markus Esser	Germany	76.27
7	András Haklits	Croatia	76.26
8	Pavel Kryvitski	Belarus	76.00
9	Nicola Vizzoni	Italy	73.70
10	Libor Charfreitag	Slovakia	72.63
11	Dilshod Nazarov	Tajikistan	71.69
12	Igor Vinichenko	Russia	-

Athlete	Throw 1	Throw 2	Throw 3	Throw 4	Throw 5	Throw 6
Primož Kozmus	75.14	79.74	77.21	79.28	80.15	80.84
Szymon Ziółkowski	77.44	79.30	77.85	77.66	78.09	76.89
Aleksey Zagornyi	76.11	X	77.42	X	75.11	78.09
Krisztián Pars	75.51	X	X	77.45	X	X
Sergej Litvinov	74.50	74.49	75.88	76.58	76.00	74.45
Markus Esser	68.07	76.27	74.07	X	X	X
András Haklits	72.60	75.12	75.09	X	74.82	76.26
Pavel Kryvitski	73.72	X	72.73	X	X	76.00
Nicola Vizzoni	X	X	73.70			
Libor Charfreitag	X	72.63	X			
Dilshod Nazarov	X	X	71.69			
Igor Vinichenko	X	X	X			

Women's Hammer

Qualification for the Final: Minimum achieved distance 72.00m or 12 best qualifiers.

Group A   20 August 2009

Position	Athlete	Country			Distance
1	Betty Heidler	Germany	CR	Q	75.27
2	Anita Wlodarczyk	Poland		Q	74.54
3	Jessica Cosby	United States		Q	72.21
4	Stéphanie Falzon	France		q	71.54
5	Aksana Miankova	Belarus			69.58
6	Jennifer Dahlgren	Argentina			68.90
7	Silvia Salis	Italy			68.55
8	Bianca Perie	Romania			68.47
9	Stilianí Papadopoúlou	Greece			67.33
10	Berta Castells	Spain			67.32
11	Jennifer Joyce	Canada			67.07
12	Andrea Bunjes	Germany			67.01
13	Iryna Sekachova	Ukraine			66.69
14	Johana Moreno	Colombia			65.05
15	Marina Marghiev	Moldova			64.83
16	Eileen O'Keeffe	Ireland			63.20
17	Lenka Ledvinová	Czech Republic			62.92
18	Vânia Silva	Portugal			62.86
19	Florence Ezeh	Togo			59.76
20	Galina Mityaeva	Tajikistan			56.31
	Paraskevi Theodorou	Cyprus			-

Athlete	Throw 1	Throw 2	Throw 3
Betty Heidler	75.27	-	-
Anita Wlodarczyk	74.54	-	-
Jessica Cosby	72.21	-	-
Stéphanie Falzon	70.35	X	71.54
Aksana Miankova	X	67.47	69.58
Jennifer Dahlgren	68.90	65.42	64.56
Silvia Salis	68.55	67.46	64.36
Bianca Perie	67.74	68.47	62.67
Stilianí Papadopoúlou	X	67.33	X
Berta Castells	67.32	X	X
Jennifer Joyce	X	66.59	67.07
Andrea Bunjes	67.01	X	-
Iryna Sekachova	X	66.69	66.26
Johana Moreno	65.05	64.35	X
Marina Marghiev	X	X	64.83
Eileen O'Keeffe	63.20	X	X
Lenka Ledvinová	62.92	X	58.72
Vânia Silva	62.66	62.86	62.67
Florence Ezeh	59.76	59.61	58.34
Galina Mityaeva	X	56.31	X
Paraskevi Theodorou	X	X	X

Women's Hammer (continued)

Group B 20 August 2009

Position	Athlete	Country		Distance
1	Wenxiu Zhang	China	Q	72.72
2	Tatyana Lysenko	Russia	q	71.73
3	Martina Hrasnová	Slovakia	q	71.50
4	Sultana Frizell	Canada	q	70.98
5	Manuela Montebrun	France	q	70.66
6	Amber Campbell	United States	q	70.54
7	Kathrin Klaas	Germany	q	70.53
8	Clarissa Claretti	Italy	q	70.01
9	Éva Orbán	Hungary		69.39
10	Darya Pchelnik	Belarus		69.30
11	Arasay Thondike	Cuba		68.97
12	Erin Gilreath	United States		68.34
13	Merja Korpela	Finland		66.72
14	Zalina Marghieva	Moldova		66.70
15	Alexándra Papayeoryíou	Greece		66.33
16	Nataliya Zolotukhina	Ukraine		65.95
17	Rosa Rodríguez	Venezuela		65.88
18	Iryna Novozhylova	Ukraine		64.90
19	Cecilia Nilsson	Sweden		63.77
	Zoe Derham	Great Britain		-

Athlete	Throw 1	Throw 2	Throw 3
Wenxiu Zhang	72.72	-	-
Tatyana Lysenko	70.16	X	71.73
Martina Hrasnová	X	70.97	71.50
Sultana Frizell	67.53	70.98	09.33
Manuela Montebrun	68.65	62.49	70.66
Amber Campbell	68.48	70.54	69.95
Kathrin Klaas	70.53	68.82	X
Clarissa Claretti	68.99	69.93	70.01
Éva Orbán	67.57	67.57	69.39
Darya Pchelnik	69.14	67.61	69.30
Arasay Thondike	X	X	68.97
Erin Gilreath	66.89	68.34	68.02
Merja Korpela	65.64	66.72	66.25
Zalina Marghieva	66.70	X	62.56
Alexándra Papayeoryíou	66.33	X	62.78
Nataliya Zolotukhina	65.95	64.88	65.71
Rosa Rodríguez	65.88	65.39	60.27
Iryna Novozhylova	62.98	X	64.90
Cecilia Nilsson	61.00	63.77	63.31
Zoe Derham	X	X	X

Women's Hammer (continued)

FINAL 22 August 2009

Position	Athlete	Country		Distance
GOLD	Anita Wlodarczyk	Poland	WR	77.96
SILVER	Betty Heidler	Germany		77.12
BRONZE	Martina Hrasnová	Slovakia		74.79
4	Kathrin Klaas	Germany		74.23
5	Wenxiu Zhang	China		72.57
6	Tatyana Lysenko	Russia		72.22
7	Jessica Cosby	United States		72.17
8	Clarissa Claretti	Italy		71.56
9	Stéphanie Falzon	France		71.40
10	Sultana Frizell	Canada		70.88
11	Amber Campbell	United States		70.08
12	Manuela Montebrun	France		69.92

Athlete	Throw 1	Throw 2	Throw 3	Throw 4	Throw 5	Throw 6
Anita Wlodarczyk	74.86	77.96	-	-	-	X
Betty Heidler	75.10	75.38	75.73	73.45	76.44	77.12
Martina Hrasnová	67.84	72.72	73.07	69.50	74.79	65.65
Kathrin Klaas	72.02	X	74.23	66.28	X	X
Wenxiu Zhang	69.42	72.57	X	71.80	70.83	71.03
Tatyana Lysenko	72.22	X	71.36	X	71.51	70.16
Jessica Cosby	X	72.17	69.94	68.10	X	71.35
Clarissa Claretti	71.56	69.42	70.97	70.91	70.24	X
Stéphanie Falzon	71.40	70.80	X			
Sultana Frizell	69.63	70.88	68.47			
Amber Campbell	64.62	70.08	X			
Manuela Montebrun	X	69.92	69.75			

Men's Javelin

Qualification for the Final: Minimum achieved distance 82.00m or 12 best qualifiers.

Group A   21 August 2009

Position	Athlete	Country		Distance
1	Yukifumi Murakami	Japan	Q	83.10
2	Guillermo Martínez	Cuba	Q	82.50
3	Tero Pitkämäki	Finland	q	81.65
4	Andreas Thorkildsen	Norway	q	80.37
5	Ainars Kovals	Latvia	q	79.76
6	Tero Järvenpää	Finland	q	79.48
7	Sergey Makarov	Russia		78.68
8	Csongor Olteán	Hungary		78.46
9	Mihkel Kukk	Estonia		78.18
10	Mike Hazle	United States		78.17
11	Jae-myong Park	South Korea		78.16
12	Qiang Qin	China		77.65
13	Roman Avramenko	Ukraine		77.44
14	Aliaksandr Ashomka	Belarus		76.85
15	Eriks Rags	Latvia		76.23
16	Vítezslav Veselý	Czech Republic		75.76
17	Jonas Lohse	Sweden		75.33
18	Melik Janoyan	Armenia		74.74
19	Adrian Markowski	Poland		74.13
20	Tino Häber	Germany		74.11
21	Stefan Müller	Switzerland		72.83
22	Thomas Smet	Belgium		70.35
23	Víctor Fatecha	Paraguay		68.65
24	Tomas Intas	Lithuania		68.40

Athlete	Throw 1	Throw 2	Throw 3
Yukifumi Murakami	74.87	83.10	-
Guillermo Martínez	X	76.69	82.50
Tero Pitkämäki	80.96	X	81.65
Andreas Thorkildsen	X	80.37	79.93
Ainars Kovals	79.76	X	X
Tero Järvenpää	77.22	X	79.48
Sergey Makarov	78.68	X	78.47
Csongor Olteán	74.75	X	78.46
Mihkel Kukk	72.63	76.70	78.18
Mike Hazle	X	76.98	78.17
Jae-myong Park	75.62	76.17	78.16
Qiang Qin	76.87	75.40	77.65
Roman Avramenko	73.85	76.46	77.44
Aliaksandr Ashomka	72.83	76.85	76.04
Eriks Rags	76.23	X	75.97
Vítezslav Veselý	75.16	75.76	69.48
Jonas Lohse	X	75.33	74.46
Melik Janoyan	68.74	74.74	72.75
Adrian Markowski	68.84	72.87	74.13
Tino Häber	73.66	74.11	73.64
Stefan Müller	71.09	71.63	72.83
Thomas Smet	70.35	X	68.23
Víctor Fatecha	66.31	68.65	65.93
Tomas Intas	68.40	X	X

Men's Javelin (continued)

Group B 21 August 2009

Position	Athlete	Country		Distance
1	Vadims Vasilevskis	Latvia	Q	86.69
2	Mark Frank	Germany	q	80.85
3	Teemu Wirkkala	Finland	q	79.84
4	Petr Frydrych	Czech Republic	q	79.57
5	Sean Furey	United States	q	79.28
6	Antti Ruuskanen	Finland	q	78.69
7	Stuart Farquhar	New Zealand		78.53
8	Fatih Avan	Turkey		78.12
9	Aleksandr Ivanov	Russia		78.00
10	Tom Goyvaerts	Belgium		77.37
11	Chris Hill	United States		77.14
12	Oleksandr Pyatnytsya	Ukraine		76.13
13	Uladzimir Kazlou	Belarus		75.38
14	Igor Janik	Poland		75.20
15	Sangjin Jung	South Korea		72.80
16	Arley Ibargüen	Colombia		72.54
17	Ilya Korotkov	Russia		71.59
18	Mohamed Ali Kebabou	Tunisia		68.75
19	Júlio César de Oliveira	Brazil		68.49
20	John Robert Oosthuizen	South Africa		67.86
21	Mervyn Luckwell	Great Britain		66.30
	Ignacio Guerra	Chile		-
	Tanel Laanmäe	Estonia		-
	Andrus Värnik	Estonia		DNS

Athlete	Throw 1	Throw 2	Throw 3
Vadims Vasilevskis	86.69	-	-
Mark Frank	79.04	80.85	-
Teemu Wirkkala	76.82	79.84	79.23
Petr Frydrych	79.57	78.14	72.73
Sean Furey	X	74.51	79.28
Antti Ruuskanen	78.61	78.69	76.82
Stuart Farquhar	72.84	74.54	78.53
Fatih Avan	78.12	X	68.12
Aleksandr Ivanov	X	77.13	78.00
Tom Goyvaerts	77.37	X	73.62
Chris Hill	70.23	75.20	77.14
Oleksandr Pyatnytsya	76.13	75.61	X
Uladzimir Kazlou	X	73.17	75.38
Igor Janik	75.20	X	X
Sangjin Jung	X	72.80	X
Arley Ibargüen	69.49	72.54	X
Ilya Korotkov	71.59	70.37	X
Mohamed Ali Kebabou	64.68	68.75	-
Júlio César de Oliveira	67.85	68.49	X
John Robert Oosthuizen	67.86	X	67.57
Mervyn Luckwell	65.02	61.42	66.30
Ignacio Guerra	X	X	X
Tanel Laanmäe	X	X	-

Men's Javelin (continued)

FINAL 23 August 2009

Position	Athlete	Country	Distance
GOLD	Andreas Thorkildsen	Norway	89.59
SILVER	Guillermo Martínez	Cuba	86.41
BRONZE	Yukifumi Murakami	Japan	82.97
4	Vadims Vasilevskis	Latvia	82.37
5	Tero Pitkämäki	Finland	81.90
6	Antti Ruuskanen	Finland	81.87
7	Ainars Kovals	Latvia	81.54
8	Mark Frank	Germany	81.32
9	Teemu Wirkkala	Finland	79.82
10	Petr Frydrych	Czech Republic	79.29
11	Tero Järvenpää	Finland	75.57
12	Sean Furey	United States	74.51

Athlete	Throw 1	Throw 2	Throw 3	Throw 4	Throw 5	Throw 6
Andreas Thorkildsen	77.80	89.59	88.95	X	-	-
Guillermo Martínez	83.43	83.28	78.22	77.27	-	86.41
Yukifumi Murakami	76.01	82.97	X	X	-	77.90
Vadims Vasilevskis	X	82.05	X	X	X	82.37
Tero Pitkämäki	81.90	81.14	80.50	X	80.17	81.14
Antti Ruuskanen	75.36	75.67	81.87	78.65	X	80.87
Ainars Kovals	X	81.54	X	X	75.98	76.39
Mark Frank	73.77	79.86	X	X		81.32
Teemu Wirkkala	79.76	X	79.82			
Petr Frydrych	78.57	X	79.29			
Tero Järvenpää	75.43	X	75.57			
Sean Furey	73.18	74.51	73.77			

Women's Javelin

Qualification for the Final: Minimum achieved distance 62.00m or 12 best qualifiers.

Group A   16 August 2009

Position	Athlete	Country		Distance
1	Maria Abakumova	Russia	Q	68.92
2	Linda Stahl	Germany	Q	63.86
3	Martina Ratej	Slovenia	Q	63.42
4	Barbora Špotáková	Czech Republic	Q	63.27
5	Steffi Nerius	Germany	q	61.73
6	Monica Stoian	Romania	q	60.29
7	Vira Rebryk	Ukraine	q	59.70
8	Sávva Líka	Greece	q	59.64
9	Goldie Sayers	Great Britain		58.98
10	Yainelis Ribiaux	Cuba		57.38
11	Mercedes Chilla	Spain		56.68
12	Maryna Novik	Belarus		56.44
13	Indré Jakubaityté	Lithuania		55.86
14	Kara Patterson	United States		52.71
15	Elisabeth Pauer	Austria		50.88
16	Serafina Akeli	Samoa		49.58

Athlete	Throw 1	Throw 2	Throw 3
Maria Abakumova	68.92	-	-
Linda Stahl	63.86	-	-
Martina Ratej	53.13	63.42	-
Barbora Špotáková	63.27	-	-
Steffi Nerius	61.00	X	61.73
Monica Stoian	59.45	60.29	55.57
Vira Rebryk	59.68	59.70	58.27
Sávva Líka	57.26	X	59.64
Goldie Sayers	56.44	58.58	58.98
Yainelis Ribiaux	57.26	57.38	56.48
Mercedes Chilla	56.68	X	X
Maryna Novik	51.56	56.44	55.01
Indré Jakubaityté	55.86	X	X
Kara Patterson	50.60	X	52.71
Elisabeth Pauer	X	49.32	50.88
Serafina Akeli	49.58	X	X

Women's Javelin (continued)

Group B   16 August 2009

Position	Athlete	Country		Distance
1	Olisdeilys Menéndez	Cuba	q	61.94
2	Christina Obergföll	Germany	q	60.74
3	Rachel Yurkovich	United States	q	59.57
4	Maria Nicoleta Negoita	Romania	q	59.46
5	Mikaela Ingberg	Finland		57.88
6	Kimberley Mickle	Australia		57.46
7	Olha Ivankova	Ukraine		56.91
8	Sunette Viljoen	South Africa		56.83
9	Urszula Piwnicka	Poland		56.49
10	Yanet Cruz	Cuba		56.19
11	Ásdís Hjálmsdóttir	Iceland		55.86
12	Yuki Ebihara	Japan		54.81
13	Moonika Aava	Estonia		53.86
14	Madara Palameika	Latvia		52.98
15	Valeriya Zabruskova	Russia		52.87

Athlete	Throw 1	Throw 2	Throw 3
Olisdeilys Menéndez	59.86	61.94	X
Christina Obergföll	60.04	59.86	60.74
Rachel Yurkovich	59.57	53.84	59.55
Maria Nicoleta Negoita	59.46	X	56.32
Mikaela Ingberg	53.86	57.88	X
Kimberley Mickle	57.46	X	56.85
Olha Ivankova	56.91	54.86	54.85
Sunette Viljoen	X	56.83	49.45
Urszula Piwnicka	56.33	56.49	55.74
Yanet Cruz	55.50	56.19	X
Ásdís Hjálmsdóttir	55.86	55.27	X
Yuki Ebihara	49.14	53.30	54.81
Moonika Aava	49.49	52.69	53.86
Madara Palameika	51.80	52.98	X
Valeriya Zabruskova	47.31	52.87	51.13

Women's Javelin (continued)

FINAL 18 August 2009

Position	Athlete	Country	Distance
GOLD	Steffi Nerius	Germany	67.30
SILVER	Barbora Špotáková	Czech Republic	66.42
BRONZE	Maria Abakumova	Russia	66.06
4	Monica Stoian	Romania	64.51
5	Christina Obergföll	Germany	64.34
6	Linda Stahl	Germany	63.23
7	Olisdeilys Menéndez	Cuba	63.11
8	Sávva Líka	Greece	60.29
9	Vira Rebryk	Ukraine	58.25
10	Maria Nicoleta Negoita	Romania	57.65
11	Martina Ratej	Slovenia	57.57
12	Rachel Yurkovich	United States	51.15

Athlete	Throw 1	Throw 2	Throw 3	Throw 4	Throw 5	Throw 6
Steffi Nerius	67.30	62.79	65.81	X	62.27	X
Barbora Špotáková	64.94	64.26	66.42	61.29	62.25	59.74
Maria Abakumova	63.01	X	65.39	X	59.71	66.06
Monica Stoian	64.51	X	61.90	59.62	61.84	61.53
Christina Obergföll	X	60.37	64.34	X	63.02	X
Linda Stahl	61.64	63.23	63.18	59.00	61.33	60.9
Olisdeilys Menéndez	63.11	X	X	X	61.56	58.27
Sávva Líka	56.55	57.33	58.80	57.29	X	60.29
Vira Rebryk	58.25	56.78	57.50			
Maria Nicoleta Negoita	57.59	57.65	X			
Martina Ratej	57.57	X	X			
Rachel Yurkovich	51.15	50.05	X			

Heptathlon - 100m Hurdles

Heat 1 15 August 2009

Position	Lane	Athlete	Country	Time	Points
1	6	Jessica Ennis	Great Britain	12.93	1135
2	2	Sara Aerts	Belgium	13.45	1058
3	7	Kamila Chudzik	Poland	13.50	1050
4	4	Diana Pickler	United States	13.50	1050
5	8	Hanna Melnychenko	Ukraine	13.60	1036
6	3	Jennifer Oeser	Germany	13.62	1033
7	1	Yvonne Wisse	Netherlands	13.66	1027
8	5	Aiga Grabuste	Latvia	13.78	1010

Heat 2 15 August 2009

Position	Lane	Athlete	Country	Time	Points
1	5	Bettie Wade	United States	13.79	1008
2	4	Lilli Schwarzkopf	Germany	13.80	1007
3	3	Natallia Dobrynska	Ukraine	13.85	1000
4	7	Sharon Day	United States	13.90	993
5	2	Kaie Kand	Estonia	13.99	980
6	8	Aryiró Stratáki	Greece	14.17	954
7	6	Sushmitha Singha Roy	India	14.55	902

Heat 3 15 August 2009

Position	Lane	Athlete	Country	Time	Points
1	6	Louise Hazel	Great Britain	13.60	1036
2	2	Karolina Tyminska	Poland	13.67	1026
3	8	Jessica Samuelsson	Sweden	13.96	984
4	5	Julia Mächtig	Germany	14.40	923
5	4	Nadja Casadei	Sweden	14.40	923
6	7	Ida Marcussen	Norway	14.51	907
7	3	Eliška Klucinová	Czech Republic	14.89	856

Heat 4 15 August 2009

Position	Lane	Athlete	Country	Time	Points
1	2	Ida Antoinette Nana Djimou	France	13.44	1059
2	7	Tatyana Chernova	Russia	13.58	1039
3	3	Lyudmyla Yosypenko	Ukraine	13.64	1030
4	5	Brianne Theisen	Canada	13.69	1023
5	4	Linda Züblin	Switzerland	13.75	1014
6	6	Marisa De Aniceto	France	13.78	1010
7	8	Yuliya Tarasova	Uzbekistan	14.23	946

Heptathlon - High Jump

Group A 15 August 2009

Position	Athlete	Country	Height	Points
1	Brianne Theisen	Canada	1.77	941
1	Ida Antoinette Nana Djimou	France	1.77	941
3	Kamila Chudzik	Poland	1.74	903
4	Kaie Kand	Estonia	1.71	867
5	Louise Hazel	Great Britain	1.71	867
6	Karolina Tyminska	Poland	1.71	867
7	Aryiró Stratáki	Greece	1.71	867
8	Yvonne Wisse	Netherlands	1.68	830
8	Nadja Casadei	Sweden	1.68	830
8	Jessica Samuelsson	Sweden	1.68	830
11	Yuliya Tarasova	Uzbekistan	1.68	830
12	Ida Marcussen	Norway	1.65	795
13	Sushmitha Singha Roy	India	1.62	759
14	Linda Züblin	Switzerland	1.62	759

Athlete	1.53	1.56	1.59	1.62	1.65	1.68	1.71	1.74	1.77	1.80
Brianne Theisen	-	-	-	-	O	XO	XO	O	XXO	XXX
Ida Antoinette Nana Djimou	-	-	-	-	O	-	O	XXO	XXO	XXX
Kamila Chudzik	-	-	-	O	O	O	XO	O	XXX	
Kaie Kand	-	-	-	O	O	O	O	XXX		
Louise Hazel	-	-	O	O	O	O	XO	XXX		
Karolina Tyminska	-	-	-	O	O	XO	XO	XXX		
Aryiró Stratáki	-	-	-	O	XXO	XO	XXO	XXX		
Yvonne Wisse	-	-	-	-	O	O	XXX			
Nadja Casadei	-	-	-	O	O	O	XXX			
Jessica Samuelsson	-	-	-	O	O	O	XXX			
Yuliya Tarasova	-	-	-	O	O	XXO	XXX			
Ida Marcussen	-	-	-	O	O	XXX				
Sushmitha Singha Roy	O	O	O	O	XXX					
Linda Züblin	-	O	O	XO	XXX					

Heptathlon - High Jump (continued)

Group B 15 August 2009

Position	Athlete	Country	Height	Points
1	Jessica Ennis	Great Britain	1.92	1132
2	Sharon Day	United States	1.89	1093
3	Lyudmyla Yosypenko	Ukraine	1.86	1054
4	Julia Mächtig	Germany	1.83	1016
4	Hanna Melnychenko	Ukraine	1.83	1016
6	Natallia Dobrynska	Ukraine	1.83	1016
7	Jennifer Oeser	Germany	1.83	1016
8	Bettie Wade	United States	1.80	978
9	Marisa De Aniceto	France	1.77	941
10	Diana Pickler	United States	1.77	941
11	Lilli Schwarzkopf	Germany	1.74	903
12	Tatyana Chernova	Russia	1.74	903
13	Eliška Klucinová	Czech Republic	1.71	867
14	Aiga Grabuste	Latvia	1.71	867
15	Sara Aerts	Belgium	1.68	830

Athlete	1.65	1.68	1.71	1.74	1.77	1.80	1.83	1.86	1.89	1.92	1.95
Jessica Ennis	-	-	-	O	-	O	O	O	O	XO	XXX
Sharon Day	-	-	O	-	-	O	O	O	XXO	XXX	
Lyudmyla Yosypenko	-	O	O	O	O	O	XO	XO	XXX		
Julia Mächtig	-	O	O	O	O	XO	O	XXX			
Hanna Melnychenko	-	O	O	O	XO	O	O	XXX			
Natallia Dobrynska	-	-	O	O	O	O	XO	XXX			
Jennifer Oeser	-	-	O	O	O	XO	XO	XXX			
Bettie Wade	-	O	O	O	O	XXO	XXX				
Marisa De Aniceto	O	-	O	O	O	XXX					
Diana Pickler	O	-	O	XO	XXO	XXX					
Lilli Schwarzkopf	O	O	O	XXO	XXX						
Tatyana Chernova	-	O	XO	XXO	XXX						
Eliška Klucinová	O	O	O	XXX							
Aiga Grabuste	-	O	XO	XXX							
Sara Aerts	XO	O	XXX								

Heptathlon - Shot Put

Group A 15 August 2009

Position	Athlete	Country	Distance	Points
1	Hanna Melnychenko	Ukraine	13.70	774
2	Sharon Day	United States	13.42	755
3	Eliška Klucinová	Czech Republic	13.40	754
4	Linda Züblin	Switzerland	13.16	738
5	Lyudmyla Yosypenko	Ukraine	13.01	728
6	Aryiró Stratáki	Greece	12.93	723
7	Kaie Kand	Estonia	12.83	716
8	Ida Marcussen	Norway	12.71	708
9	Tatyana Chernova	Russia	12.43	690
10	Marisa De Aniceto	France	12.21	675
11	Louise Hazel	Great Britain	11.62	636
12	Sushmitha Singha Roy	India	11.15	605
13	Brianne Theisen	Canada	11.07	600
	Sara Aerts	Belgium	DNS	-

Athlete	Throw 1	Throw 2	Throw 3
Hanna Melnychenko	11.94	13.23	13.70
Sharon Day	12.67	12.81	13.42
Eliška Klucinová	12.96	11.81	13.40
Linda Züblin	12.88	13.16	13.04
Lyudmyla Yosypenko	X	13.01	12.96
Aryiró Stratáki	12.27	X	12.93
Kaie Kand	12.64	X	12.83
Ida Marcussen	12.04	X	12.71
Tatyana Chernova	10.88	12.43	12.33
Marisa De Aniceto	12.21	11.39	X
Louise Hazel	11.24	10.92	11.62
Sushmitha Singha Roy	11.15	10.10	10.98
Brianne Theisen	10.57	11.07	X

Heptathlon - Shot Put (continued)

Group B 15 August 2009

Position	Athlete	Country	Distance	Points
1	Natallia Dobrynska	Ukraine	15.82	916
2	Julia Mächtig	Germany	15.21	875
3	Kamila Chudzik	Poland	15.10	868
4	Jennifer Oeser	Germany	14.29	813
5	Jessica Ennis	Great Britain	14.14	803
6	Ida Antoinette Nana Djimou	France	14.04	797
7	Karolina Tyminska	Poland	13.75	777
8	Jessica Samuelsson	Sweden	13.56	765
9	Lilli Schwarzkopf	Germany	13.43	756
10	Aiga Grabuste	Latvia	13.26	745
11	Yuliya Tarasova	Uzbekistan	12.92	722
12	Nadja Casadei	Sweden	12.92	722
13	Yvonne Wisse	Netherlands	12.53	696
14	Diana Pickler	United States	12.40	688
	Bettie Wade	United States	-	-

Athlete	Throw 1	Throw 2	Throw 3
Natallia Dobrynska	15.81	15.82	15.61
Julia Mächtig	15.21	13.97	14.82
Kamila Chudzik	14.68	X	15.10
Jennifer Oeser	14.29	X	X
Jessica Ennis	13.07	12.55	14.14
Ida Antoinette Nana Djimou	11.92	13.96	14.04
Karolina Tyminska	13.03	X	13.75
Jessica Samuelsson	13.56	13.52	X
Lilli Schwarzkopf	13.43	X	-
Aiga Grabuste	12.48	13.26	X
Yuliya Tarasova	12.92	12.71	12.65
Nadja Casadei	X	12.92	12.55
Yvonne Wisse	10.32	11.17	12.53
Diana Pickler	11.36	12.40	12.01
Bettie Wade	X	X	X

Heptathlon - 200m

Heat 1   15 August 2009

Position	Lane	Athlete	Country	Time	Points
1	7	Jessica Ennis	Great Britain	23.25	1054
2	5	Lyudmyla Yosypenko	Ukraine	23.86	994
3	4	Karolina Tyminska	Poland	23.87	993
4	2	Hanna Melnychenko	Ukraine	24.11	970
5	1	Tatyana Chernova	Russia	24.13	968
6	8	Brianne Theisen	Canada	24.62	922
7	3	Jessica Samuelsson	Sweden	24.71	914
8	6	Yvonne Wisse	Netherlands	24.78	907

Heat 2   15 August 2009

Position	Lane	Athlete	Country	Time	Points
1	5	Diana Pickler	United States	24.75	910
2	8	Nadja Casadei	Sweden	24.92	894
3	2	Marisa De Aniceto	France	25.32	858
4	4	Ida Marcussen	Norway	25.59	833
5	3	Aryiró Stratáki	Greece	25.93	803
6	7	Kaie Kand	Estonia	26.07	791
7	6	Lilli Schwarzkopf	Germany	DNS	-

Heat 3   15 August 2009

Position	Lane	Athlete	Country	Time	Points
1	3	Louise Hazel	Great Britain	24.19	963
2	8	Jennifer Oeser	Germany	24.30	952
3	7	Kamila Chudzik	Poland	24.33	949
4	2	Julia Mächtig	Germany	24.39	944
5	5	Yuliya Tarasova	Uzbekistan	24.60	924
6	4	Natallia Dobrynska	Ukraine	25.02	885
7	6	Linda Züblin	Switzerland	25.04	883

Heat 4   15 August 2009

Position	Lane	Athlete	Country	Time	Points
1	2	Ida Antoinette Nana Djimou	France	24.83	902
2	6	Bettie Wade	United States	24.98	889
3	7	Sharon Day	United States	25.15	873
4	8	Aiga Grabuste	Latvia	25.49	842
5	4	Sushmitha Singha Roy	India	25.65	828
6	3	Eliška Klucinová	Czech Republic	26.17	782
7	5	Sara Aerts	Belgium	DNS	-

Heptathlon - Long Jump

Group A 16 August 2009

Position	Athlete	Country	Wind	Distance	Points
1	Aiga Grabuste	Latvia	0.9	6.4	975
2	Ida Antoinette Nana Djimou	France	-0.7	6.32	949
3	Kaie Kand	Estonia	-0.2	5.99	846
4	Marisa De Aniceto	France	0.0	5.97	840
5	Jessica Samuelsson	Sweden	0.3	5.9	819
6	Aryiró Stratáki	Greece	1.1	5.87	810
7	Yvonne Wisse	Netherlands	0.2	5.87	810
8	Brianne Theisen	Canada	0.8	5.82	795
9	Eliška Klucinová	Czech Republic	0.9	5.78	783
10	Sharon Day	United States	-0.8	5.69	756
11	Linda Züblin	Switzerland	0.9	5.69	756
12	Sushmitha Singha Roy	India	-2.1	5.43	680
13	Ida Marcussen	Norway		-	
14	Sara Aerts	Belgium		DNS	

Athlete	Jump 1	Jump 2	Jump 3
Aiga Grabuste	6.40	4.22	6.24
Ida Antoinette Nana Djimou	6.01	6.32	6.10
Kaie Kand	X	X	5.99
Marisa De Aniceto	X	5.97	5.71
Jessica Samuelsson	X	X	5.90
Aryiró Stratáki	X	5.87	5.59
Yvonne Wisse	5.55	X	5.87
Brianne Theisen	5.82	X	5.74
Eliška Klucinová	X	5.78	X
Sharon Day	5.64	X	5.69
Linda Züblin	5.54	X	5.69
Sushmitha Singha Roy	5.43	X	4.70
Ida Marcussen	X	X	X

Heptathlon - Long Jump (continued)

Group B 16 August 2009

Position	Athlete	Country	Wind	Distance	Points
1	Kamila Chudzik	Poland	0.2	6.55	1023
2	Tatyana Chernova	Russia	-0.1	6.50	1007
3	Hanna Melnychenko	Ukraine	0.8	6.43	985
4	Jennifer Oeser	Germany	1.0	6.42	981
4	Natallia Dobrynska	Ukraine	0.6	6.41	978
6	Julia Mächtig	Germany	0.4	6.36	962
7	Jessica Ennis	Great Britain	-0.8	6.29	940
8	Diana Pickler	United States	1.5	6.24	924
9	Yuliya Tarasova	Uzbekistan	0.0	6.23	921
10	Lyudmyla Yosypenko	Ukraine	-0.6	6.20	912
11	Bettie Wade	United States	0.8	6.18	905
12	Louise Hazel	Great Britain	0.2	6.13	890
13	Nadja Casadei	Sweden	-0.3	5.78	783
14	Lilli Schwarzkopf	Germany		DNS	
15	Karolina Tyminska	Poland		DNS	

Athlete	Jump 1	Jump 2	Jump 3
Kamila Chudzik	6.31	6.37	6.55
Tatyana Chernova	6.33	6.44	6.50
Hanna Melnychenko	6.43	6.32	X
Jennifer Oeser	6.42	6.32	5.76
Natallia Dobrynska	6.24	6.41	6.33
Julia Mächtig	X	X	6.36
Jessica Ennis	6.19	6.08	6.29
Diana Pickler	6.11	6.16	6.24
Yuliya Tarasova	6.23	X	6.02
Lyudmyla Yosypenko	6.09	6.12	6.20
Bettie Wade	X	6.18	X
Louise Hazel	6.13	5.93	5.94
Nadja Casadei	X	X	5.78

Heptathlon - Javelin

Group A 16 August 2009

Position	Athlete	Country	Distance	Points
1	Linda Züblin	Switzerland	53.01	919
2	Ida Marcussen	Norway	50.02	861
3	Kamila Chudzik	Poland	48.72	835
4	Marisa De Aniceto	France	48.39	829
5	Ida Antoinette Nana Djimou	France	47.93	820
6	Lyudmyla Yosypenko	Ukraine	46.87	800
7	Brianne Theisen	Canada	43.84	741
8	Jessica Ennis	Great Britain	43.54	735
9	Aiga Grabuste	Latvia	43.52	735
10	Natallia Dobrynska	Ukraine	43.29	731
11	Hanna Melnychenko	Ukraine	42.24	710
12	Tatyana Chernova	Russia	41.88	703
13	Eliška Klucinová	Czech Republic	41.19	690
14	Julia Mächtig	Germany	40.70	681
	Lilli Schwarzkopf	Germany	DNS	-

Athlete	Throw 1	Throw 2	Throw 3
Linda Züblin	X	53.01	47.65
Ida Marcussen	50.02	X	X
Kamila Chudzik	48.72	45.20	46.60
Marisa De Aniceto	48.39	47.16	43.50
Ida Antoinette Nana Djimou	43.08	47.93	45.12
Lyudmyla Yosypenko	46.87	38.77	45.84
Brianne Theisen	41.07	42.42	43.84
Jessica Ennis	43.54	38.96	X
Aiga Grabuste	43.52	41.19	X
Natallia Dobrynska	42.38	43.29	41.96
Hanna Melnychenko	42.24	X	X
Tatyana Chernova	41.88	34.99	41.21
Eliška Klucinová	41.19	X	29.52
Julia Mächtig	40.70	39.61	40.58

Heptathlon - Javelin

Group B 16 August 2009

Position	Athlete	Country	Distance	Points
1	Jennifer Oeser	Germany	46.70	796
2	Sharon Day	United States	44.14	747
3	Louise Hazel	Great Britain	43.51	735
4	Aryiró Stratáki	Greece	42.87	722
5	Diana Pickler	United States	41.13	689
6	Yuliya Tarasova	Uzbekistan	40.88	684
7	Kaie Kand	Estonia	37.68	623
8	Jessica Samuelsson	Sweden	37.15	613
9	Bettie Wade	United States	36.70	604
10	Sushmitha Singha Roy	India	36.03	591
11	Yvonne Wisse	Netherlands	33.82	549
12	Nadja Casadei	Sweden	32.30	520
	Sara Aerts	Belgium	DNS	-
	Karolina Tyminska	Poland	DNS	-

Athlete	Throw 1	Throw 2	Throw 3
Jennifer Oeser	X	46.70	46.01
Sharon Day	40.43	44.14	X
Louise Hazel	43.41	42.90	43.51
Aryiró Stratáki	42.87	41.49	X
Diana Pickler	38.85	41.13	X
Yuliya Tarasova	39.55	40.88	X
Kaie Kand	32.93	X	37.68
Jessica Samuelsson	34.03	34.50	37.15
Bettie Wade	X	36.70	X
Sushmitha Singha Roy	35.07	36.03	X
Yvonne Wisse	33.48	33.82	32.68
Nadja Casadei	28.02	X	32.30

Heptathlon - 800m

Heat 1 16 August 2009

Position	Lane	Athlete	Country	Time	Points
1	5	Nadja Casadei	Sweden	2:12.66	926
2	3	Ida Marcussen	Norway	2:13.81	910
3	7	Yvonne Wisse	Netherlands	2:15.58	885
4	6	Eliška Klucinová	Czech Republic	2:23.79	773
5	4	Bettie Wade	United States	2:25.50	750
6	8	Sushmitha Singha Roy	India	2:36.13	618

Heat 2 16 August 2009

Position	Lane	Athlete	Country	Time	Points
1	7	Jessica Samuelsson	Sweden	2:10.34	960
2	4	Kaie Kand	Estonia	2:11.92	937
3	8	Brianne Theisen	Canada	2:12.62	927
4	3	Aryiró Stratáki	Greece	2:16.72	869
5	6	Linda Züblin	Switzerland	2:17.01	865
6	5	Yuliya Tarasova	Uzbekistan	2:35.05	631

Heat 3 16 August 2009

Position	Lane	Athlete	Country	Time	Points
1	8	Tatyana Chernova	Russia	2:09.11	978
2	7	Sharon Day	United States	2:13.84	909
3	5	Marisa De Aniceto	France	2:14.80	896
4	3	Diana Pickler	United States	2:15.60	884
5	6	Louise Hazel	Great Britain	2:15.85	881
6	4	Aiga Grabuste	Latvia	2:17.43	859

Heat 4 16 August 2009

Position	Lane	Athlete	Country	Time	Points
1	4	Jessica Ennis	Great Britain	2:12.22	932
2	8	Hanna Melnychenko	Ukraine	2:12.85	923
3	5	Natallia Dobrynska	Ukraine	2:13.22	918
4	3	Jennifer Oeser	Germany	2:14.34	902
5	7	Lyudmyla Yosypenko	Ukraine	2:14.64	898
6	1	Julia Mächtig	Germany	2:17.07	864
7	2	Ida Antoinette Nana Djimou	France	2:17.72	855
8	6	Kamila Chudzik	Poland	2:18.58	843

Heptathlon - Final Standings

Position	Athlete	Country	Points
GOLD	Jessica Ennis	Great Britain	6731
SILVER	Jennifer Oeser	Germany	6493
BRONZE	Kamila Chudzik	Poland	6471
4	Natallia Dobrynska	Ukraine	6444
5	Lyudmyla Yosypenko	Ukraine	6416
6	Hanna Melnychenko	Ukraine	6414
7	Ida Antoinette Nana Djimou	France	6323
8	Tatyana Chernova	Russia	6288
9	Julia Mächtig	Germany	6265
10	Sharon Day	United States	6126
11	Diana Pickler	United States	6086
12	Marisa De Aniceto	France	6049
13	Aiga Grabuste	Latvia	6033
14	Louise Hazel	Great Britain	6008
15	Brianne Theisen	Canada	5949
16	Linda Züblin	Switzerland	5934
17	Jessica Samuelsson	Sweden	5885
18	Kaie Kand	Estonia	5760
19	Aryiró Stratáki	Greece	5748
20	Yvonne Wisse	Netherlands	5704
21	Yuliya Tarasova	Uzbekistan	5658
22	Nadja Casadei	Sweden	5598
23	Eliška Klucinová	Czech Republic	5505
24	Bettie Wade	United States	5134
25	Ida Marcussen	Norway	5014
26	Sushmitha Singha Roy	India	4983
	Karolina Tyminska	Poland	DNF
	Sara Aerts	Belgium	DNF
	Lilli Schwarzkopf	Germany	DNF

Decathlon - 100m

Heat 1   19 August 2009

Position	Lane	Athlete	Country	Time	Points
1	4	Alexey Sysoev	Russia	10.85	894
2	6	Dmitriy Karpov	Kakakhstan	11.02	856
3	5	Nadir El Fassi	France	11.12	834
4	7	Vasiliy Kharlamov	Russia	11.22	812
5	8	Atis Vaisjuns	Latvia	11.27	801
6	3	Mateo Sossah	France	11.57	738
7	2	Roland Schwarzl	Austria	11.69	713

Heat 2   19 August 2009

Position	Lane	Athlete	Country	Time	Points
1	7	Aleksandr Pogorelov	Russia	10.95	872
2	3	Moritz Cleve	Germany	11.06	847
3	8	Roman Šebrle	Czech Republic	11.16	825
4	2	Daisuke Ikeda	Japan	11.16	825
5	4	Andrei Krauchanka	Belarus	11.18	821
6	6	Eugene Martineau	Netherlands	11.18	821
7	5	Agustín Félix	Spain	11.32	791

Heat 3   19 August 2009

Position	Lane	Athlete	Country	Time	Points
1	5	Trey Hardee	United States	10.45	987
2	2	Ashton Eaton	United States	10.53	968
3	8	Yordani García	Cuba	10.60	952
4	6	Oleksiy Kasyanov	Ukraine	10.63	945
5	4	Yunior Díaz	Cuba	10.66	938
0	1	Larbi Bouraada	Algeria	10.68	933
7	3	Andres Raja	Estonia	10.82	901
8	7	Maurice Smith	Jamaica	29.42	-

Heat 4   19 August 2009

Position	Lane	Athlete	Country	Time	Points
1	1	Ingmar Vos	Netherlands	10.90	883
2	4	Pascal Behrenbruch	Germany	10.92	878
3	6	Daniel Almgren	Sweden	10.92	878
4	7	Norman Müller	Germany	11.01	858
5	2	Simon Walter	Switzerland	11.05	850
6	5	Eelco Sintnicolaas	Netherlands	11.05	850
7	3	Mikk-Mihkel Arro	Estonia	11.11	836
8	8	Leonel Suárez	Cuba	11.13	832

Heat 5   19 August 2009

Position	Lane	Athlete	Country	Time	Points
1	2	Willem Coertzen	South Africa	10.89	885
2	1	Nicklas Wiberg	Sweden	10.96	870
3	6	Mikk Pahapill	Estonia	11.01	858
4	3	Jake Arnold	United States	11.01	858
5	5	Yevhen Nikitin	Ukraine	11.04	852
6	7	Brent Newdick	New Zealand	11.11	836
7	4	Romain Barras	France	11.14	830
8	8	Attila Szabó	Hungary	11.15	827

Decathlon - Long Jump

Group A   19 August 2009

Position	Athlete	Country	Wind	Distance	Points
1	Ashton Eaton	United States	0.9	7.85	1022
2	Trey Hardee	United States	1.9	7.83	1017
3	Oleksiy Kasyanov	Ukraine	0.9	7.80	1010
4	Roman Šebrle	Czech Republic	0.7	7.80	1010
5	Yunior Díaz	Cuba	-0.3	7.72	990
6	Andrei Krauchanka	Belarus	0.2	7.62	965
7	Eugene Martineau	Netherlands	0.8	7.41	913
8	Andres Raja	Estonia	0.4	7.38	905
9	Vasiliy Kharlamov	Russia	-0.8	7.38	905
10	Larbi Bouraada	Algeria	0.5	7.35	898
11	Norman Müller	Germany	0.8	7.35	898
12	Willem Coertzen	South Africa	0.4	7.35	891
13	Nicklas Wiberg	Sweden	-0.4	7.32	874
14	Leonel Suárez	Cuba	-0.3	7.25	871
15	Ingmar Vos	Netherlands	-0.4	7.24	864
16	Agustín Félix	Spain	-0.5	7.19	859
17	Yordani García	Cuba	1.0	7.05	826
18	Mikk-Mihkel Arro	Estonia	0.4	6.94	799
	Roland Schwarzl	Austria		-	-

Athlete	Jump 1	Jump 2	Jump 3
Ashton Eaton	7.85	7.54	7.79
Trey Hardee	7.80	7.77	7.83
Oleksiy Kasyanov	7.80	X	7.76
Roman Šebrle	7.72	7.80	7.71
Yunior Díaz	7.72	7.45	7.69
Andrei Krauchanka	7.62	X	X
Eugene Martineau	7.15	7.41	-
Andres Raja	7.38	7.11	X
Vasiliy Kharlamov	7.38	6.99	X
Larbi Bouraada	7.29	7.35	X
Norman Müller	7.23	7.35	X
Willem Coertzen	X	7.32	7.26
Nicklas Wiberg	X	7.20	7.25
Leonel Suárez	6.76	X	7.24
Ingmar Vos	7.21	6.97	7.20
Agustín Félix	X	7.17	7.19
Yordani García	X	6.63	7.05
Mikk-Mihkel Arro	X	6.84	6.94
Roland Schwarzl	X	-	-

Decathlon - Long Jump (continued)

Group B   19 August 2009

Position	Athlete	Country	Wind	Distance	Points
1	Aleksandr Pogorelov	Russia	-0.4	7.49	932
2	Brent Newdick	New Zealand	1.9	7.42	915
3	Daniel Almgren	Sweden	0.0	7.29	883
4	Moritz Cleve	Germany	-0.3	7.27	878
4	Nadir El Fassi	France	0.2	7.26	876
6	Simon Walter	Switzerland	0.9	7.21	864
7	Eelco Sintnicolaas	Netherlands	-0.7	7.16	852
8	Attila Szabó	Hungary	1.0	7.09	835
9	Daisuke Ikeda	Japan	0.8	7.09	835
10	Pascal Behrenbruch	Germany	1.6	7.09	835
11	Romain Barras	France	0.1	7.04	823
12	Mateo Sossah	France	-0.4	7.04	823
13	Atis Vaisjuns	Latvia	0.0	6.94	799
14	Yevhen Nikitin	Ukraine	0.6	6.92	795
15	Alexey Sysoev	Russia	1.0	6.87	783
16	Dmitriy Karpov	Kazakhstan	0.2	6.86	781
17	Jake Arnold	United States	2.0	6.73	750
	Mikk Pahapill	Estonia		-	
	Maurice Smith	Jamaica		DNS	

Athlete	Jump 1	Jump 2	Jump 3
Aleksandr Pogorelov	7.29	7.26	7.49
Brent Newdick	7.27	X	7.42
Daniel Almgren	7.29	X	X
Moritz Cleve	6.80	7.27	X
Nadir El Fassi	7.22	7.26	7.26
Simon Walter	7.21	7.01	-
Eelco Sintnicolaas	7.10	7.16	7.09
Attila Szabó	7.03	7.09	X
Daisuke Ikeda	6.53	6.99	7.09
Pascal Behrenbruch	X	7.09	X
Romain Barras	7.04	X	7.01
Mateo Sossah	7.04	X	-
Atis Vaisjuns	6.73	X	6.94
Yevhen Nikitin	6.92	X	6.67
Alexey Sysoev	6.83	6.87	6.60
Dmitriy Karpov	X	6.86	6.78
Jake Arnold	6.41	6.73	6.35
Mikk Pahapill	X	X	X
Maurice Smith			

Decathlon - Shot Put

Group A 19 August 2009

Position	Athlete	Country	Distance	Points
1	Trey Hardee	United States	15.33	810
2	Nicklas Wiberg	Sweden	14.99	789
3	Andres Raja	Estonia	14.55	762
4	Mikk-Mihkel Arro	Estonia	14.42	754
5	Moritz Cleve	Germany	14.12	736
6	Andrei Krauchanka	Belarus	13.96	726
7	Ingmar Vos	Netherlands	13.78	715
8	Nadir El Fassi	France	13.62	705
9	Daisuke Ikeda	Japan	13.43	693
10	Daniel Almgren	Sweden	13.43	693
11	Agustín Félix	Spain	13.23	681
12	Willem Coertzen	South Africa	13.16	677
13	Eelco Sintnicolaas	Netherlands	12.80	655
14	Simon Walter	Switzerland	12.80	655
15	Eugene Martineau	Netherlands	12.66	647
16	Larbi Bouraada	Algeria	12.30	625
17	Ashton Eaton	United States	12.26	622
18	Mateo Sossah	France	11.97	605
	Roland Schwarzl	Austria	DNS	

Athlete	Throw 1	Throw 2	Throw 3
Trey Hardee	14.20	15.33	-
Nicklas Wiberg	14.46	14.13	14.99
Andres Raja	14.55	14.55	X
Mikk-Mihkel Arro	12.74	14.24	14.42
Moritz Cleve	13.84	14.12	X
Andrei Krauchanka	13.62	13.96	13.72
Ingmar Vos	13.05	13.44	13.78
Nadir El Fassi	13.37	13.41	13.62
Daisuke Ikeda	13.22	13.43	13.41
Daniel Almgren	X	13.40	13.43
Agustín Félix	12.09	13.23	X
Willem Coertzen	13.16	12.68	12.65
Eelco Sintnicolaas	12.80	12.28	12.60
Simon Walter	12.49	12.51	12.80
Eugene Martineau	12.36	12.47	12.66
Larbi Bouraada	12.30	X	10.37
Ashton Eaton	12.26	12.22	X
Mateo Sossah	X	11.97	X

Decathlon - Shot Put (continued)

Group B   19 August 2009

Position	Athlete	Country	Distance	Points
1	Aleksandr Pogorelov	Russia	16.65	891
2	Alexey Sysoev	Russia	16.17	862
3	Pascal Behrenbruch	Germany	15.77	837
4	Oleksiy Kasyanov	Ukraine	15.72	834
5	Dmitriy Karpov	Kazakhstan	15.27	806
6	Leonel Suárez	Cuba	15.20	802
7	Yordani García	Cuba	15.15	799
8	Roman Šebrle	Czech Republic	14.98	788
9	Vasiliy Kharlamov	Russia	14.95	787
10	Norman Müller	Germany	14.93	785
11	Romain Barras	France	14.78	776
12	Yevhen Nikitin	Ukraine	14.69	771
13	Yunior Díaz	Cuba	14.54	761
14	Mikk Pahapill	Estonia	14.38	752
15	Brent Newdick	New Zealand	14.35	750
16	Atis Vaisjuns	Latvia	14.07	733
17	Jake Arnold	United States	13.97	727
18	Attila Szabó	Hungary	13.92	723
	Maurice Smith	Jamaica	DNS	

Athlete	Throw 1	Throw 2	Throw 3
Aleksandr Pogorelov	16.55	16.36	16.65
Alexey Sysoev	15.61	16.17	X
Pascal Behrenbruch	15.74	15.77	X
Oleksiy Kasyanov	15.09	15.02	15.72
Dmitriy Karpov	15.27	X	15.12
Leonel Suárez	15.20	14.49	14.51
Yordani García	15.15	13.34	14.64
Roman Šebrle	14.98	14.91	X
Vasiliy Kharlamov	X	14.95	14.52
Norman Müller	14.93	14.70	X
Romain Barras	X	14.78	X
Yevhen Nikitin	14.07	14.69	X
Yunior Díaz	14.15	14.42	14.54
Mikk Pahapill	X	13.62	14.38
Brent Newdick	13.19	13.80	14.35
Atis Vaisjuns	12.98	14.07	X
Jake Arnold	13.97	X	13.90
Attila Szabó	13.86	13.47	13.92
Maurice Smith			

Decathlon - High Jump

Group A 19 August 2009

Position	Athlete	Country	Height	Points
1	Oleksiy Kasyanov	Ukraine	2.05	850
1	Pascal Behrenbruch	Germany	2.02	822
3	Yunior Díaz	Cuba	2.02	822
4	Andres Raja	Estonia	1.99	794
5	Atis Vaisjuns	Latvia	1.99	794
6	Eugene Martineau	Netherlands	1.99	794
7	Brent Newdick	New Zealand	1.99	794
8	Daniel Almgren	Sweden	1.99	794
8	Vasiliy Kharlamov	Russia	1.93	740
8	Yevhen Nikitin	Ukraine	1.93	740
11	Simon Walter	Switzerland	1.93	740
12	Mikk-Mihkel Arro	Estonia	1.90	714
13	Moritz Cleve	Germany	1.87	687
14	Daisuke Ikeda	Japan	1.87	687
15	Attila Szabó	Hungary	1.84	661
16	Eelco Sintnicolaas	Netherlands	1.81	636
	Roland Schwarzl	Austria	DNS	
	Mikk Pahapill	Estonia	DNS	
	Maurice Smith	Jamaica	DNS	

Athlete	1.75	1.78	1.81	1.84	1.87	1.90	1.93	1.96	1.99	2.02	2.05	2.08
Oleksiy Kasyanov	-	-	-	-	O	-	O	O	O	O	XXO	XXX
Pascal Behrenbruch	-	-	-	O	O	O	O	O	XO	XXO	XXX	
Yunior Díaz	-	-	O	O	O	O	O	XO	XXO	XXO	XXX	
Andres Raja	-	-	-	-	O	O	O	XXO	XO	XXX		
Atis Vaisjuns	-	-	-	-	O	-	O	O	XXO	XXX		
Eugene Martineau	-	-	-	-	-	O	O	O	XXO	XXX		
Brent Newdick	-	-	-	O	-	O	XO	XXO	XXO	XXX		
Daniel Almgren	-	-	-	-	O	XO	XO	XXO	XXO	XXX		
Vasiliy Kharlamov	-	-	-	O	-	o	O	XXX				
Yevhen Nikitin	-	-	O	-	O	XO	XO	XXX				
Simon Walter	-	-	-	-	O	XXO	XXO	XXX				
Mikk-Mihkel Arro	-	-	-	O	O	XO	XXX					
Moritz Cleve	-	-	O	O	O	XXX						
Daisuke Ikeda	O	O	O	O	O	XXX						
Attila Szabó	-	-	O	O	XXX							
Eelco Sintnicolaas	-	-	XXO	-	-	XX-						

Decathlon - High Jump (continued)

Group B 19 August 2009

Position	Athlete	Country	Height	Points
1	Roman Šebrle	Czech Republic	2.11	906
2	Leonel Suárez	Cuba	2.11	906
3	Andrei Krauchanka	Belarus	2.11	906
4	Yordani García	Cuba	2.08	878
4	Aleksandr Pogorelov	Russia	2.08	878
6	Agustín Félix	Spain	2.08	878
7	Mateo Sossah	France	2.05	850
8	Dmitriy Karpov	Kazakhstan	2.05	850
9	Larbi Bouraada	Algeria	2.05	850
10	Nicklas Wiberg	Sweden	2.05	850
11	Ingmar Vos	Netherlands	2.02	822
12	Willem Coertzen	South Africa	2.02	822
13	Alexey Sysoev	Russia	2.02	822
14	Ashton Eaton	United States	2.02	822
15	Romain Barras	France	1.99	794
16	Nadir El Fassi	France	1.99	794
17	Norman Müller	Germany	1.99	794
18	Trey Hardee	United States	1.99	794
19	Jake Arnold	United States	1.96	767

Athlete	1.81	1.84	1.87	1.90	1.93	1.96	1.99	2.02	2.05	2.08	2.11	2.14
Roman Šebrle	-	-	-	-	-	O	-	O	O	O	O	XXX
Leonel Suárez	-	-	-	-	-	O	-	XO	O	O	O	XX
Andrei Krauchanka	-	-	-	-	-	O	O	O	O	O	XO	XXX
Yordani García	-	-	-	-	-	O	O	O	O	O	XXX	
Aleksandr Pogorelov	-	-	-	-	-	O	-	O	XO	XO	XXX	
Agustín Félix	-	O	-	O	O	XXO	O	XO	O	XO	XXX	
Mateo Sossah	-	-	-	O	-	O	O	XO	O	XXX		
Dmitriy Karpov	-	-	-	O	O	O	XO	XXO	O	XXX		
Larbi Bouraada	-	-	-	XO	O	XO	O	XXO	O	XXX		
Nicklas Wiberg	-	-	-	-	-	O	XXO	XO	XO	XXX		
Ingmar Vos	-	-	-	-	-	XO	XO	O	XXX			
Willem Coertzen	-	-	-	O	-	O	O	XO	XXX			
Alexey Sysoev	-	-	XO	O	O	O	O	XO	X			
Ashton Eaton	-	O	-	O	-	O	XXO	XXO	XXX			
Romain Barras	-	-	O	O	O	O	O	XXX				
Nadir El Fassi	O	O	-	O	XO	O	XO	XXX				
Norman Müller	-	O	-	O	XO	O	XO	XXX				
Trey Hardee	-	-	-	O	-	XXO	XXO	XXX				
Jake Arnold	-	-	-	O	XO	XXO	XXX					

Decathlon - 400m

Heat 1 19 August 2009

Position	Lane	Athlete	Country	Time	Points
1	4	Daisuke Ikeda	Japan	49.28	848
2	5	Alexey Sysoev	Russia	49.32	846
3	7	Attila Szabó	Hungary	49.79	824
4	3	Atis Vaisjuns	Latvia	49.88	820
5	6	Ingmar Vos	Netherlands	49.99	815
6	8	Brent Newdick	New Zealand	50.10	810
7	2	Roman Šebrle	Czech Republic	50.42	795

Heat 2 19 August 2009

Position	Lane	Athlete	Country	Time	Points
1	8	Yunior Díaz	Cuba	46.15	1001
2	3	Daniel Almgren	Sweden	47.68	925
3	6	Ashton Eaton	United States	47.75	921
4	5	Oleksiy Kasyanov	Ukraine	47.85	916
5	4	Leonel Suárez	Cuba	48.00	909
6	2	Larbi Bouraada	Algeria	48.58	881
7	7	Simon Walter	Switzerland	49.67	830
	1	Eelco Sintnicolaas	Netherlands	DNS	

Heat 3 19 August 2009

Position	Lane	Athlete	Country	Time	Points
1	5	Norman Müller	Germany	48.20	899
2	8	Pascal Behrenbruch	Germany	48.72	875
3	2	Andres Raja	Estonia	49.00	861
4	6	Jake Arnold	United States	49.07	858
5	3	Vasiliy Kharlamov	Russia	49.44	841
6	4	Yevhen Nikitin	Ukraine	49.50	838
7	7	Mateo Sossah	France	49.60	833

Heat 4 19 August 2009

Position	Lane	Athlete	Country	Time	Points
1	5	Trey Hardee	United States	48.13	903
2	3	Yordani García	Cuba	48.34	893
3	2	Willem Coertzen	South Africa	48.63	879
4	4	Nicklas Wiberg	Sweden	48.73	874
5	6	Andrei Krauchanka	Belarus	48.77	872
6	8	Moritz Cleve	Germany	49.17	853
7	7	Romain Barras	France	49.66	830

Heat 5 19 August 2009

Position	Lane	Athlete	Country	Time	Points
1	7	Dmitriy Karpov	Kazakhstan	49.45	840
2	8	Eugene Martineau	Netherlands	50.26	803
3	4	Aleksandr Pogorelov	Russia	50.27	802
4	2	Mikk-Mihkel Arro	Estonia	51.28	757
5	3	Nadir El Fassi	France	51.35	753
6	5	Agustín Félix	Spain	52.41	707
	6	Mikk Pahapill	Estonia	DNS	

Decathlon - 110m Hurdles

Heat 1   20 August 2009

Position	Lane	Athlete	Country	Time	Points
1	8	Aleksandr Pogorelov	Russia	14.19	950
2	6	Yunior Díaz	Cuba	14.56	903
3	5	Norman Müller	Germany	14.59	900
4	2	Yevhen Nikitin	Ukraine	14.87	865
5	3	Daisuke Ikeda	Japan	14.90	862
6	7	Eugene Martineau	Netherlands	14.91	860
	4	Eelco Sintnicolaas	Netherlands	DNS	

Heat 2   20 August 2009

Position	Lane	Athlete	Country	Time	Points
1	1	Trey Hardee	United States	13.86	993
2	4	Yordani García	Cuba	14.08	964
3	7	Andres Raja	Estonia	14.22	946
4	2	Pascal Behrenbruch	Germany	14.24	944
5	5	Ashton Eaton	United States	14.28	939
6	6	Jake Arnold	United States	14.40	924
7	8	Leonel Suárez	Cuba	14.45	917
	3	Mikk Pahapill	Estonia	DNS	

Heat 3   20 August 2009

Position	Lane	Athlete	Country	Time	Points
1	4	Andrei Krauchanka	Belarus	14.13	958
2	6	Willem Coertzen	South Africa	14.26	941
3	8	Romain Barras	France	14.27	940
4	7	Oleksiy Kasyanov	Ukraine	14.44	918
5	2	Roman Šebrle	Czech Republic	14.44	918
6	5	Moritz Cleve	Germany	14.54	906
7	3	Brent Newdick	New Zealand	14.82	871

Heat 4   20 August 2009

Position	Lane	Athlete	Country	Time	Points
1	4	Dmitriy Karpov	Kazakhstan	14.46	916
2	8	Attila Szabó	Hungary	14.65	892
3	2	Simon Walter	Switzerland	14.83	870
4	5	Nadir El Fassi	France	14.9	862
5	6	Alexey Sysoev	Russia	14.97	853
6	3	Daniel Almgren	Sweden	15.14	833
7	7	Atis Vaisjuns	Latvia	15.27	817

Heat 5   20 August 2009

Position	Lane	Athlete	Country	Time	Points
1	4	Ingmar Vos	Netherlands	14.51	910
2	5	Larbi Bouraada	Algeria	14.57	902
3	7	Nicklas Wiberg	Sweden	14.75	880
4	8	Agustín Félix	Spain	14.8	874
5	3	Mikk-Mihkel Arro	Estonia	14.82	871
6	2	Mateo Sossah	France	14.83	870
7	6	Vasiliy Kharlamov	Russia	14.83	870

Decathlon - Discus

Group A 20 August 2009

Position	Athlete	Country	Distance	Points
1	Yunior Díaz	Cuba	43.52	736
2	Agustín Félix	Spain	42.81	722
3	Andres Raja	Estonia	42.75	721
4	Willem Coertzen	South Africa	42.40	713
5	Ingmar Vos	Netherlands	42.39	713
6	Nicklas Wiberg	Sweden	42.28	711
7	Nadir El Fassi	France	42.25	710
8	Andrei Krauchanka	Belarus	42.24	710
9	Atis Vaisjuns	Latvia	42.02	706
10	Mikk-Mihkel Arro	Estonia	41.83	702
11	Norman Müller	Germany	41.21	689
12	Daisuke Ikeda	Japan	39.72	659
13	Moritz Cleve	Germany	39.62	657
14	Larbi Bouraada	Algeria	37.83	621
15	Ashton Eaton	United States	37.15	607
16	Daniel Almgren	Sweden	34.33	550
	Eelco Sintnicolaas	Netherlands	DNS	

Athlete	Throw 1	Throw 2	Throw 3
Yunior Díaz	43.52	X	X
Agustín Félix	42.81	X	X
Andres Raja	39.29	42.75	40.88
Willem Coertzen	37.76	42.40	42.09
Ingmar Vos	40.90	42.39	X
Nicklas Wiberg	X	40.13	42.28
Nadir El Fassi	40.33	42.25	40.23
Andrei Krauchanka	42.24	X	40.67
Atis Vaisjuns	X	40.85	42.02
Mikk-Mihkel Arro	40.82	40.19	41.83
Norman Müller	40.09	X	41.21
Daisuke Ikeda	37.52	39.72	36.51
Moritz Cleve	39.62	38.60	39.54
Larbi Bouraada	37.83	X	33.87
Ashton Eaton	X	37.15	X
Daniel Almgren	34.33	33.93	X

Decathlon - Discus (continued)

Group B   20 August 2009

Position	Athlete	Country	Distance	Points
1	Alexey Sysoev	Russia	53.03	934
2	Dmitriy Karpov	Kazakhstan	48.93	848
3	Aleksandr Pogorelov	Russia	48.46	838
4	Trey Hardee	United States	48.08	830
5	Pascal Behrenbruch	Germany	48.06	830
6	Oleksiy Kasyanov	Ukraine	46.70	802
7	Roman Šebrle	Czech Republic	46.30	794
8	Vasiliy Kharlamov	Russia	46.24	792
9	Romain Barras	France	45.62	780
10	Eugene Martineau	Netherlands	44.94	766
11	Leonel Suárez	Cuba	44.71	761
12	Yordani García	Cuba	44.40	754
13	Attila Szabó	Hungary	43.75	741
14	Brent Newdick	New Zealand	43.60	738
15	Jake Arnold	United States	43.23	730
16	Yevhen Nikitin	Ukraine	42.71	720
17	Simon Walter	Switzerland	42.48	715
18	Mateo Sossah	France	41.25	690

Athlete	Throw 1	Throw 2	Throw 3
Alexey Sysoev	48.86	52.53	53.03
Dmitriy Karpov	X	48.93	X
Aleksandr Pogorelov	48.46	X	46.42
Trey Hardee	46.04	48.08	47.33
Pascal Behrenbruch	48.06	44.60	X
Oleksiy Kasyanov	45.22	46.32	46.70
Roman Šebrle	X	46.30	X
Vasiliy Kharlamov	42.91	46.24	X
Romain Barras	45.62	X	44.46
Eugene Martineau	42.56	44.94	43.56
Leonel Suárez	42.70	42.37	44.71
Yordani García	X	43.93	44.40
Attila Szabó	40.18	43.12	43.75
Brent Newdick	42.01	41.34	43.60
Jake Arnold	42.78	43.23	43.08
Yevhen Nikitin	42.71	39.59	X
Simon Walter	42.00	41.09	42.48
Mateo Sossah	40.78	X	41.25

Decathlon - Pole Vault

Group A 20 August 2009

Position	Athlete	Country	Height	Points
1	Nadir El Fassi	France	4.80	849
2	Andres Raja	Estonia	4.80	849
3	Brent Newdick	New Zealand	4.80	849
3	Oleksiy Kasyanov	Ukraine	4.80	849
5	Pascal Behrenbruch	Germany	4.80	849
6	Larbi Bouraada	Algeria	4.70	819
7	Willem Coertzen	South Afrca	4.60	790
8	Daisuke Ikeda	Japan	4.60	790
9	Yevhen Nikitin	Ukraine	4.60	790
10	Yunior Díaz	Cuba	4.60	790
11	Mikk-Mihkel Arro	Estonia	4.50	760
12	Nicklas Wiberg	Sweden	4.50	760
13	Mateo Sossah	France	4.40	731
13	Atis Vaisjuns	Latvia	4.40	731
13	Ingmar Vos	Netherlands	4.40	731
16	Attila Szabó	Hungary	4.40	731
17	Daniel Almgren	Sweden	4.30	702

Athlete	3.80	3.90	4.00	4.10	4.20	4.30	4.40	4.50	4.60	4.70	4.80	4.90
Nadir El Fassi	-	-	-	-	O	-	O	XXO	O	XXO	O	XXX
Andres Raja	-	-	-	-	-	-	O	-	XO	O	XO	XXX
Brent Newdick	-	-	-	-	-	O	-	O	O	XO	XXO	XXX
Oleksiy Kasyanov	-	-	-	-	-	-	O	O	XO	O	XXO	XXX
Pascal Behrenbruch	-	-	-	-	O	O	O	O	XO	XO	XXO	XXX
Larbi Bouraada	-	-	-	-	-	-	O	O	O	O	XXX	
Willem Coertzen	-	-	O	-	O	XXO	O	O	O	XXX		
Daisuke Ikeda	-	-	-	-	O	O	O	O	XXO	XXX		
Yevhen Nikitin	-	-	-	-	XO	-	O	-	XXO	XXX		
Yunior Díaz	-	-	O	O	O	XO	O	XO	XXO	XXX		
Mikk-Mihkel Arro	-	-	-	-	O	-	XXO	O	XXX			
Nicklas Wiberg	-	XO	O	O	O	O	XO	XO	XXX			
Mateo Sossah	-	-	O	-	O	-	O	XXX				
Atis Vaisjuns	-	-	-	-	-	-	O	-	XXX			
Ingmar Vos	-	-	O	O	O	O	O	XXX				
Attila Szabó	-	-	-	O	XO	O	O	XXX				
Daniel Almgren	XO	-	O	O	XXO	XXO	XXX					

Decathlon - Pole Vault (continued)

Group B 20 August 2009

Position	Athlete	Country	Height	Points
1	Trey Hardee	United States	5.20	972
2	Alexey Sysoev	Russia	5.10	941
3	Aleksandr Pogorelov	Russia	5.10	941
4	Simon Walter	Switzerland	5.00	910
5	Vasiliy Kharlamov	Russia	5.00	910
5	Ashton Eaton	United States	5.00	910
7	Romain Barras	France	5.00	910
8	Leonel Suárez	Cuba	5.00	910
9	Andrei Krauchanka	Belarus	4.90	880
10	Agustín Félix	Spain	4.90	880
11	Dmitriy Karpov	Kazakhstan	4.80	849
12	Eugene Martineau	Netherlands	4.80	849
13	Norman Müller	Germany	4.80	849
14	Jake Arnold	United States	4.70	819
15	Yordani García	Cuba	4.70	819
16	Roman Šebrle	Czech Republic	4.60	790
16	Moritz Cleve	Germany	4.60	790
	Eelco Sintnicolaas	Netherlands	DNS	

Athlete	4.30	4.40	4.50	4.60	4.70	4.80	4.90	5.00	5.10	5.20	5.30
Trey Hardee	-	-	-	-	O	-	O	O	O	O	XXX
Alexey Sysoev	-	O	-	O	O	XO	O	XXO	O	XXX	
Aleksandr Pogorelov	-	-	-	-	-	O	-	O	XXO	XXX	
Simon Walter	-	-	O	-	O	XO	XXO	O	XXX		
Vasiliy Kharlamov	-	XO	-	O	O	O	O	XO	XXX		
Ashton Eaton	O	-	O	XO	-	O	O	XO	XXX		
Romain Barras	-	-	-	O	-	XO	O	XXO	XXX		
Leonel Suárez	-	-	O	-	O	XXO	O	XXO	XXX		
Andrei Krauchanka	-	-	-	O	-	O	O	XXX			
Agustín Félix	-	XO	-	O	O	XO	O	XXX			
Dmitriy Karpov	-	-	-	XO	-	O	XXX				
Eugene Martineau	-	-	-	XO	-	XO	XX-				
Norman Müller	-	O	-	XXO	O	XO	XXX				
Jake Arnold	-	-	-	-	O	-	XXX				
Yordani García	-	O	O	O	XO	XXX					
Roman Šebrle	-	O	-	O	-	XXX					
Moritz Cleve	O	O	O	O	XXX						

Decathlon - Javelin

Group A   20 August 2009

Position	Athlete	Country	Distance	Points
1	Nicklas Wiberg	Sweden	75.02	966
2	Eugene Martineau	Netherlands	70.14	892
3	Yordani García	Cuba	69.37	880
4	Roman Šebrle	Czech Republic	65.61	823
5	Ingmar Vos	Netherlands	64.27	802
6	Andrei Krauchanka	Belarus	60.71	749
7	Mateo Sossah	France	59.67	733
8	Attila Szabó	Hungary	59.56	731
9	Atis Vaisjuns	Latvia	57.50	700
10	Norman Müller	Germany	57.40	699
11	Jake Arnold	United States	57.37	698
12	Daniel Almgren	Sweden	56.69	688
13	Mikk-Mihkel Arro	Estonia	56.21	681
14	Moritz Cleve	Germany	54.26	652
15	Dmitriy Karpov	Kazakhstan	51.38	609
16	Agustín Félix	Spain	50.10	590

Athlete	Throw 1	Throw 2	Throw 3
Nicklas Wiberg	75.02	-	-
Eugene Martineau	67.56	70.14	X
Yordani García	69.37	67.00	66.95
Roman Šebrle	61.80	62.74	65.61
Ingmar Vos	61.49	64.27	61.52
Andrei Krauchanka	60.07	60.71	X
Mateo Sossah	53.84	59.67	56.08
Attila Szabó	58.94	56.36	59.56
Atis Vaisjuns	57.50	X	X
Norman Müller	56.20	54.45	57.40
Jake Arnold	56.04	X	57.37
Daniel Almgren	46.51	56.62	56.69
Mikk-Mihkel Arro	55.29	54.77	56.21
Moritz Cleve	53.93	54.06	54.26
Dmitriy Karpov	51.38	50.74	47.77
Agustín Félix	X	50.10	X

Decathlon - Javelin

Group B 20 August 2009

Position	Athlete	Country	Distance	Points
1	Leonel Suárez	Cuba	75.19	969
2	Pascal Behrenbruch	Germany	69.72	885
3	Trey Hardee	United States	68.00	859
4	Willem Coertzen	South Africa	65.46	820
5	Alexey Sysoev	Russia	64.55	807
6	Aleksandr Pogorelov	Russia	63.95	797
7	Daisuke Ikeda	Japan	63.73	794
8	Larbi Bouraada	Algeria	62.53	776
9	Romain Barras	France	61.24	757
10	Yunior Díaz	Cuba	60.09	739
11	Vasiliy Kharlamov	Russia	59.93	737
12	Andres Raja	Estonia	57.73	704
13	Nadir El Fassi	France	57.65	703
14	Simon Walter	Switzerland	54.91	662
15	Yevhen Nikitin	Ukraine	54.73	659
16	Brent Newdick	New Zealand	51.52	611
17	Ashton Eaton	United States	50.87	601
18	Oleksiy Kasyanov	Ukraine	49.00	574

Athlete	Throw 1	Throw 2	Throw 3
Leonel Suárez	69.01	73.96	75.19
Pascal Behrenbruch	69.72	67.28	66.87
Trey Hardee	65.22	66.86	68.00
Willem Coertzen	65.46	61.98	63.05
Alexey Sysoev	59.65	64.55	61.70
Aleksandr Pogorelov	63.95	60.94	X
Daisuke Ikeda	62.71	63.73	62.05
Larbi Bouraada	62.53	57.84	54.78
Romain Barras	60.72	61.24	60.68
Yunior Díaz	48.10	56.35	60.09
Vasiliy Kharlamov	58.69	59.93	X
Andres Raja	57.73	56.00	54.82
Nadir El Fassi	56.34	54.72	57.65
Simon Walter	54.91	49.92	49.20
Yevhen Nikitin	48.28	54.73	50.69
Brent Newdick	51.52	-	-
Ashton Eaton	46.59	45.24	50.87
Oleksiy Kasyanov	35.82	45.02	49.00

Decathlon - 1500m

Heat 1 20 August 2009

Position	Athlete	Country	Time	Points
1	Larbi Bouraada	Algeria	4:12.15	866
2	Daniel Almgren	Sweden	4:13.47	857
3	Nadir El Fassi	France	4:16.51	836
4	Mateo Sossah	France	4:20.40	809
5	Daisuke Ikeda	Japan	4:22.39	795
6	Moritz Cleve	Germany	4:25.96	771
7	Ingmar Vos	Netherlands	4:28.51	754
8	Brent Newdick	New Zealand	4:30.57	741
9	Eugene Martineau	Netherlands	4:35.27	710
10	Jake Arnold	United States	4:35.93	706
11	Yevhen Nikitin	Ukraine	4:40.12	680
12	Mikk-Mihkel Arro	Estonia	4:44.14	654
13	Attila Szabó	Hungary	4:45.64	645
14	Atis Vaisjuns	Latvia	4:52.08	606
15	Dmitriy Karpov	Kazakhstan	4:53.61	597
16	Agustín Félix	Spain	5:00.50	557
17	Simon Walter	Switzerland	5:01.12	553

Heat 2 20 August 2009

Position	Athlete	Country	Time	Points
1	Nicklas Wiberg	Sweden	4:17.05	832
2	Oleksiy Kasyanov	Ukraine	4:24.52	781
3	Romain Barras	France	4:27.04	764
4	Leonel Suárez	Cuba	4:27.25	763
5	Willem Coertzen	South Africa	4:32.57	728
6	Norman Müller	Germany	4:33.02	725
7	Alexey Sysoev	Russia	4:34.97	712
8	Andrei Krauchanka	Belarus	4:37.77	694
9	Pascal Behrenbruch	Germany	4:39.45	684
10	Yunior Díaz	Cuba	4:40.58	677
11	Andres Raja	Estonia	4:40.73	676
12	Vasiliy Kharlamov	Russia	4:41.54	671
13	Ashton Eaton	United States	4:45.03	649
14	Aleksandr Pogorelov	Russia	4:48.70	627
15	Trey Hardee	United States	4:48.91	625
16	Yordani García	Cuba	4:49.45	622
17	Roman Šebrle	Czech Republic	4:50.33	617

Decathlon - Final Standings

Position	Athlete	Country	Points
GOLD	Trey Hardee	United States	8790
SILVER	Leonel Suárez	Cuba	8640
BRONZE	Aleksandr Pogorelov	Russia	8528
4	Oleksiy Kasyanov	Ukraine	8479
5	Alexey Sysoev	Russia	8454
6	Pascal Behrenbruch	Germany	8439
7	Nicklas Wiberg	Sweden	8406
8	Yordani García	Cuba	8387
9	Yunior Díaz	Cuba	8357
10	Andrei Krauchanka	Belarus	8281
11	Roman Šebrle	Czech Republic	8266
12	Romain Barras	France	8204
13	Larbi Bouraada	Algeria	8171
14	Willem Coertzen	South Africa	8146
15	Andres Raja	Estonia	8119
16	Norman Müller	Germany	8096
17	Vasiliy Kharlamov	Russia	8065
18	Ashton Eaton	United States	8061
19	Eugene Martineau	Netherlands	8055
20	Ingmar Vos	Netherlands	8009
21	Dmitriy Karpov	Kazakhstan	7952
22	Nadir El Fassi	France	7922
23	Brent Newdick	New Zealand	7915
24	Jake Arnold	United States	7837
25	Daniel Almgren	Sweden	7803
26	Daisuke Ikeda	Japan	7788
27	Moritz Cleve	Germany	7777
28	Yevhen Nikitin	Ukraine	7710
29	Mateo Sossah	France	7682
30	Simon Walter	Switzerland	7649
31	Attila Szabó	Hungary	7610
32	Agustín Félix	Spain	7539
33	Mikk-Mihkel Arro	Estonia	7528
34	Atis Vaisjuns	Latvia	7507
	Roland Schwarzl	Austria	DNF
	Maurice Smith	Jamaica	DNF
	Mikk Pahapill	Estonia	DNF
	Eelco Sintnicolaas	Netherlands	DNF

Men's 20 Kilometres Walk

FINAL 15 August 2009

Position	Athlete	Country	Time
GOLD	Valeriy Borchin	Russia	1:18.41
SILVER	Hao Wang	China	1:19.06
BRONZE	Eder Sánchez	Mexico	1:19.22
4	Giorgio Rubino	Italy	1:19.50
5	Luis López	Colombia	1:20.03
6	Jared Tallent	Australia	1:20.27
7	Erik Tysse	Norway	1:20.38
8	Jesús Sánchez	Mexico	1:20.52
9	Matej Tóth	Slovakia	1:21.13
10	João Vieira	Portugal	1:21.43
11	Koichiro Morioka	Japan	1:21.48
12	Jianbo Li	China	1:21.54
13	Yafei Zhu	China	1:21.56
14	André Höhne	Germany	1:21.59
15	Robert Heffernan	Ireland	1:22.09
16	José Ignacio Díaz	Spain	1:22.12
17	Andrey Krivov	Russia	1:22.19
18	Luke Adams	Australia	1:22.37
19	Hassanine Sebei	Tunisia	1:22.52
20	Babubhai Panucha	India	1:23.06
21	Jean-Jacques Nkouloukidi	Italy	1:23.07
22	Dzianis Simanovich	Belarus	1:23.36
23	Rolando Saquipay	Ecuador	1:23.51
24	Juan Manuel Molina	Spain	1:24.00
25	Chil-sung Park	South Korea	1:24.01
26	Artur Brzozowski	Poland	1:24.17
27	Sérgio Vieira	Portugal	1:24.32
28	Pedro Daniel Gómez	Mexico	1:24.39
29	Yerko Araya	China	1:24.49
30	Isamu Fujisawa	Japan	1:25.12
31	Petr Trofimov	Russia	1:26.02
32	David Kimutai Rotich	Kenya	1:26.35
33	Ruslan Dmytrenko	Ukraine	1:27.01
34	Hyunsub Kim	South Korea	1:27.08
35	Predrag Filipovic	Serbia	1:27.44
36	Pavel Chihuan	Peru	1:27.54
37	Rustam Kuvatov	Kazakhstan	1:28.47
38	Jakub Jelonek	Poland	1:28.59
39	Andrés Chocho	Ecuador	1:29.14
40	Juan Manuel Cano	Argentina	1:29.20
41	Allan Segura	Costa Rica	1:29.52
42	Yusuke Suzuki	Japan	1:30.21
43	Youngjun Byun	South Korea	1:30.35
44	Mauricio Arteaga	Ecuador	1:32.25
45	Vilius Mikelionis	Lithuania	1:32.53
	Adam Rutter	Australia	DQ
	Moacir Zimmermann	Brazil	DQ
	José Alessandro Bagio	Brazil	DNF
	Francisco Javier Fernández	Spain	DNF
	Ivano Brugnetti	Italy	DNF

Women's 20 Kilometres Walk

FINAL 16 August 2009

Position	Athlete	Country	Time
GOLD	Olga Kaniskina	Russia	1:28.09
SILVER	Olive Loughnane	Ireland	1:28.58
BRONZE	Hong Liu	China	1:29.10
4	Anisya Kirdyapkina	Russia	1:30.09
5	Vera Santos	Portugal	1:30.35
6	Beatriz Pascual	Spain	1:30.40
7	Masumi Fuchise	Japan	1:31.15
8	Kristina Saltanovic	Lithuania	1:31.23
9	Elisa Rigaudo	Italy	1:31.52
10	Susana Feitor	Portugal	1:32.42
11	Inês Henriques	Portugal	1:32.51
12	Kumi Otoshi	Japan	1:33.05
13	Larisa Emelyanova	Russia	1:34.31
14	Vera Sokolova	Russia	1:34.55
15	Sniazhana Yurchanka	Belarus	1:34.57
16	Ana Maria Groza	Romania	1:35.19
17	Valentina Trapletti	Italy	1:35.33
18	Mingxia Yang	China	1:35.42
19	Zuzana Schindlerová	Czech Republic	1:35.47
20	Tania Regina Spindler	Brazil	1:35.51
21	Evaggelía Xinoú	Greece	1:35.56
22	Jess Rothwell	Australia	1:36.01
23	Claudia Stef	Romania	1:36.09
24	Brigita Virbalyté	Lithuania	1:36.28
25	Marie Polli	Switzerland	1:36.44
26	Zuzana Malíková	Slovakia	1:37.47
27	Claire Tallent	Australia	1:38.12
28	Agnieszka Dygacz	Poland	1:38.36
29	Alessandra Picagevicz	Brazil	1:38.50
30	Geovana Irusta	Bolivia	1:00.16
31	Chaima Trabelsi	Tunisia	1:39.50
32	Svetlana Tolstaya	Kazakhstan	1:40.41
33	Johana Ordóñez	Ecuador	1:42.57
34	Anamaria Greceanu	Romania	1:43.35
35	Rachel Lavallée	Canada	1:45.45
36	Olha Yakovenko	Ukraine	1:45.55
37	Cristina López	El Salvador	1:47.33
	Cheryl Webb	Australia	DQ
	Yawei Yang	China	DQ
	Johanna Jackson	Great Britain	DQ
	María Hatzipanayiotídou	Greece	DQ
	Mayumi Kawasaki	Japan	DQ
	Kjersti Plätzer	Norway	DQ
	Monica Svensson	Sweden	DQ
	María Vasco	Spain	DNF
	Sabine Krantz	Germany	DNF
	Mária Gáliková	Slovakia	DNF
	Teresa Vaill	United States	DNF

Men's 50 Kilometres Walk

FINAL 21 August 2009

Position	Athlete	Country	Time
GOLD	Sergey Kirdyapkin	Russia	3:38.35
SILVER	Trond Nymark	Norway	3:41.16
BRONZE	Jesús Angel García	Spain	3:41.37
4	Grzegorz Sudol	Poland	3:42.34
5	André Höhne	Germany	3:43.19
6	Luke Adams	Australia	3:43.39
7	Jared Tallent	Australia	3:44.50
8	Marco De Luca	Italy	3:46.31
9	Jarkko Kinnunen	Finland	3:47.36
10	Matej Tóth	Slovakia	3:48.35
11	Faguang Xu	China	3:48.52
12	Yohan Diniz	France	3:49.03
13	Jesús Sánchez	Mexico	3:50.55
14	Donatas Škarnulis	Lithuania	3:50.56
15	Chengliang Zhao	China	3:53.06
16	Oleksiy Shelest	Ukraine	3:54.03
17	Tadas Šuškevicius	Lithuania	3:54.29
18	Koichiro Morioka	Japan	3:56.21
19	Horacio Nava	Mexico	3:56.26
20	Herve Davaux	France	3:57.10
21	Andreas Gustafsson	Sweden	3:57.53
22	Rafal Augustyn	Poland	3:58.30
23	Augusto Cardoso	Portugal	3:59.10
24	Miloš Bátovský	Slovakia	3:59.39
25	Lei Li	China	4:00.13
26	Mikel Odriozola	Spain	4:00.54
27	Cedric Houssaye	France	4:02.44
28	Diego Cafagna	Italy	4:08.04
29	José Alejandro Cambil	Spain	4:13.14
30	Magno Mesías Zapata	Ecuador	4:15.28
31	Luis Fernando García	Guatemala	4:18.13
	Takayuki Tanii	Japan	DQ
	Yuki Yamazaki	Japan	DQ
	Omar Zepeda	Mexico	DQ
	Mario José dos Santos Jr	Brazil	DNF
	Marco Benavides	El Salvador	DNF
	Konstadínos Stefanópoulos	Greece	DNF
	Jamie Costin	Ireland	DNF
	Colin Griffin	Ireland	DNF
	Alex Schwazer	Italy	DNF
	Ingus Janevics	Latvia	DNF
	Erik Tysse	Norway	DNF
	Rafal Fedaczynski	Poland	DNF
	António Pereira	Portugal	DNF
	Yuriy Andronov	Russia	DNF
	Denis Nizhegorodov	Russia	DNF
	Nenad Filipovic	Serbia	DNF

Men's 4x100m Relay

Qualification for the Final: first two in each heat plus the next two fastest finishers.

Heat 1   21 August 2009

Position	Lane	Athletes	Country		Time
1	7	Darrel Brown, Marc Burns, Keston Bledman, Richard Thompson	Trinidad & Tobago	Q	38.47
2	3	Masashi Eriguchi, Naoki Tsukahara, Shinji Takahira, Kenji Fujimitsu	Japan	Q	38.53
3	5	Ronald Pognon, Martial Mbandjock, Pierre-Alexis Pessonneaux, Christophe Lemaître	France	q	38.59
4	8	Vicente de Lima, Sandro Viana, Basílio de Moraes, José Carlos Moreira	Brazil	q	38.72
5	6	Pascal Mancini, Marc Schneeberger, Reto Schenkel, Marco Cribari	Switzerland		39.47
6	4	Hannes Dreyer, Leigh Julius, Thuso Mpuang, Louis van Zyl	South Africa		39.71

Heat 2   21 August 2009

Position	Lane	Athletes	Country		Time
1	6	Simeon Williamson, Tyrone Edgar, Marlon Devonish, Harry Aikines-Aryeetey	Great Britain	Q	38.11
2	3	Hank Palmer, Oluseyi Smith, Jared Connaughton, Bryan Barnett	Canada	Q	38.60
3	8	Gregory Sedoc, Caimin Douglas, Guus Hoogmoed, Patrick van Luijk	Netherlands		38.95
4	5	Dany Gonçalves, Arnaldo Abrantes, Ricardo Monteiro, Francis Obikwelu	Portugal		39.25
5	4	Nana Kofi Camm, Tanko Braimah, Seth Amoo, Aziz Zakari	Ghana		39.61
	7	Terrence Trammell, Mike Rodgers, Shawn Crawford, Darvis Patton	United States		DQ

Heat 3   21 August 2009

Position	Lane	Athletes	Country		Time
1	7	Roberto Donati, Simone Collio, Emanuele Di Gregorio, Fabio Cerutti	Italy	Q	38.52
2	3	Lerone Clarke, Michael Frater, Steve Mullings, Dwight Thomas	Jamaica	Q	38.6
3	4	Anthony Alozie, Joshua Ross, Aaron Rouge-Serret, Matt Davies	Australia		38.93
4	5	Apinan Sukaphai, Wachara Sondee, Suppachai Chimdee, Sittichai Suwonprateep	Thailand		39.73
	8	Tobias Unger, Marius Broening, Alexander Kosenkow, Martin Keller	Germany		DNF
		Michal Bielczyk, Dariusz Kuc, Mikolaj Lewanski, Robert Kubaczyk	Poland		DNS

Men's 4x100m Relay (continued)

FINAL 22 August 2009

Position	Lane	Athletes	Country		Time
GOLD	7	Steve Mullings, Michael Frater, Usain Bolt, Asafa Powell	Jamaica	CR	37.31
SILVER	6	Darrel Brown, Marc Burns, Emmanuel Callander, Richard Thompson	Trinidad & Tobago		37.62
BRONZE	3	Simeon Williamson, Tyrone Edgar, Marlon Devonish, Harry Aikines-Aryeetey	Great Britain		38.02
4	5	Masashi Eriguchi, Naoki Tsukahara, Shinji Takahira, Kenji Fujimitsu	Japan		38.30
5	8	Sam Effah, Oluseyi Smith, Jared Connaughton, Bryan Barnett	Canada		38.39
6	4	Roberto Donati, Simone Collio, Emanuele Di Gregorio, Fabio Cerutti	Italy		38.54
7	2	Vicente de Lima, Sandro Viana, Basílio de Moraes, José Carlos Moreira	Brazil		38.56
8	1	Ronald Pognon, Martial Mbandjock, Eddy De Lepine, Christophe Lemaître	France		39.21

Women's 4x100m Relay

Qualification for the Final: first two in each heat plus the next two fastest finishers.

Heat 1 22 August 2009

Position	Lane	Athletes	Country		Time
1	4	Simone Facey, Shelly-Ann Fraser, Aleen Bailey, Kerron Stewart	Jamaica	Q	41.88
2	3	Sheniqua Ferguson, Chandra Sturrup, Christine Amertil, Debbie Ferguson-McKenzie	Bahamas	Q	42.66
3	6	Reyare Thomas, Kelly-Ann Baptiste, Ayanna Hutchinson, Semoy Hackett	Trinidad & Tobago	q	43.22
4	8	Olena Chebanu, Nataliya Pohrebnyak, Mariya Ryemyen, Hrystyna Stuy	Ukraine		43.77
5	5	Tanika Liburd, Meritzer Williams, Tameka Williams, Virgil Hodge	St Kitts & Nevis		43.98
6	7	Olivia Borlee, Hanna Mariën, Elodie Ouédraogo, Anne Zagre	Belgium		43.99

Heat 2 22 August 2009

Position	Lane	Athletes	Country		Time
1	7	Marion Wagner, Anne Möllinger, Cathleen Tschirch, Verena Sailer	Germany	Q	42.96
2	4	Yomara Hinestroza, Felipa Palacios, Darlenis Obregón, Norma González	Colombia	Q	43.30
3	8	Laura Turner, Montell Douglas, Emily Freeman, Emma Ania	Great Britain	q	43.34
4	6	Hanna Bahdanovich, Aksana Drahun, Alena Kievich, Yulia Nestsiarenka	Belarus		44.12
5	3	Sangwan Jaksunin, Orranut Klomdee, Jutamass Tawoncharoen, Jintara Seangdee	Thailand		44.59
	5	Olutoyin Augustus, Halimat Ismaila, Seun Adigun, Oludamola Osayomi	Nigeria		DQ

Women's 4x100m Relay (continued)

Heat 3   22 August 2009

Position	Lane	Athletes	Country		Time
1	6	Rosemar Maria Neto, Lucimar Aparecida de Moura, Thaissa Presti, Vanda Gomes	Brazil	Q	43.07
2	7	Evgeniya Polyakova, Aleksandra Fedoriva, Yulia Gushchina, Natalia Rusakova	Russia	Q	43.18
3	4	Iwona Ziółkowska, Marta Jeschke, Dorota Jedrusinska, Iwona Brzezinska	Poland		43.63
4	3	Chisato Fukushima, Momoko Takahashi, Mayumi Watanabe, Maki Wada	Japan		44.24
	5	Lauryn Williams, Alexandria Anderson, Muna Lee, Carmelita Jeter	United States		DNF

FINAL   22 August 2009

Position	Lane	Athletes	Country	Time
GOLD	5	Simone Facey, Shelly-Ann Fraser, Aleen Bailey, Kerron Stewart	Jamaica	42.06
SILVER	3	Sheniqua Ferguson, Chandra Sturrup, Christine Amertil, Debbie Ferguson-McKenzie	Bahamas	42.29
BRONZE	4	Marion Wagner, Anne Möllinger, Cathleen Tschirch, Verena Sailer	Germany	42.87
4	8	Evgeniya Polyakova, Aleksandra Fedoriva, Yulia Gushchina, Yuliya Chermoshanskaya	Russia	43.00
5	6	Rosemar Maria Neto, Lucimar Aparecida de Moura, Thaissa Presti, Vanda Gomes	Brazil	43.13
6	1	Laura Turner, Montell Douglas, Emily Freeman, Emma Ania	Great Britain	43.16
7	2	Reyare Thomas, Kelly-Ann Baptiste, Ayanna Hutchinson, Semoy Hackett	Trinidad & Tobago	43.43
8	7	Yomara Hinestroza, Felipa Palacios, Darlenis Obregón, Norma González	Colombia	43.71

Men's 4x400m Relay

Qualification for the Final: first three in each heat plus the next two fastest finishers.

Heat 1   22 August 2009

Position	Lane	Athletes	Country		Time
1	5	Lionel Larry, Kerron Clement, Bershawn Jackson, Angelo Taylor	United States	Q	3:01.40
2	7	Leslie Djhone, Teddy Venel, Yannick Fonsat, Yoann Décimus	France	Q	3:01.65
3	8	Conrad Williams, Robert Tobin, David Greene, Martyn Rooney	Great Britain	Q	3:01.91
4	4	Joel Milburn, Tristan Thomas, Ben Offereins, Sean Wroe	Australia	q	3:02.04
5	6	Saul Welgopwa, Noah Akwu, Amaechi Morton, Bola Gee Lawal	Nigeria	q	3:02.36
6	3	Maksim Dyldin, Valentin Kruglyakov, Konstantin Svechkar, Aleksandr Derevyagin	Russia		3:02.78

Heat 2   22 August 2009

Position	Lane	Athletes	Country		Time
1	7	Antoine Gillet, Cedric van Branteghem, Nils Duerinck, Kévin Borlée	Belgium	Q	3:02.13
2	4	Gustavo Cuesta, Arismendy Peguero, Yoel Tapia, Felix Sánchez	Dominican Republic	Q	3:02.76
3	2	Piotr Klimczak, Marcin Marciniszyn, Rafal Wieruszewski, Jan Ciepiela	Poland	Q	3:03.23
4	6	Martin Grothkopp, Kamghe Gaba, Eric Krüger, Ruwen Faller	Germany		3:03.52
5	5	Leford Green, Ricardo Chambers, Isa Phillips, Jermaine Gonzales	Jamaica		3:04.45
6	8	Ofentse Mogawane, Jacob Mothsodi Ramokoka, Sibusiso Sishi, Pieter Smith	South Africa		3:07.88
	3	Ramon Miller, Avard Moncur, Latoy Williams, Nathaniel McKinney	Bahamas		DQ

FINAL   23 August 2009

Position	Lane	Athletes	Country	Time
GOLD	4	Angelo Taylor, Jeremy Wariner, Kerron Clement, LaShawn Merritt	United States	2:57.86
SILVER	7	Conrad Williams, Michael Bingham, Robert Tobin, Martyn Rooney	Great Britain	3:00.53
BRONZE	2	John Steffensen, Ben Offereins, Tristan Thomas, Sean Wroe	Australia	3:00.90
4	5	Antoine Gillet, Kévin Borlée, Nils Duerinck, Cedric van Branteghem	Belgium	3:01.88
5	8	Marcin Marciniszyn, Piotr Klimczak, Kacper Kozlowski, Jan Ciepiela	Poland	3:02.23
6	6	Arismendy Peguero, Yon Soriano, Yoel Tapia, Felix Sánchez	Dominican Republic	3:02.47
7	3	Leslie Djhone, Teddy Venel, Yannick Fonsat, Yoann Décimus	France	3:02.65
8	1	Saul Welgopwa, Noah Akwu, Amaechi Morton, Bola Gee Lawal	Nigeria	3:02.73

Women's 4x400m Relay

Qualification for the Final: first three in each heat plus the next two fastest finishers.

Heat 1   22 August 2009

Position	Lane	Athletes	Country		Time
1	3	Debbie Dunn, Natasha Hastings, Jessica Beard, Sanya Richards	United States	Q	3:29.31
2	5	Endurance Abinuwa, Muizat Ajoke Odumosu, Josephine Ehigie, Folasade Abugan	Nigeria	Q	3:29.60
3	6	Virginie Michanol, Aurélie Kamga, Symphora Béhi, Solen Désert-Mariller	France	Q	3:29.60
4	4	Pirrenee Steinert, Madeleine Pape, Caitlin Willis-Pincott, Tamsyn Lewis	Australia		3:30.80
5	1	Marta Milani, Daniela Reina, Maria Enrica Spacca, Libania Grenot	Italy		3:31.05
6	7	Geisa Aparecida Coutinho, Emmilly Pinheiro, Sheila Ferreira, Jailma de Lima	Brazil		3:31.42
7	8	Alejandra Cherizola, Nallely Vela, Ruth Grajeda, Karla Dueñas	Mexico		3:40.03
	2	Sasha Rolle, Shakeitha Henfield, Rashan Brown, Katrina Seymour	Bahamas		DQ

Heat 2   22 August 2009

Position	Lane	Athletes	Country		Time
1	3	Natalya Nazarova, Tatyana Firova, Natalya Antyukh, Lyudmila Litvinova	Russia	Q	3:23.80
2	6	Kaliese Spencer, Shereefa Lloyd, Rosemarie Whyte, Novlene Williams-Mills	Jamaica	Q	3:24.72
3	7	Fabienne Kohlmann, Sorina Nwachukwu, Esther Cremer, Claudia Hoffmann	Germany	Q	3:25.08
4	1	Nicola Sanders, Vicki Barr, Jennifer Meadows, Lee McConnell	Great Britain	q	3:25.23
5	4	Susana A Clement, Daisurami Bonne, Zulia Calatayud, Indira Terrero	Cuba	q	3:27.36
6	8	Esther Akinsulie, Adrienne Power, Jenna Martin, Carline Muir	Canada		3:29.17
7	5	Yuliya Baraley, Tetiana Petlyuk, Anastasiya Rabchenyuk, Antonina Yefremova	Ukraine		3:30.76
8	2	Sayaka Aoki, Asami Tanno, Mayu Sato, Satomi Kubokura	Japan		3:34.46

FINAL   23 August 2009

Position	Lane	Athletes	Country	Time
GOLD	5	Debbie Dunn, Allyson Felix, Lashinda Demus, Sanya Richards	United States	3:17.83
SILVER	6	Rosemarie Whyte, Novlene Williams-Mills, Shereefa Lloyd, Shericka Williams	Jamaica	3:21.15
BRONZE	4	Anastasiya Kapachinskaya, Tatyana Firova, Lyudmila Litvinova, Antonina Krivoshapka	Russia	3:21.64
4	2	Lee McConnell, Christine Ohuruogu, Vicki Barr, Nicola Sanders	Great Britain	3:25.16
5	8	Fabienne Kohlmann, Sorina Nwachukwu, Esther Cremer, Claudia Hoffmann	Germany	3:27.61
6	3	Endurance Abinuwa, Muizat Ajoke Odumosu, Josephine Ehigie, Folasade Abugan	Nigeria	3:28.55
7	7	Virginie Michanol, Aurélie Kamga, Symphora Béhi, Solen Désert-Mariller	France	3:30.16
8	1	Diosmely Peña, Daisurami Bonne, Zulia Calatayud, Indira Terrero	Cuba	3:36.99

Athlete Index

Forenames	Surname	Born	Country	Event(s)	Prev Apps
Annemette	Aagaard	05/08/1973	Denmark	Marathon (w)	07
Moonika	Aava	19/06/1979	Estonia	Javelin (w)	05
Maria	Abakumova	15/01/1986	Russia	Javelin (w)	07
Yeoryía	Abatzídou	19/04/1969	Greece	Marathon (w)	07
Abdalla	Abdelgadir	12/09/1988	Sudan	1500 (m)	0
Youcef	Abdi	07/12/1977	Australia	3000m SC (m)	03 07
Ali	Abdosh	28/08/1987	Ethiopia	5000m (m)	0
Halim Abdul Hakeem	Abdul	09/12/1987	Singapore	110m Hurdles	07
Ruky	Abdulai	08/08/1985	Canada	Long Jump (w)	0
Ahmad Hassan	Abdullah	29/07/1981	Qatar	10000m (m)	03 07
Haider Naser	Abdulshaheed	13/01/1981	Iraq	Discus (m)	0
Elvan	Abeylegesse	11/09/1982	Turkey	5000m (w), 10000m (w)	01 03 07
Shehan	Abeypitiyage	17/01/1990	Sri Lanka	100m (m)	0
Endurance	Abinuwa	31/07/1987	Nigeria	4x400m (w)	0
Joseph G	Abraham	11/09/1981	India	400m Hurdles (m)	07
Yuriy	Abramov	09/12/1976	Russia	Marathon (m)	0
Arnaldo	Abrantes	27/11/1986	Portugal	100m (m), 200m (m), 4x100m (m)	07
Sanaa	Abubkheet	07/12/1984	Palestine	800m (w)	0
Folasade	Abugan	17/12/1990	Nigeria	400m (w), 4x400m (w)	07
Omar	Abusaid	29/10/1985	Palestine	5000m (m)	0
Onochie	Achike	31/01/1975	Great Britain	Triple Jump (m)	99 01
Amy	Acuff	14/07/1975	United States	High Jump (w)	99 01 03 05 07
Muna Jabir	Adam	06/01/1987	Sudan	400m Hurdles (w)	07
Luke	Adams	22/10/1976	Australia	20km Walk (m), 50km Walk	03 05 07
Seun	Adigun	03/01/1987	Nigeria	100m Hurdles, 4x100m (w)	0
Elisângela	Adriano	27/07/1972	Brazil	Discus (w)	99 01 03 05 07
Sara	Aerts	25/01/1984	Belgium	Heptathlon	0
Kseniya	Agafonova	25/06/1983	Russia	10000m (w)	0
Naroa	Agirre	15/05/1979	Spain	Pole Vault (w)	03 05 07
Alessandra	Aguilar	01/07/1978	Spain	Marathon (w)	0
Zemzem	Ahmed	27/12/1984	Ethiopia	3000m SC (w)	07
Harry	Aikines-Aryeetey	29/08/1988	Great Britain	4x100m (m)	0
Michael	Aish	24/07/1976	New Zealand	Marathon (m)	03 07
Marina	Aitova	13/09/1982	Kazakhstan	High Jump (w)	03 07
Yukiko	Akaba	18/10/1979	Japan	Marathon (w)	0
Serafina	Akeli	07/12/1984	Samoa	Javelin (w)	05 07
Esther	Akinsulie	22/04/1984	Canada	400m (w), 4x400m (w)	0
Noah	Akwu	23/09/1990	Nigeria	4x400m (m)	0
Mohamed Salman	Al Khuwalidi	18/06/1981	Saudi Arabia	Long Jump (m)	05 07
Mohammad	Al-Azemi	16/06/1982	Kuwait	800m (m)	05 07
Hamed Hamdan	AlBishi	03/03/1982	Saudi Arabia	200m (m)	03 05
Kyle	Alcorn	18/03/1985	United States	3000m SC (m)	0
Yamilé	Aldama	14/08/1972	Sudan	Triple Jump (w)	99 05 07
Ali	Al-Deraan	17/04/1990	Saudi Arabia	800m (m)	0
Nadezhda	Alekhina	22/09/1978	Russia	Triple Jump (w)	03 05
Virgilijus	Alekna	13/02/1972	Lithuania	Discus (m)	99 01 03 05 07
David	Alerte	18/09/1984	France	200m (m)	05 07
Kineke	Alexander	21/02/1986	St Vincent & Grenadines	400m (w)	05 07
Annie	Alexander	28/08/1987	Trinidad & Tobago	Shot Put (w)	0
Mohamad	Al-Garni	02/07/1992	Qatar	1500 (m)	0
Rakia	Al-Gassra	06/09/1982	Brunei	100m (w), 200m (w)	07
Sultan Abdulmajeed	Alhabashi	31/01/1985	Saudi Arabia	Shot Put (m)	07
Hussain Jamaan	Alhamdah	04/08/1983	Saudi Arabia	5000m (m)	0
Khalil	Al-Hanahneh	11/05/1980	Jordan	200m (m)	03 07
Barakat	Al-Harthi	15/06/1988	Oman	100m (m)	0
Liqat	Ali	06/08/1983	Pakistan	100m (m)	0
Belal Mansoor	Ali	17/10/1988	Brunei	800m (m), 1500m (m)	05 07
Abubakr Nagmeldin	Ali	22/02/1986	Sudan	400m (m)	03 05 07
Hamza	Alic	20/01/1979	Bosnia & Herzegovina	Shot Put (m)	05 07
Daniel	Almgren	30/11/1979	Sweden	Decathlon	0
Anna	Alminova	17/01/1985	Russia	1500 (w)	0
Anthony	Alozie	18/08/1986	Australia	4x100m (m)	0
Rania	Alqebali	09/01/1991	Jordan	400m (w)	0
Hussein Taher	Al-Sabee	13/11/1979	Saudi Arabia	Long Jump (m)	99 01 03 07
Omar Jouma Bilal	Al-Salfa	15/10/1989	United Arab Emirates	200m (m)	0

Athlete Index

Forenames	Surname	Born	Country	Event(s)	Prev Apps
Mohammed	Al-Salhi	11/05/1986	Saudi Arabia	800m (m)	03 05 07
Ali Mohamed	Al-Zinkawi	27/02/1984	Kuwait	Hammer (m)	05 07
Doreen	Amata	06/05/1988	Nigeria	High Jump (w)	0
Morhad	Amdouni	21/06/1988	France	5000m (m)	0
Christine	Amertil	18/08/1979	Bahamas	400m (w), 4x100m (w)	01 03 05 07
Vida	Amin	07/12/1983	Ghana	200m (w)	03 05 07
Seth	Amoo	20/03/1983	Ghana	200m (m), 4x100m (m)	07
Lindsey	Anderson	23/05/1985	United States	3000m SC (w)	07
Alexandria	Anderson	28/01/1987	United States	4x100m (w)	0
Leonid	Andreev	06/10/1983	Uzbekistan	Pole Vault (m)	05 07
Yuriy	Andronov	06/11/1971	Russia	50km Walk	0
Emma	Ania	07/02/1980	Great Britain	4x100m (w)	0
Vida	Anim	07/12/1983	Ghana	100m (w)	03 05 07
Justin	Anlezark	14/08/1977	Australia	Shot Put (m)	01 03
Seema	Antil	27/07/1983	India	Discus (w)	07
Olena	Antonova	16/06/1972	Ukraine	Discus (w)	99 01 03 05 07
Natalya	Antyukh	26/06/1981	Russia	400m Hurdles (w), 4x400m (w)	01 05 07
Sayaka	Aoki	15/12/1986	Japan	400m Hurdles (w), 4x400m (w)	0
Esref	Apak	03/01/1982	Turkey	Hammer (m)	05 07
Ronalds	Arajs	29/11/1987	Latvia	200m (m)	0
Daisuke	Arakawa	19/09/1981	Japan	Long Jump (m)	07
Yerko	Araya	14/02/1986	China	20km Walk (m)	0
Tiraa	Arere	16/10/1984	Cook Islands	100m (m)	0
Yarianny	Argüelles	14/04/1984	Cuba	Long Jump (w)	0
Eva	Arias	08/10/1980	Spain	3000m SC (w)	0
Aaron	Armstrong	14/10/1977	Trinidad & Tobago	200m (m)	05
Dylan	Armstrong	15/01/1981	Canada	Shot Put (m)	01 07
Jake	Arnold	03/01/1984	United States	Decathlon	07
Mikk-Mihkel	Arro	28/03/1984	Estonia	Decathlon	0
Mauricio	Arteaga	08/08/1988	Ecuador	20km Walk (m)	0
Eleni	Artymata	16/05/1986	Cyprus	100m (w), 200m (w)	0
Aliaksandr	Ashomka	18/02/1984	Belarus	Javelin (m)	0
Yared	Asmerom	04/02/1980	Eritrea	Marathon (m)	05 07
Meskerem	Assefa	28/09/1986	Ethiopia	1500 (w)	03
Sofia	Assefa	14/11/1987	Ethiopia	3000m SC (w)	0
Nikolay	Atanasov	11/12/1974	Bulgaria	Long Jump (m)	99 03 07
Derrick	Atkins	05/01/1984	Bahamas	100m (m)	05 07
Jessica	Augusto	08/11/1981	Portugal	3000m SC (w)	05 07
Olutoyin	Augustus	24/12/1979	Nigeria	100m Hurdles, 4x100m (w)	07
Rafal	Augustyn	14/05/1984	Poland	50km Walk	07
Fatih	Avan	01/01/1989	Turkey	Javelin (m)	0
Anna	Avdeeva	06/04/1985	Russia	Shot Put (w)	07
Roman	Avramenko	23/03/1988	Ukraine	Javelin (m)	0
Wude	Ayalew	04/07/1987	Ethiopia	10000m (w)	0
Simon	Ayeko	10/05/1987	Uganda	3000m SC (m)	0
Tatyana	Azarova	02/12/1985	Kazakhstan	400m Hurdles (w)	07
Masoud	Azizi	02/02/1985	Afghanistan	100m (m)	0
Mehdi	Baala	17/08/1978	France	1500 (m)	99 01 03 05 07
Samir	Baala	11/11/1974	France	Marathon (m)	0
Jaroslav	Bába	02/09/1984	Czech Republic	High Jump (m)	03 05 07
Andrew	Baddeley	20/06/1982	Great Britain	1500 (m)	07
Ndiss Kaba	Badji	21/09/1983	Senegal	Long Jump (m)	07
José Alessandro	Bagio	16/04/1981	Brazil	20km Walk (m)	0
Oumar Bella	Bah	11/09/1986	Guinea	100m (m)	0
Mariama	Bah	11/07/1988	Guinea	100m (w)	0
Hanna	Bahdanovich	14/10/1983	Belarus	4x100m (w)	0
Xue	Bai	13/12/1988	China	Marathon (w)	0
Daniel	Bailey	09/09/1986	Antigua & Barbuda	100m (m)	05
Aleen	Bailey	25/11/1980	Jamaica	100m (w), 4x100m (w)	03 05 07
Jade	Bailey	10/06/1983	Barbados	200m (w)	0
Alain	Bailey	14/08/1987	Jamaica	Long Jump (m)	0
Zivilé	Balciūnaité	03/04/1979	Lithuania	Marathon (w)	07
Maria Zeferina	Baldaia	29/08/1972	Brazil	Marathon (w)	0
Jorge	Balliengo	05/01/1978	Argentina	Discus (m)	05
Ksenija	Balta	01/11/1986	Estonia	Long Jump (w)	0

Athlete Index

Forenames	Surname	Born	Country	Event(s)	Prev Apps
Konstadínos	Baniótis	06/11/1986	Greece	High Jump (m)	0
Kelly-Ann	Baptiste	14/01/2008	Trinidad & Tobago	100m (w), 200m (w), 4x100m (w)	05
Yuliya	Baraley	25/04/1990	Ukraine	4x400m (w)	0
Aleesha	Barber	16/05/1987	Trinidad & Tobago	100m Hurdles	0
Bryan	Barnett	10/02/1987	Canada	100m (m), 4x100m (m)	07
Vicki	Barr	14/04/1982	Great Britain	4x400m (w)	0
Romain	Barras	01/08/1980	France	Decathlon	05 07
Jennifer	Barringer	23/08/1986	United States	3000m SC (w)	07
Juan Luis	Barrios	24/06/1983	Mexico	5000m (m), 10000m (m)	07
Yarelis	Barrios	12/07/1983	Cuba	Discus (w)	07
Marisa	Barros	25/02/1980	Portugal	Marathon (w)	0
Trevor	Barry	14/06/1983	Bahamas	High Jump (m)	0
Ralf	Bartels	21/02/1978	Germany	Shot Put (m)	01 03 05 07
Rondell	Bartholomew	07/04/1990	Grenada	400m (m)	0
Trish	Bartholomew	23/10/1986	Grenada	400m (w)	0
Dimitri	Bascou	20/07/1987	France	110m Hurdles	0
Adriano	Bastos	22/02/1978	Brazil	Marathon (m)	0
Makelesi	Batimala	23/10/1977	Fiji	200m (w), 400m (w)	03 07
Ser-Od	Bat-Ochir	07/10/1981	Mongolia	Marathon (m)	03 05 07
Miloš	Bátovský	26/05/1979	Slovakia	50km Walk	05 07
Anna	Battke	03/01/1985	Germany	Pole Vault (w)	0
Melanie	Bauschke	14/07/1986	Germany	Long Jump (w)	0
Sebastian	Bayer	11/06/1986	Germany	Long Jump (m)	0
Getuli	Bayo	07/06/1980	Tanzania	Marathon (m)	05 07
Atsede	Baysa	16/04/1987	Ethiopia	Marathon (w)	0
Mario	Bazán	01/08/1997	Peru	3000m SC (m)	0
Jessica	Beard	08/01/1989	United States	400m (w), 4x400m (w)	0
Martin	Beckmann	15/07/1977	Germany	Marathon (m)	07
Sylwester	Bednarek	28/04/1989	Poland	High Jump (m)	0
Vera	Begic	17/03/1982	Croatia	Discus (w)	0
Amy Yoder	Begley	11/01/1978	United States	10000m (w)	0
Symphora	Béhi	22/03/1986	France	4x400m (w)	0
Pascal	Behrenbruch	19/01/1985	Germany	Decathlon	0
Ruth	Beitia	01/04/1979	Spain	High Jump (w)	03 05 07
Alemitu	Bekele	17/09/1977	Turkey	1500 (w), 5000m (w)	0
Kenenisa	Bekele	13/06/1982	Ethiopia	5000m (m), 10000m (m)	03 05 07
Bezunesh	Bekele	29/01/1983	Ethiopia	Marathon (w)	05
Mimi	Belete	09/06/1988	Brunei	1500 (w)	0
Kenta	Bell	16/03/1977	United States	Triple Jump (m)	03 05 07
Fadil	Bellaabouss	15/06/1986	France	400m Hurdles (m)	07
Marco	Benavides	02/05/1986	El Salvador	50km Walk	0
Hasna	Benhassi	01/06/1978	Morocco	800m (w)	99 03 05 07
Yvonne	Bennett	29/07/1990	Northern Mariana Is	100m (w)	07
Eline	Berings	28/05/1986	Belgium	100m Hurdles	07
Antoine	Berlin	02/08/1989	Monaco	1500 (m)	0
Javier	Bermejo	23/12/1978	Spain	High Jump (m)	07
Jeimy	Bernárdez	03/09/1986	Honduras	100m Hurdles	05 07
Neisha	Bernard-Thomas	21/01/1981	Grenada	800m (w)	05
Yahya	Berrabah	13/10/1981	Morocco	Long Jump (m)	03 05 07
Yoandris	Betanzos	15/02/1982	Cuba	Triple Jump (m)	03 05 07
Alemayehu	Bezabeh	01/01/1986	Spain	5000m (m)	0
Yury	Bialou	20/03/1981	Belarus	Shot Put (m)	03 05 07
Michal	Bielczyk	05/06/1984	Poland	4x100m (m)	0
Alevtina	Biktimirova	10/09/1982	Russia	Marathon (w)	0
Cindy	Billaud	11/03/1986	France	100m Hurdles	0
Wilfried	Bingangoye	25/03/1985	Gabon	100m (m)	05 07
Michael	Bingham	13/04/1986	Great Britain	400m (m), 4x400m (m)	0
Collis	Birmingham	27/12/1984	Australia	5000m (m), 10000m (m)	0
Etienne	Bizimana	01/01/1986	Burundi	5000m (m)	0
José Luis	Blanco	03/06/1975	Spain	3000m SC (m)	01 03 05 07
Keston	Bledman	08/03/1988	Trinidad & Tobago	4x100m (m)	07
Ancuta	Bobocel	03/10/1987	Romania	3000m SC (w)	07
Ihor	Bodrov	09/07/1987	Ukraine	200m (m)	0
Sechaba	Bohosi	01/11/1982	Lesotho	Marathon (m)	0
Svetlana	Bolshakova	14/10/1984	Belgium	Triple Jump (w)	0

Athlete Index

Forenames	Surname	Born	Country	Event(s)	Prev Apps
Yelena	Bolsun	25/06/1982	Russia	200m (w)	05 07
Usain	Bolt	21/08/1986	Jamaica	100m (m), 200m (m), 4x100m (m)	03 05 07
Daisurami	Bonne	09/03/1988	Cuba	4x400m (w)	0
Valeriy	Borchin	11/09/1986	Russia	20km Walk (m)	07
Cleopatra	Borel-Brown	03/10/1979	Trinidad & Tobago	Shot Put (w)	05 07
Evgeniy	Borisov	07/03/1984	Russia	110m Hurdles	0
Olivia	Borlee	10/04/1986	Belgium	200m (w), 4x100m (w)	05
Kévin	Borlée	22/02/1988	Belgium	400m (m), 4x400m (m)	0
Jérôme	Bortoluzzi	20/05/1982	France	Hammer (m)	0
Yuriy	Borzakovskiy	12/04/1981	Russia	800m (m)	03 05 07
Béranger Aymard	Bosse	13/03/1985	Central African Rep	100m (m)	05 07
Chakir	Boujattaoui	16/01/1983	Morocco	5000m (m)	0
Tarek	Boukensa	19/11/1981	Algeria	1500 (m)	03 05 07
Larbi	Bouraada	10/05/1988	Algeria	Decathlon	0
Tanko	Braimah	12/05/1979	Ghana	4x100m (m)	0
Nathan	Brannen	08/09/1982	Canada	1500 (m)	01 05
Ryan	Brathwaite	06/06/1988	Barbados	110m Hurdles	07
Becky	Breisch	16/03/1983	United States	Discus (w)	05 07
Nery	Brenes	25/09/1985	Costa Rica	400m (m)	05 07
James	Brewer	18/06/1988	Great Britain	1500 (m)	0
Stephanie	Briand	27/05/1972	France	Marathon (w)	0
Marius	Broening	24/10/1983	Germany	4x100m (m)	0
Damien	Broothaerts	13/03/1983	Belgium	110m Hurdles	0
Chris	Brown	15/10/1978	Bahamas	400m (m)	01 03 05 07
Darrel	Brown	11/10/1984	Trinidad & Tobago	4x100m (m)	03 05
Rashan	Brown	27/11/1983	Bahamas	4x400m (w)	0
Ryan	Brown	17/09/1984	United States	800m (m)	0
Stephanie	Brown Trafton	01/12/1979	United States	Discus (w)	07
Daniel	Browne	24/06/1975	United States	Marathon (m)	99 03
Ivano	Brugnetti	01/09/1976	Italy	20km Walk (m)	99 05 07
Anna Giordano	Bruno	13/12/1980	Italy	Pole Vault (w)	0
Elizaveta	Bryzhina	28/11/1989	Ukraine	200m (w)	0
Iwona	Brzezinska	24/05/1986	Poland	4x100m (w)	0
Artur	Brzozowski	29/03/1985	Poland	20km Walk (m)	0
Boštjan	Buc	13/04/1980	Slovenia	3000m SC (m)	03 05 07
Ivano	Bucci	01/12/1986	San Marino	100m (m)	07
Nicole	Büchler	17/12/1983	Switzerland	Pole Vault (w)	07
Stéphane	Buckland	20/01/1977	Mauritius	200m (m)	99 01 03 05
Matthias	Bühler	02/09/1986	Germany	110m Hurdles	0
Cristina	Bujin	12/04/1988	Romania	Triple Jump (w)	0
Spas	Bukhalov	14/11/1980	Bulgaria	Pole Vault (m)	03 07
Michaël	Bultheel	30/06/1986	Belgium	400m Hurdles (m)	0
Andrea	Bunjes	05/02/1976	Germany	Hammer (w)	03
Gelete	Burka	23/01/1986	Ethiopia	1500 (w)	05 07
Marian	Burnett	22/02/1976	Guyana	800m (w)	05 07
Marc	Burns	07/01/1983	Trinidad & Tobago	100m (m), 4x100m (m)	03 05 07
Janeth Jepkosgei	Busienei	13/12/1983	Kenya	800m (w)	07
Deirdre	Byrne	21/09/1982	Ireland	1500 (w)	0
Youngjun	Byun	20/03/1984	South Korea	20km Walk (m)	0
Erik	Cadee	15/02/1984	Netherlands	Discus (m)	07
Diego	Cafagna	09/07/1975	Italy	50km Walk	05 07
Asli	Cakir	20/08/1985	Turkey	3000m SC (w)	0
Zulia	Calatayud	09/11/1979	Cuba	800m (w), 4x400m (w)	99 01 05 07
Emmanuel	Callander	10/05/1984	Trinidad & Tobago	100m (m), 200m (m), 4x100m (m)	0
Jillian	Camarena	02/08/1982	United States	Shot Put (w)	07
José Alejandro	Cambil	26/01/1975	Spain	50km Walk	07
Ibrahin	Camejo	28/06/1982	Cuba	Long Jump (m)	05
Amber	Campbell	05/06/1981	United States	Hammer (w)	05
Veronica	Campbell-Brown	15/05/1982	Jamaica	100m (w), 200m (w)	05 07
Juan Manuel	Cano	12/12/1987	Argentina	20km Walk (m)	0
Christian	Cantwell	30/09/1980	United States	Shot Put (m)	03 05 07
Andrés	Capellán	10/06/1985	Spain	Triple Jump (m)	0
Dayron	Capetillo	11/09/1987	Cuba	110m Hurdles	0
Augusto	Cardoso	13/12/1970	Portugal	50km Walk	99 07
Michelle	Carey	20/03/1981	Ireland	400m Hurdles (w)	07

Athlete Index

Forenames	Surname	Born	Country	Event(s)	Prev Apps
Héctor	Carrasquillo	30/09/1987	Puerto Rico	400m (m)	0
Dominic	Carroll	15/11/1983	Gibraltar	100m (m)	03
Michelle	Carter	12/10/1985	United States	Shot Put (w)	0
Nadja	Casadei	03/04/1983	Sweden	Heptathlon	0
Arturo	Casado	26/01/1983	Spain	1500 (m)	05 07
Yennifer Frank	Casañas	18/10/1978	Spain	Discus (m)	03 05
Cristina	Casandra	01/02/1977	Romania	3000m SC (w)	05 07
Berta	Castells	24/01/1984	Spain	Hammer (w)	03 05 07
Carles	Castillejo	18/08/1978	Spain	10000m (m)	0
Jessica	Cérival	20/01/1982	France	Shot Put (w)	0
Juan Ignacio	Cerra	16/10/1976	Argentina	Hammer (m)	99 01 03 05
Fabio	Cerutti	26/09/1985	Italy	100m (m), 4x100m (m)	0
Noengrothai	Chaipetch	01/12/1982	Thailand	High Jump (w)	0
Dwain	Chambers	05/04/1978	Great Britain	100m (m), 200m (m)	99 01 03
Ricardo	Chambers	07/10/1984	Jamaica	400m (m), 4x400m (m)	07
Thomas	Chamney	16/04/1984	Ireland	800m (m), 1500m (m)	0
Chia-Che	Chang	22/04/1983	Chinese Taipei	Marathon (m)	07
Libor	Charfreitag	11/09/1977	Slovakia	Hammer (m)	99 01 03 05 07
Jamel	Chatbi	30/04/1984	Morocco	3000m SC (m)	0
Olena	Chebanu	04/01/1981	Ukraine	4x100m (w)	07
Abdelatif	Chemlal	11/01/1982	Morocco	3000m SC (m)	0
Iness Chepkesis	Chenonge	01/02/1982	Kenya	5000m (w)	0
Abraham	Chepkirwok	18/11/1988	Uganda	800m (m)	07
Vincent Kiprop	Chepkok	05/07/1988	Kenya	5000m (m)	0
Daniel Kipkorir	Chepyegon	01/06/1986	Uganda	Marathon (m)	0
Alejandra	Cherizola	18/10/1990	Mexico	4x400m (w)	0
Yuliya	Chermoshanskaya	06/01/1986	Russia	4x100m (w)	07
Tatyana	Chernova	29/01/1988	Russia	Heptathlon	07
Damu	Cherry	29/11/1977	United States	100m Hurdles	07
Vivian	Cheruiyot	11/09/1983	Kenya	5000m (w)	07
Robert Kipkoech	Cheruiyot	26/09/1978	Kenya	Marathon (m)	0
Milcah Chemos	Cheywa	24/02/1986	Kenya	3000m SC (w)	0
Anna	Chicherova	22/07/1982	Russia	High Jump (w)	03 05 07
Pavel	Chihuan	19/01/1986	Peru	20km Walk (m)	0
Hugo	Chila	22/07/1987	Ecuador	Long Jump (m), Triple Jump (m)	0
Eilidh	Child	20/02/1987	Great Britain	400m Hurdles (w)	0
Mercedes	Chilla	19/01/1980	Spain	Javelin (w)	05 07
Suppachai	Chimdee	05/01/1991	Thailand	4x100m (m)	0
Deressa	Chimsa	21/11/1976	Ethiopia	Marathon (m)	0
Viktor	Chistiakov	09/02/1975	Russia	Pole Vault (m)	99 01 03
Andrés	Chocho	04/11/1983	Ecuador	20km Walk (m)	07
Augustine Kiprono	Choge	21/01/1987	Kenya	1500 (m)	05
Lidia	Chojecka	15/07/1984	Poland	1500 (w)	0
Brendan	Christian	11/12/1983	Antigua & Barbuda	200m (m)	07
Kamila	Chudzik	12/09/1986	Poland	Heptathlon	07
Elena	Churakova	16/12/1986	Russia	400m Hurdles (w)	0
Javier	Cienfuegos	15/07/1990	Spain	Hammer (m)	0
Jan	Ciepiela	21/01/1989	Poland	4x400m (m)	0
Falk	Cierpinski	17/05/1978	Germany	Marathon (m)	0
Giulio	Ciotti	05/10/1976	Italy	High Jump (m)	0
Omar	Cisneros	19/11/1989	Cuba	400m Hurdles (m)	0
James Kwalia	C'Kurui	12/06/1984	Qatar	5000m (m)	05
Mattias	Claesson	26/07/1986	Sweden	800m (m)	07
Clarissa	Claretti	07/10/1980	Italy	Hammer (w)	03 05 07
Charles	Clark	10/08/1987	United States	200m (m)	0
Hazel	Clark	03/10/1977	United States	800m (w)	01 05 07
Lerone	Clarke	06/12/1981	Jamaica	4x100m (m)	0
Sarah	Claxton	23/09/1979	Great Britain	100m Hurdles	05
Kerron	Clement	31/10/1985	United States	400m Hurdles (m), 4x400m (m)	05 07
Susana	Clement	18/08/1989	Cuba	4x400m (w)	0
Moritz	Cleve	18/02/1987	Germany	Decathlon	0
Helen	Clitheroe	02/01/1974	Great Britain	3000m SC (w)	99 01 05 07
Willem	Coertzen	30/12/1982	South Africa	Decathlon	0
Brendan	Cole	29/05/1981	Australia	400m Hurdles (m)	0
Yarisley	Collado	30/04/1985	Cuba	Discus (w)	0

Athlete Index

Forenames	Surname	Born	Country	Event(s)	Prev Apps
William	Collazo	31/08/1986	Cuba	400m (m)	07
Kim	Collins	05/04/1976	St Kitts & Nevis	100m (m), 200m (m)	99 01 03 05 07
Simone	Collio	27/12/1979	Italy	100m (m), 4x100m (m)	05 07
Rocío	Comba	14/07/1987	Argentina	Discus (w)	0
Jared	Connaughton	20/07/1985	Canada	200m (m), 4x100m (m)	0
Reid	Coolsaet	29/07/1979	Canada	Marathon (m)	05
Alexis	Copello	12/08/1985	Cuba	Triple Jump (m)	0
Carlos	Cordero	07/01/1977	Mexico	Marathon (m)	0
Jessica	Cosby	31/05/1982	United States	Hammer (w)	07
Keila	Costa	06/02/1983	Brazil	Long Jump (w)	07
Jamie	Costin	01/06/1977	Ireland	50km Walk	01 03 07
Héctor	Cotto	08/08/1984	Puerto Rico	110m Hurdles	0
Geisa Aparecida	Coutinho	01/06/1980	Brazil	4x400m (w)	03
Kurt	Couto	14/05/1985	Mozambique	400m Hurdles (m)	05 07
Alistair Ian	Cragg	13/06/1980	Ireland	5000m (m)	07
Shawn	Crawford	14/01/1978	United States	200m (m), 4x100m (m)	01 05
Esther	Cremer	29/03/1988	Germany	4x400m (w)	0
Marco	Cribari	07/07/1985	Switzerland	200m (m), 4x100m (m)	07
Olga	Cristea	13/12/1987	Moldova	800m (w)	0
Johan	Cronje	13/04/1982	South Africa	1500 (m)	05
Shireen	Crumpton	10/10/1970	New Zealand	Marathon (w)	05
Yanet	Cruz	08/02/1988	Cuba	Javelin (w)	0
Nelson	Cruz	31/12/1977	Cape Verde	Marathon (m)	0
Gustavo	Cuesta	14/11/1988	Dominican Republic	4x400m (m)	0
Julie	Culley	10/09/1981	United States	5000m (w)	0
Javier	Culson	25/07/1984	Puerto Rico	400m Hurdles (m)	07
Luke	Cutts	13/02/1988	Great Britain	Pole Vault (m)	0
Adriana Aparecida	Da Silva	22/07/1981	Brazil	Marathon (w)	0
Fábio Gomes	Da Silva	04/08/1983	Brazil	Pole Vault (m)	07
Bekana	Daba	29/07/1988	Ethiopia	5000m (m)	07
Petia	Dacheva	10/03/1985	Bulgaria	Triple Jump (w)	0
Henry	Dagmil	07/12/1981	Philippines	Long Jump (m)	0
Jennifer	Dahlgren	21/04/1984	Argentina	Hammer (w)	05 07
Naoyuki	Daigo	18/01/1981	Japan	High Jump (m)	05 07
Naiel	d'Almeida	20/10/1986	São Tomé & Príncipe	400m (m)	0
Johanna	Danois	04/04/1987	France	200m (w)	0
Garfield	Darien	22/12/1987	France	110m Hurdles	0
Herve	Davaux	22/08/1978	France	50km Walk	0
Kleberson	Davide	20/07/1985	Brazil	800m (m)	07
Matt	Davies	18/04/1985	Australia	4x100m (m)	0
Mary	Davies	27/08/1982	New Zealand	Marathon (w)	0
Desireé	Davila	26/07/1983	United States	Marathon (w)	0
Elisabeth	Davin	03/06/1981	Belgium	100m Hurdles	0
Kia	Davis	23/05/1976	Liberia	400m (w)	0
Walter	Davis	02/07/1979	United States	Triple Jump (m)	01 03 05 07
Christine	Day	23/08/1986	Jamaica	400m (w)	0
Sharon	Day	09/06/1985	United States	Heptathlon, High Jump (w)	0
Marisa	De Aniceto	11/11/1986	France	Heptathlon	0
Eddy	De Lepine	30/03/1984	France	200m (m), 4x100m (m)	03 07
Vicente	De Lima	04/06/1977	Brazil	4x100m (m)	99 07
Jailma	De Lima	31/12/1986	Brazil	4x400m (w)	0
Jessé	De Lima	16/02/1981	Brazil	High Jump (m)	07
Marco	De Luca	12/05/1981	Italy	50km Walk	05 07
Basílio	De Moraes	11/05/1982	Brazil	100m (m), 4x100m (m)	05 07
Lucimar Aparecida	De Moura	22/03/1974	Brazil	100m (w), 4x100m (w)	99 05 07
Júlio César	De Oliveira	04/02/1986	Brazil	Javelin (m)	0
Gisele	De Oliveira	01/08/1980	Brazil	Triple Jump (w)	0
José	De Souza	22/04/1971	Brazil	Marathon (m)	07
Yoann	Décimus	30/11/1987	France	4x400m (m)	0
Meseret	Defar	19/11/1983	Ethiopia	5000m (w), 10000m (w)	03 05 07
Adrien	Deghelt	10/05/1985	Belgium	110m Hurdles	07
Chahyd Hind	Déhiba	17/03/1979	France	1500 (w)	05
Tatyana	Dektyareva	08/05/1981	Russia	100m Hurdles	0
Salome	Dell	21/03/1983	Papua New Guinea	800m (w)	0
Lashinda	Demus	10/03/1983	United States	400m Hurdles (w), 4x400m (w)	05

Athlete Index

Forenames	Surname	Born	Country	Event(s)	Prev Apps
Katja	Demut	21/12/1983	Germany	Triple Jump (w)	0
Serhiy	Demydyuk	05/06/1982	Ukraine	110m Hurdles	05 07
Kate	Dennison	07/05/1984	Great Britain	Pole Vault (w)	07
Martin	Dent	08/02/1979	Australia	Marathon (m)	0
Aleksandr	Derevyagin	24/03/1979	Russia	400m Hurdles (m), 4x400m (m)	07
Zoe	Derham	24/11/1980	Great Britain	Hammer (w)	0
Solen	Désert-Mariller	02/08/1982	France	400m (w), 4x400m (w)	03 05 07
Pieter	Desmet	07/06/1983	Belgium	3000m SC (m)	05 07
Marlon	Devonish	01/06/1976	Great Britain	200m (m), 4x100m (m)	99 01 05 07
Ahmed Mohamed	Dheeb	29/09/1985	Qatar	Discus (m)	0
Emanuele	Di Gregorio	13/12/1980	Italy	100m (m), 4x100m (m)	0
Antonietta	Di Martino	01/06/1978	Italy	High Jump (w)	01 07
Ana	Dias	15/01/1974	Portugal	10000m (w)	99 01 05
José Ignacio	Díaz	22/11/1979	Spain	20km Walk (m)	05 07
Yunior	Díaz	28/04/1987	Cuba	Decathlon	0
Genzebe	Dibaba	08/02/1991	Ethiopia	5000m (w)	0
Franka	Dietzsch	22/01/1968	Germany	Discus (w)	99 01 03 05 07
Mantas	Dilys	30/03/1984	Lithuania	Triple Jump (m)	0
Yohan	Diniz	01/01/1978	France	50km Walk	05 07
Abebe	Dinkesa	06/03/1984	Ethiopia	10000m (m)	05
Gloria	Diogo	13/01/1983	São Tomé & Príncipe	100m (w)	05 07
Dieudonné	Disi	24/11/1980	Rwanda	Marathon (m)	05 07
Leslie	Djhone	18/03/1981	France	400m (m), 4x400m (m)	03 05 07
Boampouguini	Djigban	01/01/1979	Togo	1500 (m)	0
Ida Antoinette Nana	Djimou	02/08/1985	France	Heptathlon	07
Nomvula	Dlamini	11/07/1984	Swaziland	200m (w)	0
Norman	Dlomo	18/04/1975	South Africa	Marathon (m)	07
Ruslan	Dmytrenko	22/03/1986	Ukraine	20km Walk (m)	0
Teresa	Dobija	09/10/1982	Poland	Long Jump (w)	0
Lisa	Dobriskey	23/12/1983	Great Britain	1500 (w)	07
Natallia	Dobrynska	29/05/1982	Ukraine	Heptathlon, Long Jump (w)	05 07
Fiona	Docherty	01/09/1975	New Zealand	Marathon (w)	0
Marta	Domínguez	03/11/1975	Spain	3000m SC (w)	99 01 03 05 07
Roberto	Donati	15/03/1983	Italy	4x100m (m)	0
Fabrizio	Donato	14/08/1976	Italy	Triple Jump (m)	03 07
Marilson	Dos Santos	06/08/1977	Brazil	Marathon (m)	05
Leonardo Elisiario	Dos Santos	07/05/1984	Brazil	Triple Jump (m)	07
Mario José	Dos Santos Jr	10/09/1979	Brazil	50km Walk	0
Damiel	Dossévi	03/02/1983	France	Pole Vault (m)	07
Caimin	Douglas	11/05/1977	Netherlands	4x100m (m)	01
Montell	Douglas	24/01/1986	Great Britain	4x100m (w)	07
Nathan	Douglas	04/12/1982	Great Britain	Triple Jump (m)	05
Stacy	Dragila	25/03/1971	United States	Pole Vault (w)	99 01 03 05
Aksana	Drahun	19/05/1981	Belarus	4x100m (w)	0
Hannes	Dreyer	13/01/1985	South Africa	4x100m (m)	0
Danny	D'Souza	14/11/1987	Seychelles	100m (m)	0
Sophie	Duarte	31/07/1981	France	3000m SC (w)	07
Natalia	Ducó	31/01/1989	Chile	Shot Put (w)	0
Karla	Dueñas	31/03/1989	Mexico	4x400m (w)	0
Nils	Duerinck	20/03/1984	Belgium	4x400m (m)	0
Debbie	Dunn	26/03/1978	United States	400m (w), 4x400m (w)	0
Adrian	Durant	16/10/1984	US Virgin Islands	100m (m)	03
Nadiya	Dusanova	17/11/1987	Uzbekistan	High Jump (w)	0
Johnny	Dutch	20/01/1989	United States	400m Hurdles (m)	0
Agnieszka	Dygacz	18/07/1985	Poland	20km Walk (w)	0
Maksim	Dyldin	19/05/1987	Russia	400m (m), 4x400m (m)	0
Dzmitry	Dziatsuk	09/04/1985	Belarus	Triple Jump (m)	0
Brian	Dzingai	29/04/1981	Zimbabwe	200m (m)	03 05 07
Ashton	Eaton	21/01/1988	United States	Decathlon	0
Stefan	Eberhardt	12/01/1985	Germany	1500 (m)	0
Yuki	Ebihara	28/10/1985	Japan	Javelin (w)	0
Joseph	Ebuya	20/06/1987	Kenya	5000m (m)	07
Tyrone	Edgar	29/03/1982	Great Britain	100m (m), 4x100m (m)	07
Alonso	Edward	08/12/1989	Panama	200m (m)	0
Monzavous	Edwards	07/05/1981	United States	100m (m)	0

Athlete Index

Forenames	Surname	Born	Country	Event(s)	Prev Apps
Sam	Effah	29/12/1988	Canada	200m (m), 4x100m (m)	0
Josephine	Ehigie	01/12/1985	Nigeria	4x400m (w)	0
Sylwia	Ejdys	17/07/1984	Poland	1500 (w)	0
Sentayehu	Ejigu	28/06/1985	Ethiopia	5000m (w)	03 05
Yevgeniy	Ektov	01/09/1986	Kazakhstan	Triple Jump (m)	0
Mohsen	El Anany	21/05/1985	Egypt	Hammer (m)	05 07
Nadir	El Fassi	23/09/1983	France	Decathlon	0
Omar Ahmed	El Ghazaly	09/02/1984	Egypt	Discus (m)	07
Driss	El Himer	04/04/1974	France	Marathon (m)	01 03
Nawal	El Jack	17/10/1988	Sudan	400m (w)	05 07
Ali Mabrouk	El Zaidi	13/01/1978	Libya	Marathon (m)	99 01 07
Larisa	Emelyanova	06/01/1980	Russia	20km Walk (w)	0
Helena	Engman	16/06/1976	Sweden	Shot Put (w)	07
Adil	Ennani	30/06/1980	Morocco	Marathon (m)	0
Jessica	Ennis	28/01/1986	Great Britain	Heptathlon, 100m Hurdles	07
Delloreen	Ennis-London	05/03/1975	Jamaica	100m Hurdles	99 03 05 07
Benjamín	Enzema	25/03/1989	Equatorial Guinea	1500 (m)	0
Masashi	Eriguchi	17/12/1988	Japan	100m (m), 4x100m (m)	0
Sandra	Eriksson	04/06/1989	Finland	3000m SC (w)	0
Jesús	España	21/08/1978	Spain	5000m (m)	05 07
Markus	Esser	03/02/1980	Germany	Hammer (m)	05 07
Reyes	Estévez	02/08/1976	Spain	1500 (m)	99 01 03 05 07
Mbango	Etone Françoise	14/04/1976	Cameroon	Triple Jump (w)	99 01 03 05
Natalya	Evdokimova	17/03/1978	Russia	1500 (w)	03
Tommi	Evilä	06/04/1980	Finland	Long Jump (m)	05
Nelson	Évora	20/04/1984	Portugal	Triple Jump (m)	05 07
Florence	Ezeh	29/12/1977	Togo	Hammer (w)	99 01 03
Simone	Facey	07/05/1985	Jamaica	200m (w), 4x100m (w)	07
Martin	Fagan	26/06/1983	Ireland	10000m (m)	0
Mohamed	Faisal	26/12/1987	Brunei	100m (m)	0
Alice	Falaiye	24/12/1978	Canada	Long Jump (w)	01
Fatou Bintou	Fall	23/08/1981	Senegal	400m (w)	03 05
Ruwen	Faller	22/07/1980	Germany	4x400m (m)	0
Stéphanie	Falzon	07/01/1983	France	Hammer (w)	07
Yasser Ibrahim	Farag	02/05/1984	Egypt	Shot Put (m)	0
Mohammed	Farah	23/03/1983	Great Britain	5000m (m)	07
Mahamoud	Farah	04/09/1988	Djibouti	800m (m)	0
Terani	Faremiro	04/05/1988	French Polynesia	100m (w)	0
Stuart	Farquhar	15/03/1982	New Zealand	Javelin (m)	07
Olusoji	Fasuba	09/07/1984	Nigeria	100m (m)	05 07
Víctor	Fatecha	10/03/1988	Paraguay	Javelin (m)	07
Rafal	Fedaczynski	03/12/1980	Poland	50km Walk	05 07
Denys	Fedas	24/08/1985	Ukraine	Pole Vault (m)	0
Aleksandra	Fedoriva	13/09/1988	Russia	4x100m (w)	0
Luís	Feiteira	21/04/1973	Portugal	Marathon (m)	01 07
Susana	Feitor	28/01/1975	Portugal	20km Walk (w)	99 01 03 05 07
Perdita	Felicien	29/08/1980	Canada	100m Hurdles	01 03 05
Allyson	Felix	18/11/1985	United States	200m (w), 4x400m (w)	03 05 07
Ana Dulce	Félix	23/10/1982	Portugal	10000m (w)	0
Agustín	Félix	14/03/1979	Spain	Decathlon	07
Sheniqua	Ferguson	24/11/1989	Bahamas	100m (w), 200m (w), 4x100m (w)	0
Debbie	Ferguson-McKenzie	16/01/1976	Bahamas	100m (w), 200m (w), 4x100m (w)	03 05 07
Nuria	Fernández	16/08/1976	Spain	1500 (w)	99 01 03 05
Francisco Javier	Fernández	06/03/1977	Spain	20km Walk (m)	99 01 03 05 07
Yania	Ferrales	28/07/1977	Cuba	Discus (w)	05 07
Sheila	Ferreira	11/12/1980	Brazil	4x400m (w)	0
Ahamada	Feta	24/06/1987	Comoros	100m (w)	0
Eléni	Filándra	12/01/1984	Greece	800m (w)	0
Predrag	Filipovic	05/10/1978	Serbia	20km Walk (m)	03 07
Nenad	Filipovic	05/10/1978	Serbia	50km Walk	07
Konstadínos	Filippídis	26/11/1986	Greece	Pole Vault (m)	05
Tatyana	Firova	10/10/1982	Russia	4x400m (w)	0
Silje	Fjørtoft	23/06/1987	Norway	3000m SC (w)	07
Shalane	Flanagan	08/07/1981	United States	10000m (w)	05 07
Natalya	Fokina-Semenova	07/07/1982	Ukraine	Discus (w)	05 07

Athlete Index

Forenames	Surname	Born	Country	Event(s)	Prev Apps
Yannick	Fonsat	16/06/1988	France	400m (m), 4x400m (m)	0
Laia	Forcadell	06/06/1982	Spain	400m Hurdles (w)	0
Marco	Fortes	26/09/1982	Portugal	Shot Put (m)	0
Brigitte	Foster-Hylton	07/11/1974	Jamaica	100m Hurdles	01 03 05
Lehann	Fourie	16/02/1987	South Africa	110m Hurdles	0
Samuel	Francis	27/03/1987	Qatar	100m (m)	07
Bridget	Franek	08/11/1987	United States	3000m SC (w)	0
Mark	Frank	21/06/1977	Germany	Javelin (m)	05
Gianni	Frankis	16/04/1988	Great Britain	110m Hurdles	0
Shelly-Ann	Fraser	27/12/1986	Jamaica	100m (w), 4x100m (w)	0
Michael	Frater	06/10/1982	Jamaica	100m (m), 4x100m (m)	03 05
Emily	Freeman	24/11/1980	Great Britain	200m (w), 4x100m (w)	07
Thomas	Freeman	05/11/1980	United States	Hammer (m)	0
Charles Michael	Friedek	26/08/1971	Germany	Triple Jump (m)	99 05
Ariane	Friedrich	10/01/1984	Germany	High Jump (w)	0
Jesper	Fritz	13/09/1985	Sweden	Pole Vault (m)	07
Sultana	Frizell	24/10/1984	Canada	Hammer (w)	0
Oskari	Frösén	24/01/1976	Finland	High Jump (m)	03 05 07
Petr	Frydrych	13/01/1988	Czech Republic	Javelin (m)	0
Masumi	Fuchise	02/09/1986	Japan	20km Walk (w)	07
Iris	Fuentes-Pila	10/08/1980	Spain	1500 (w)	07
Kenji	Fujimitsu	01/05/1986	Japan	200m (m), 4x100m (m)	0
Yoshiko	Fujinaga	15/08/1981	Japan	Marathon (w)	99
Isamu	Fujisawa	12/10/1987	Japan	20km Walk (m)	0
Arata	Fujiwara	12/09/1981	Japan	Marathon (m)	0
Kayoko	Fukushi	25/03/1982	Japan	10000m (w)	03 05 07
Chisato	Fukushima	27/06/1988	Japan	100m (w), 200m (w), 4x100m (w)	0
Sean	Furey	31/08/1982	United States	Javelin (m)	0
Kamghe	Gaba	13/01/1984	Germany	4x400m (m)	0
Arne	Gabius	22/03/1981	Germany	5000m (m)	07
Matt	Gabrielson	28/06/1978	United States	Marathon (m)	0
Kristina	Gadschiew	03/07/1984	Germany	Pole Vault (w)	0
Mária	Gáliková	21/08/1980	Slovakia	20km Walk (w)	05 07
Gulnara	Galkina	09/07/1978	Russia	3000m SC (w)	03 07
Geena	Gall	18/01/1987	United States	800m (w)	0
Natalia	Gallego	28/09/1980	Andorra	800m (w)	07
Matteo	Galvan	20/04/1988	Italy	400m (m)	0
Shuying	Gao	28/10/1979	China	Pole Vault (w)	01 03 05 07
Jesús Angel	García	17/10/1969	Spain	50km Walk	99 01 03 05 07
Luis Fernando	García	13/09/1974	Guatemala	50km Walk	99 01 03 05
Rosibel	García	13/02/1981	Colombia	800m (w)	07
Yordani	García	21/11/1988	Cuba	Decathlon	07
José Amado	García	13/09/1977	Guatemala	Marathon (m)	05
Gable	Garenamotse	28/02/1977	Botswana	Long Jump (m)	99 03 07
Roba	Gary	12/04/1982	Ethiopia	3000m SC (m)	07
Tyson	Gay	09/08/1982	United States	100m (m), 200m (m)	05 07
Mabel	Gay	05/05/1983	Cuba	Triple Jump (w)	03 05
Majed Aldin	Gazal	01/01/1988	Syria	High Jump (m)	0
Magdaliní	Gazéa	30/06/1977	Greece	Marathon (w)	0
Stanley	Gbagbeke	24/07/1989	Nigeria	Long Jump (m)	0
Gebre-egziabher	Gebremariam	10/09/1984	Ethiopia	10000m (m)	03 05 07
Mekonnen	Gebremedhin	11/10/1988	Ethiopia	1500 (m)	07
Anna	Geflikh	01/02/1983	Russia	100m (w)	0
Venera	Getova	13/12/1980	Bulgaria	Discus (w)	0
Kalkidan	Gezahegne	08/05/1991	Ethiopia	1500 (w)	0
Jaouad	Gharib	22/05/1972	Morocco	Marathon (m)	01 03 05 07
Habiba	Ghribi	09/04/1984	Tunisia	3000m SC (w)	05
Giuseppe	Gibilisco	05/01/1979	Italy	Pole Vault (m)	01 03 05
Antoine	Gillet	22/03/1988	Belgium	4x400m (m)	0
David	Gillick	09/07/1983	Ireland	400m (m)	05 07
Erin	Gilreath	11/08/1980	United States	Hammer (w)	05 07
Arnie David	Girat	26/08/1984	Cuba	Triple Jump (m)	03 05 07
Ramon	Gittens	20/07/1987	Barbados	100m (m), 200m (m)	0
Vanessa	Gladone	03/06/1982	France	Triple Jump (w)	0
Zaneta	Glanc	11/03/1983	Poland	Discus (w)	0

Athlete Index

Forenames	Surname	Born	Country	Event(s)	Prev Apps
Brianna	Glenn	18/04/1980	United States	Long Jump (w)	07
Olga	Glok	16/12/1982	Russia	Marathon (w)	0
Mathieu	Gnanligo	13/12/1986	Benin	400m (m)	07
James	Godday	09/01/1984	Nigeria	400m (m)	05
Lacena	Golding-Clarke	20/03/1975	Jamaica	100m Hurdles	03 07
Yuliya	Golubchikova	27/03/1983	Russia	Pole Vault (w)	07
Vanda	Gomes	07/11/1988	Brazil	4x100m (w)	0
Naide	Gomes	20/11/1979	Portugal	Long Jump (w)	05 07
Pedro Daniel	Gómez	31/12/1990	Mexico	20km Walk (m)	0
Zoila	Gómez	07/06/1979	United States	Marathon (w)	07
Sandra	Gomis	21/11/1983	France	100m Hurdles	0
Kafétien	Gomis	23/03/1980	France	Long Jump (m)	0
Dany	Gonçalves	14/03/1985	Portugal	4x100m (m)	0
Lijiao	Gong	24/01/1989	China	Shot Put (w)	07
Jermaine	Gonzales	26/11/1984	Jamaica	4x400m (m)	0
Norma	González	11/08/1982	Colombia	400m (w), 4x400m (w), 4x100m (w)	0
Misleydis	González	19/06/1978	Cuba	Shot Put (w)	05 07
Nicholas	Gordon	17/09/1988	Jamaica	Long Jump (m)	0
Jehue	Gordon	15/12/1991	Trinidad & Tobago	400m Hurdles (m)	0
Kara	Goucher	09/07/1978	United States	Marathon (w)	07
Abderrahim	Goumri	21/05/1976	Morocco	Marathon (m)	01 03 05 07
Tom	Goyvaerts	20/03/1984	Belgium	Javelin (m)	0
Aiga	Grabuste	24/03/1988	Latvia	Heptathlon	07
Ruth	Grajeda	31/07/1980	Mexico	4x400m (w)	0
Nicoleta	Grasu	11/09/1971	Romania	Discus (w)	99 01 05 07
Anamaria	Greceanu	12/06/1989	Romania	20km Walk (w)	0
Elizaveta	Grechishnikova	12/12/1983	Russia	5000m (w)	0
Daniele	Greco	01/03/1989	Italy	Triple Jump (m)	0
Leford	Green	14/11/1986	Jamaica	4x400m (m)	0
Emma	Green	08/12/1984	Sweden	High Jump (w)	05 07
David	Greene	11/04/1986	Great Britain	400m Hurdles (m), 4x400m (m)	07
Jadel	Gregório	16/09/1980	Brazil	Triple Jump (m)	01 03 05 07
Ryan	Gregson	26/04/1990	Australia	1500 (m)	0
Libania	Grenot	12/07/1983	Italy	400m (w), 4x400m (w)	05
Colin	Griffin	03/08/1982	Ireland	50km Walk	07
Adrian	Griffith	11/11/1984	Bahamas	100m (m)	0
Aleksandr	Gripich	29/09/1986	Russia	Pole Vault (m)	0
Hanna	Grobler	15/01/1981	Finland	High Jump (w)	05
Martin	Grothkopp	21/06/1986	Germany	4x400m (m)	0
Karoline Bjerkeli	Grøvdal	14/06/1990	Norway	3000m SC (w)	07
Ana Maria	Groza	01/06/1976	Romania	20km Walk (w)	05
Daniel	Grueso	30/07/1985	Colombia	100m (m)	07
Élodie	Guégan	19/12/1985	France	800m (w)	07
Ignacio	Guerra	15/09/1987	Chile	Javelin (m)	0
Ramil	Guliyev	29/05/1990	Azerbaijan	200m (m)	0
Desislav	Gunev	21/01/1986	Bulgaria	100m (m), 200m (m)	0
Yulia	Gushchina	04/03/1983	Russia	200m (w), 4x100m (w)	05 07
Andreas	Gustafsson	10/08/1981	Sweden	50km Walk	07
Robe	Guta	12/10/1986	Ethiopia	Marathon (w)	07
Tino	Häber	06/10/1982	Germany	Javelin (m)	0
Halima	Hachlaf	06/09/1988	Morocco	800m (w)	0
Semoy	Hackett	27/11/1988	Trinidad & Tobago	100m (w), 4x100m (w)	0
Susanne	Hahn	23/04/1978	Germany	Marathon (w)	07
András	Haklits	23/09/1977	Croatia	Hammer (m)	99 05 07
Hussain	Haleem	27/11/1982	Maldives	100m (m)	0
Yochai	Halevi	10/05/1982	Israel	Long Jump (m), Triple Jump (m)	0
Nikki	Hamblin	20/05/1988	New Zealand	800m (w), 1500m (w)	0
Mickael	Hanany	25/03/1983	France	High Jump (m)	05
Trey	Hardee	07/12/1984	United States	Decathlon	0
Chris	Harmse	31/05/1973	South Africa	Hammer (m)	99 05 07
Dawn	Harper	13/05/1984	United States	100m Hurdles	0
Benn	Harradine	14/10/1982	Australia	Discus (m)	0
Tahesia	Harrigan	15/02/1982	British Virgin Islands	100m (w)	05 07
Adam	Harris	21/07/1987	Guyana	100m (m), 200m (m)	0
Tora	Harris	21/09/1978	United States	High Jump (m)	03

Athlete Index

Forenames	Surname	Born	Country	Event(s)	Prev Apps
Alvin	Harrison	20/01/1974	Dominican Republic	400m (m)	0
Robert	Harting	18/10/1984	Germany	Discus (m)	05 07
Jana	Hartmann	23/05/1981	Germany	800m (w)	0
Natasha	Hastings	23/07/1986	United States	4x400m (w)	07
María	Hatzipanayiotídou	17/01/1982	Greece	20km Walk (w)	0
Minori	Hayakari	29/11/1972	Japan	3000m SC (w)	05 07
Louise	Hazel	06/10/1985	Great Britain	Heptathlon	0
Ahmad	Hazer	04/09/1989	Lebanon	110m Hurdles	0
Mike	Hazle	22/03/1979	United States	Javelin (m)	0
Kristin	Heaston	23/11/1975	United States	Shot Put (w)	03 05 07
Robert	Heffernan	28/02/1978	Ireland	20km Walk (m)	01 05 07
Betty	Heidler	14/10/1983	Germany	Hammer (w)	03 05 07
Jussi	Heikkilä	21/03/1983	Finland	400m Hurdles (m)	0
Sabine	Heitling	02/07/1987	Brazil	3000m SC (w)	07
Zuzana	Hejnová	19/12/1986	Czech Republic	400m Hurdles (w)	05 07
Anca	Heltne	01/01/1978	Romania	Shot Put (w)	07
Bunting	Hem	12/12/1985	Cambodia	1500 (m)	07
Kelsie	Hendry	29/06/1982	Canada	Pole Vault (w)	05
Shakeitha	Henfield	13/07/1983	Bahamas	4x400m (w)	0
Inês	Henriques	01/05/1980	Portugal	20km Walk (w)	01 05 07
Tabarie	Henry	01/12/1987	US Virgin Islands	400m (m)	0
Robert	Hering	14/06/1990	Germany	200m (m)	0
Adrienne	Herzog	30/09/1985	Netherlands	1500 (w)	0
Paul	Hession	27/01/1983	Ireland	200m (m)	05 07
Paige	Higgins	12/07/1982	United States	Marathon (w)	0
Juan Carlos	Higuero	03/08/1978	Spain	1500 (m)	01 03 05 07
Siham	Hilali	02/05/1986	Morocco	1500 (w)	07
Chris	Hill	26/02/1988	United States	Javelin (m)	0
Andrew	Hinds	25/04/1994	Barbados	100m (m), 200m (m)	0
Yomara	Hinestroza	20/05/1988	Colombia	100m (w), 4x100m (w)	0
Denise	Hinrichs	07/06/1987	Germany	Shot Put (w)	0
Hideyuki	Hirose	20/07/1989	Japan	400m (m)	0
Ásdís	Hjálmsdóttir	28/10/1985	Iceland	Javelin (w)	0
Virgil	Hodge	17/11/1983	St Kitts & Nevis	100m (w), 200m (w), 4x100m (w)	03 07
Reese	Hoffa	08/10/1977	United States	Shot Put (m)	03 07
Claudia	Hoffmann	10/12/1982	Germany	4x400m (w)	0
André	Höhne	10/03/1978	Germany	20km Walk (m), 50km Walk	01 03 05 07
Lucian Disdery	Hombo	01/01/1979	Tanzania	Marathon (m)	0
Amanmurad	Hommadov	28/01/1989	Turkmenistan	Hammer (m)	0
Guus	Hoogmoed	27/09/1981	Netherlands	4x100m (m)	05 07
Marshevet	Hooker	25/09/1984	United States	200m (w)	0
Steven	Hooker	16/07/1982	Australia	Pole Vault (m)	05 07
Peter	Horák	07/12/1983	Slovakia	High Jump (m)	07
Cedric	Houssaye	13/12/1979	France	50km Walk	0
Adriatik	Hoxha	09/03/1990	Albania	Shot Put (m)	0
Martina	Hrasnová	21/03/1983	Slovakia	Hammer (w)	01 07
Ivan	Hryshyn	26/07/1988	Ukraine	Discus (m)	0
Xiaoxiao	Huang	03/03/1983	China	400m Hurdles (w)	05 07
Daniel	Huling	16/07/1983	United States	3000m SC (m)	0
Erison	Hurtault	29/12/1984	Dominica	400m (m)	0
Ayanna	Hutchinson	18/02/1978	Trinidad & Tobago	100m (w), 4x100m (w)	0
Junhyeon	Hwang	25/05/1987	South Korea	Marathon (m)	0
Kemar	Hyman	11/10/1989	Cayman Islands	100m (m)	0
Periklís	Iakovákis	24/03/1979	Greece	400m Hurdles (m)	99 01 03 05 07
Natalia	Iastrebova	12/10/1984	Ukraine	Triple Jump (w)	0
Caterine	Ibargüen	12/02/1984	Colombia	High Jump (w)	05
Arley	Ibargüen	17/10/1982	Colombia	Javelin (m)	0
Phillips	Idowu	30/12/1978	Great Britain	Triple Jump (m)	01 05 07
Zougari Khalid	Idrissi	24/01/1988	Morocco	200m (m)	0
Rafael	Iglesias	05/07/1979	Spain	Marathon (m)	0
Abdalaati	Iguider	25/03/1987	Morocco	1500 (m)	07
Reinhold Ndalikokule	Iita	01/01/1975	Namibia	Marathon (m)	0
Daisuke	Ikeda	15/04/1986	Japan	Decathlon	0
David	Ilariani	20/01/1981	Georgia	110m Hurdles	01 03 05 07
Anna	Iljuštšenko	12/10/1985	Estonia	High Jump (w)	0

Athlete Index

Forenames	Surname	Born	Country	Event(s)	Prev Apps
Mikaela	Ingberg	29/07/1974	Finland	Javelin (w)	99 01 03 05
Tomas	Intas	15/09/1981	Lithuania	Javelin (m)	05
Kyriakos	Ioannou	26/07/1984	Cyprus	High Jump (m)	05 07
Satoshi	Irifune	14/12/1975	Japan	Marathon (m)	99 05
Jack	Iroqa	29/09/1986	Solomon Islands	100m (m)	0
Geovana	Irusta	26/09/1975	Bolivia	20km Walk (w)	99 01 03 05 07
Christopher	Isengwe	22/02/1976	Tanzania	Marathon (m)	05
Merjen	Ishangulyyeva	21/01/1988	Turkmenistan	400m Hurdles (w)	0
Elena	Isinbaeva	03/06/1982	Russia	Pole Vault (w)	03 05 07
Ismail Ahmed	Ismail	10/09/1984	Sudan	800m (m)	03 05 07
Halimat	Ismaila	13/07/1984	Nigeria	100m (w), 4x100m (w)	0
Märt	Israel	23/09/1983	Estonia	Discus (m)	07
Korahubsh	Itaa	28/02/1992	Ethiopia	3000m SC (w)	0
Quaski	Itaia	03/12/1984	Nauru	100m (m)	0
Olha	Ivankova	07/01/1973	Ukraine	Javelin (w)	05 07
Aleksandr	Ivanov	25/05/1982	Russia	Javelin (m)	01 03 05 07
Georgi	Ivanov	13/03/1985	Bulgaria	Shot Put (m)	0
Natalya	Ivanova	25/06/1981	Russia	400m Hurdles (w)	07
Svetlana	Ivanova-Saykina	10/07/1985	Russia	Discus (w)	0
Natalya	Ivoninskaya	22/02/1985	Kazakhstan	100m Hurdles	07
Yuki	Iwai	30/12/1982	Japan	10000m (m)	0
Yoshitaka	Iwamizu	20/06/1979	Japan	3000m SC (m)	01 03 05 07
Johanna	Jackson	17/01/1985	Great Britain	20km Walk (w)	07
Bershawn	Jackson	08/05/1983	United States	400m Hurdles (m), 4x400m (m)	03 05 07
Per	Jacobsen	30/12/1977	Sweden	3000m SC (m)	0
Ezekiel	Jafari	17/08/1985	Tanzania	10000m (m)	0
Evan	Jager	08/03/1989	United States	5000m (m)	0
Sangwan	Jaksunin	10/12/1984	Thailand	4x100m (w)	0
Indré	Jakubaityté	24/01/1976	Lithuania	Javelin (w)	07
Maryam Yusuf	Jamal	16/09/1984	Brunei	1500 (w)	05 07
Ingus	Janevics	29/04/1986	Latvia	50km Walk	07
Igor	Janik	18/01/1983	Poland	Javelin (m)	07
Melik	Janoyan	24/03/1985	Armenia	Javelin (m)	0
Jovanee	Jarrett	15/01/1983	Jamaica	Long Jump (w)	0
Yacob	Jarso	05/02/1988	Ethiopia	3000m SC (m)	0
Tero	Järvenpää	02/10/1984	Finland	Javelin (m)	07
Dorota	Jedrusinska	04/02/1982	Poland	4x100m (w)	0
Irene	Jelagat	10/12/1988	Kenya	1500 (w)	0
Pamela	Jelimo	05/12/1989	Kenya	800m (w)	0
Jakub	Jelonek	07/07/1985	Poland	20km Walk (m)	0
Alhaji	Jeng	13/12/1981	Sweden	Pole Vault (m)	07
Nate	Jenkins	06/10/1980	United States	Marathon (m)	0
Morten	Jensen	02/12/1982	Denmark	Long Jump (m)	05 07
Marta	Jeschke	02/06/1986	Poland	4x100m (w)	0
Anna	Jesien	10/12/1978	Poland	400m Hurdles (w)	01 03 05 07
Carmelita	Jeter	24/11/1979	United States	100m (w), 4x100m (w)	07
Olivera	Jevtic	24/07/1977	Serbia	10000m (w)	99 01 03
Wei	Ji	05/02/1984	China	110m Hurdles	0
Youngjun	Ji	15/10/1981	South Korea	Marathon (m)	03
Funmi	Jimoh	29/05/1984	United States	Long Jump (w)	0
Helalia	Johannes	13/08/1980	Namibia	Marathon (w)	0
Ulrika	Johansson	09/02/1975	Sweden	3000m SC (w)	0
Alexander	John	03/05/1986	Germany	110m Hurdles	0
Brian	Johnson	05/03/1980	United States	Long Jump (m)	05 07
Chelsea	Johnson	20/12/1983	United States	Pole Vault (w)	0
Rosa Mystique	Jones	07/11/1990	Nauru	100m (w)	05 07
Alwyn	Jones	28/02/1985	Australia	Triple Jump (m)	0
LaVerne	Jones-Ferrette	16/09/1981	US Virgin Islands	200m (w)	05 07
Yong-Ok	Jong	24/01/1971	North Korea	Marathon (w)	03 05
Carlos	Jorge	24/09/1986	Dominican Republic	100m (m), Long Jump (m)	0
Marco	Joseph	12/08/1989	Tanzania	5000m (m)	0
Moise	Joseph	27/12/1981	Haiti	800m (m)	03 05
Janice	Josephs	31/03/1982	South Africa	Long Jump (w)	05 07
Jennifer	Joyce	25/09/1980	Canada	Hammer (w)	05
Leigh	Julius	25/03/1985	South Africa	4x100m (m)	05

Athlete Index

Forenames	Surname	Born	Country	Event(s)	Prev Apps
Sangjin	Jung	16/04/1984	South Korea	Javelin (m)	0
Soon-ok	Jung	23/04/1983	South Korea	Long Jump (w)	07
Oxana	Juravel	23/02/1986	Moldova	3000m SC (w)	0
Dmitrijs	Jurkevics	07/01/1987	Latvia	800m (m)	0
Abubaker	Kaki	21/06/1989	Sudan	800m (m)	07
Abubaker Ali	Kamal	01/01/1983	Qatar	3000m SC (m)	03 07
Stephen Loruo	Kamar	26/01/1978	Brunei	Marathon (m)	0
Yusuf Saad	Kamel	29/03/1983	Brunei	800m (m), 1500m (m)	05 07
Aurélie	Kamga	11/08/1985	France	4x400m (w)	0
Kaie	Kand	31/03/1984	Estonia	Heptathlon	07
Yuzo	Kanemaru	18/09/1987	Japan	400m (m)	07
Olga	Kaniskina	19/01/1985	Russia	20km Walk (w)	07
Yuri	Kano	27/10/1978	Japan	Marathon (w)	0
Gerd	Kanter	06/05/1979	Estonia	Discus (m)	03 05 07
Anastasiya	Kapachinskaya	21/11/1979	Russia	400m (w), 4x400m (w)	01 03
Bianca	Kappler	08/08/1977	Germany	Long Jump (w)	03 05 07
Momchil	Karailiev	21/05/1982	Bulgaria	Triple Jump (m)	05
Mohamed Masudul	Karim	12/12/1977	Bangladesh	100m (m)	0
Olli-Pekka	Karjalainen	07/03/1980	Finland	Hammer (m)	99 01 03 05 07
Dmitriy	Karpov	23/07/1981	Kakakhstan	Decathlon	03 05 07
Kateryna	Karsak	26/12/1985	Ukraine	Discus (w)	07
Aurore	Kassambara	26/10/1979	France	400m Hurdles (w)	0
Oleksiy	Kasyanov	26/08/1985	Ukraine	Decathlon	0
Tioiti	Katutu	18/11/1989	Kiribati	100m (w)	0
Mayumi	Kawasaki	10/05/1980	Japan	20km Walk (w)	05 07
Tamás	Kazi	16/05/1985	Hungary	800m (m)	0
Uladzimir	Kazlou	20/04/1985	Belarus	Javelin (m)	0
Mohamed Ali	Kebabou	27/06/1988	Tunisia	Javelin (m)	0
Tsegay	Kebede	15/01/1987	Ethiopia	Marathon (m)	0
Héni	Kechi	31/08/1980	France	400m Hurdles (m)	0
Khoury	Keita	02/03/1985	Mauritania	400m (w)	0
Haron	Keitany	17/12/1983	Kenya	1500 (m)	0
Roman	Kejžar	11/02/1966	Slovenia	Marathon (m)	99 01 03
Johannes	Kekana	25/04/1972	South Africa	Marathon (m)	0
Martin	Keller	26/09/1986	Germany	100m (m), 4x100m (m)	0
Nicholas	Kemboi	25/11/1983	Qatar	10000m (m)	05
Ezekiel	Kemboi	25/05/1982	Kenya	3000m SC (m)	03 05 07
Fanuel	Kenosi	29/09/1986	Botswana	200m (m)	0
Clayton	Kenty	22/02/1991	Northern Mariana Is	100m (m)	0
Renalda	Kergyte	25/08/1985	Lithuania	Marathon (w)	0
Jukka	Keskisalo	27/03/1981	Finland	3000m SC (m)	03 05
Mariam	Kevkhishvili	17/09/1985	Georgia	Shot Put (w)	0
Kabelo	Kgosiemang	07/01/1986	Botswana	High Jump (m)	07
Ani	Khachikyan	16/03/1991	Armenia	100m (w)	0
Alice	Khan	05/03/1990	Seychelles	100m (w)	0
Vasiliy	Kharlamov	08/01/1986	Russia	Decathlon	0
Phyo Thet	Khin	30/07/1989	Myanmar	400m (w)	0
Mohamed Ashour	Khouaja	01/11/1987	Libya	400m (w)	0
Guzel	Khubbieva	02/05/1976	Uzbekistan	100m (w), 200m (w)	03 07
Moses	Kibet	23/03/1991	Uganda	5000m (m)	0
Sylvia Jebiwott	Kibet	28/03/1984	Kenya	5000m (w)	07
Viola Jelagat	Kibiwot	22/12/1983	Kenya	1500 (w)	07
Alena	Kievich	16/10/1987	Belarus	200m (w), 4x100m (w)	0
Yonas	Kifle	05/11/1977	Eritrea	Marathon (m)	99 01 05
Gary	Kikaya	04/02/1980	Dem Rep of Congo	400m (m)	03 05 07
Hyunsub	Kim	31/05/1985	South Korea	20km Walk (m)	07
Deokhyeon	Kim	08/12/1985	South Korea	Long Jump (m), Triple Jump (m)	07
Chol Sun	Kim	21/03/1983	North Korea	Marathon (w)	0
Kum-Ok	Kim	09/12/1988	North Korea	Marathon (w)	0
Yoo Suk	Kim	19/01/1982	South Korea	Pole Vault (m)	05
Risper Jemeli	Kimaiyo	26/06/1979	Kenya	Marathon (w)	0
Moumouni	Kimba	06/08/1987	Niger	400m (m)	0
Delivert Arsene	Kimbembe	14/09/1994	Congo	100m (m)	07
Shintaro	Kimura	30/06/1987	Japan	100m (m)	0
Jarkko	Kinnunen	19/01/1984	Finland	50km Walk	07

Athlete Index

Forenames	Surname	Born	Country	Event(s)	Prev Apps
Eliud	Kipchoge	05/11/1984	Kenya	5000m (m)	03 05 07
Gladys Jerotich	Kipkemoi	15/10/1986	Kenya	3000m SC (w)	0
Florence Jebet	Kiplagat	27/02/1987	Kenya	10000m (w)	0
Benjamin	Kiplagat	04/03/1989	Uganda	3000m SC (m)	07
Nicholas	Kiprono	07/11/1987	Uganda	Marathon (m)	0
Asbel	Kiprop	30/06/1989	Kenya	800m (m), 1500m (m)	07
Brimin Kiprop	Kipruto	31/07/1985	Kenya	3000m SC (m)	05 07
Moses Ndiema	Kipsiro	02/09/1986	Uganda	5000m (m)	05 07
Benjamin Kolum	Kiptoo	01/01/1979	Kenya	Marathon (m)	0
Bernard Kiprop	Kipyego	16/07/1986	Kenya	10000m (m)	0
Sergey	Kirdyapkin	18/06/1980	Russia	50km Walk	05 07
Anisya	Kirdyapkina	23/10/1989	Russia	20km Walk (w)	0
Nikoléta	Kiriakopoúlou	21/03/1986	Greece	Pole Vault (w)	0
Tsvetelina	Kirilova	14/07/1977	Bulgaria	400m Hurdles (w)	99 01 07
Helena Loshanyang	Kirop	09/09/1976	Kenya	Marathon (w)	0
Abel	Kirui	04/06/1982	Kenya	Marathon (m)	0
Aleksandra	Kiryashova	21/08/1985	Russia	Pole Vault (w)	0
Rachid	Kisri	02/08/1975	Morocco	Marathon (m)	07
Dániel	Kiss	12/02/1982	Hungary	110m Hurdles	0
Sirkka-Liisa	Kivine	22/06/1977	Estonia	Long Jump (w)	0
Jackson Mumbwa	Kivuva	11/08/1989	Kenya	800m (m)	0
Kathrin	Klaas	08/02/1984	Germany	Hammer (w)	05 07
Laurence	Klein	22/01/1969	France	Marathon (w)	0
Nadine	Kleinert	20/10/1975	Germany	Shot Put (w)	99 01 03 05 07
Piotr	Klimczak	18/01/1980	Poland	4x400m (m)	0
Lucia	Klocová	20/11/1983	Slovakia	800m (w)	03 05 07
Orranut	Klomdee	01/06/1980	Thailand	4x100m (w)	0
Eliška	Klucinová	14/04/1988	Czech Republic	Heptathlon	0
Svetlana	Klyuka	27/12/1978	Russia	800m (w)	03 05 07
Yuriko	Kobayashi	12/12/1988	Japan	5000m (w)	0
Joanna	Kocielnik	11/03/1983	Poland	100m Hurdles	0
Paul Kipsiele	Koech	10/11/1981	Kenya	3000m SC (m)	05
Elena	Kofanova	08/08/1988	Russia	800m (w)	0
Micah Kipkemboi	Kogo	30/06/1986	Kenya	10000m (m)	0
Fabienne	Kohlmann	06/11/1989	Germany	4x400m (w)	0
Yah Soucko	Koïta	23/09/1980	Mali	100m (w)	99 05
Iríni	Kokkinaríou	14/02/1981	Greece	3000m SC (w)	07
Valeriy	Kokoyev	22/07/1988	Russia	Shot Put (m)	0
Nina	Kolaric	12/12/1986	Slovenia	Long Jump (w)	0
Asmir	Kolašinac	15/10/1984	Serbia	Shot Put (m)	0
Martha	Komu	23/03/1983	Kenya	Marathon (w)	0
Yuliya	Kondakova	04/12/1981	Russia	100m Hurdles	0
Takayo	Kondo	17/11/1975	Japan	Pole Vault (w)	05 07
Mariya	Konovalova	14/08/1974	Russia	10000m (w)	07
Oleksandr	Korchmid	22/01/1982	Ukraine	Pole Vault (m)	07
Ilya	Korotkov	06/12/1983	Russia	Javelin (m)	0
Merja	Korpela	15/05/1981	Finland	Hammer (w)	05 07
Alexander	Kosenkow	14/03/1977	Germany	200m (m), 4x100m (m)	01 03
Zoltán	Kövágó	10/04/1979	Hungary	Discus (m)	01 03 05 07
Ainars	Kovals	21/11/1981	Latvia	Javelin (m)	05 07
Yoann	Kowal	07/10/1980	France	1500 (m)	0
Katarzyna	Kowalska	07/04/1985	Poland	3000m SC (w)	07
Kacper	Kozlowski	07/12/1986	Poland	4x400m (m)	0
Primož	Kozmus	30/09/1979	Slovenia	Hammer (m)	03 07
Kazai Suzanne	Kragbé	22/12/1981	Ivory Coast	Discus (w)	0
Irina	Krakoviak	16/11/1977	Lithuania	800m (w), 1500m (w)	01 05 07
Sabine	Krantz	06/02/1981	Germany	20km Walk (w)	03 05 07
Andrei	Krauchanka	04/01/1986	Belarus	Decathlon	07
Yuliya	Krevsun	04/11/1977	Ukraine	800m (w)	0
Bjørnar Ustad	Kristensen	26/01/1982	Norway	3000m SC (m)	07
Antonina	Krivoshapka	21/07/1987	Russia	400m (w), 4x400m (w)	0
Andrey	Krivov	14/11/1985	Russia	20km Walk (m)	0
Meike	Kröger	21/07/1986	Germany	High Jump (w)	0
Frantz	Kruger	22/05/1975	Finland	Discus (m)	99 01 03 05 07
Alfred	Kruger	18/02/1979	United States	Hammer (m)	05 07

Athlete Index

Forenames	Surname	Born	Country	Event(s)	Prev Apps
Eric	Krüger	21/03/1988	Germany	4x400m (m)	0
Valentin	Kruglyakov	28/08/1985	Russia	4x400m (m)	0
Yuriy	Krymarenko	11/08/1983	Ukraine	High Jump (m)	05 07
Pavel	Kryvitski	17/04/1984	Belarus	Hammer (m)	0
Adam	Kszczot	02/09/1989	Poland	800m (m)	0
Robert	Kubaczyk	04/08/1986	Poland	4x100m (m)	0
Satomi	Kubokura	27/04/1982	Japan	400m Hurdles (w), 4x400m (w)	07
Dariusz	Kuć	24/04/1986	Poland	100m (m), 4x100m (m)	07
Olga	Kucherenko	05/11/1985	Russia	Long Jump (w)	0
Jan	Kudlicka	29/04/1988	Czech Republic	Pole Vault (m)	0
Stine	Kufaas	07/04/1986	Norway	High Jump (w)	0
Susan	Kuijken	08/07/1986	Netherlands	1500 (w)	0
Mihkel	Kukk	08/10/1983	Estonia	Javelin (m)	0
Oleg	Kulkov	06/03/1978	Russia	Marathon (m)	0
Liliya	Kulyk	27/01/1987	Ukraine	Triple Jump (w)	0
Yeliz	Kurt	15/01/1984	Turkey	800m (w)	0
Lajos	Kürthy	22/10/1986	Hungary	Shot Put (m)	07
Geoffrey	Kusuro	12/02/1989	Uganda	5000m (m)	0
Rustam	Kuvatov	09/11/1977	Kazakhstan	20km Walk (m)	0
Viktor	Kuznyetsov	17/07/1986	Ukraine	Long Jump (m)	0
Pauline	Kwalea	29/02/1988	Solomon Islands	100m (w)	05
Amine	Laalou	13/05/1982	Morocco	800m (m), 1500m (m)	03 05 07
Tanel	Laanmäe	29/09/1989	Estonia	Javelin (m)	0
Iulio	Lafai	20/12/1989	Samoa	800m (m)	0
Bernard	Lagat	12/12/1974	United States	1500 (m), 5000m (m)	01 03 07
Samyr	Laine	17/07/1984	Haiti	Triple Jump (m)	0
Btissam	Lakhouad	07/12/1980	Morocco	1500 (w)	0
Ivet	Lalova	18/05/1984	Bulgaria	100m (w), 200m (w)	07
Ayad	Lamdassem	11/10/1981	Spain	10000m (m)	0
Legese	Lamiso	13/01/1990	Ethiopia	3000m SC (m)	0
Thomas	Lancashire	02/07/1985	Great Britain	1500 (m)	0
Nancy Jebet	Langat	22/08/1981	Kenya	1500 (w)	05
Elis	Lapenmal	06/09/1987	Vanuatu	100m (w)	07
Fabrice	Lapierre	17/10/1983	Australia	Long Jump (m)	0
Lionel	Larry	14/09/1986	United States	400m (m), 4x400m (m)	07
Sofia	Larsson	22/07/1988	Sweden	Discus (w)	0
Anabelle	Lascar	25/04/1985	Mauritius	800m (w)	0
Jeff	Lastennet	26/08/1987	France	800m (m)	0
Clayton	Latham	18/04/1980	St Vincent & Grenadines	Long Jump (m)	0
Germán	Lauro	02/04/1984	Argentina	Shot Put (m), Discus (m)	07
Rachel	Lavallée	14/01/1986	Canada	20km Walk (w)	0
Cédric	Lavanne	13/11/1980	France	110m Hurdles	05
Renaud	Lavillenie	18/09/1986	France	Pole Vault (m)	0
Elena Mirela	Lavric	17/02/1991	Romania	800m (w)	0
Bola Gee	Lawal	26/06/1976	Nigeria	4x400m (m)	0
Isabel	Le Roux	23/01/1987	South Africa	200m (w)	0
Tatyana	Lebedeva	21/07/1976	Russia	Long Jump (w), Triple Jump (w)	99 01 03 05 07
Lenka	Ledvinová	11/08/1985	Czech Republic	Hammer (w)	07
Muna	Lee	30/10/1981	United States	100m (w), 200m (w), 4x100m (w)	05
Jung-joon	Lee	26/03/1984	South Korea	110m Hurdles	0
Myong-Ki	Lee	14/08/1979	South Korea	Marathon (m)	03 07
Myongseung	Lee	10/10/1983	South Korea	Marathon (m)	0
Sun-young	Lee	20/04/1984	South Korea	Marathon (w)	0
Henok	Legesse	01/01/1980	Ethiopia	1500 (m)	0
Lauri	Leis	07/10/1978	Estonia	Triple Jump (m)	0
Mikhail	Lemaev	23/11/1986	Russia	Marathon (m)	0
Christophe	Lemaître	11/06/1990	France	100m (m), 4x100m (m)	0
Irina	Lenskiy	12/06/1971	Israel	100m Hurdles	01 03
Constantino	León	12/04/1974	Peru	Marathon (m)	0
Éloyse	Lesueur	15/07/1988	France	Long Jump (w)	0
Loïc	Letellier	01/10/1976	France	Marathon (m)	0
Andrew	Letherby	19/09/1973	Australia	Marathon (m)	03
Vladimir	Letnicov	07/10/1981	Moldova	Triple Jump (m)	0
Marcin	Lewandowski	13/06/1987	Poland	800m (m)	0
Mikolaj	Lewanski	31/08/1986	Poland	4x100m (m)	0

Athlete Index

Forenames	Surname	Born	Country	Event(s)	Prev Apps
Tamsyn	Lewis	20/07/1978	Australia	4x400m (w)	99 03 07
Steven	Lewis	20/05/1986	Great Britain	Pole Vault (m)	07
Randy	Lewis	15/11/1978	Grenada	Triple Jump (m)	05 07
Jianbo	Li	14/11/1986	China	20km Walk (m)	0
Lei	Li	29/11/1987	China	50km Walk	0
Wen-Hua	Li	03/12/1989	Taipei	Discus (w)	0
Jinzhe	Li	01/09/1989	China	Long Jump (m)	0
Ling	Li	06/07/1989	China	Pole Vault (w)	0
Meiju	Li	03/10/1979	China	Shot Put (w)	03 05 07
Yanxi	Li	26/06/1983	China	Triple Jump (w)	05 07
Tanika	Liburd	20/05/1982	St Kitts & Nevis	4x100m (w)	0
Sávva	Líka	27/06/1970	Greece	Javelin (w)	05 07
Eun-ji	Lim	02/04/1989	South Korea	Pole Vault (w)	0
Irene	Limika	28/08/1979	Kenya	Marathon (w)	0
Iryna	Lishchynska	15/01/1976	Ukraine	1500 (w)	99 01 03 07
Irina	Litvinenko	08/01/1987	Kazakhstan	Triple Jump (w)	0
Sergej	Litvinov	27/01/1986	Germany	Hammer (m)	0
Lyudmila	Litvinova	08/06/1985	Russia	400m (w), 4x400m (w)	0
Hong	Liu	12/05/1987	China	20km Walk (w)	07
Xiangrong	Liu	06/06/1988	China	Shot Put (w)	0
Shereefa	Lloyd	02/09/1982	Jamaica	4x400m (w)	07
Jonas	Lohse	15/05/1987	Sweden	Javelin (m)	0
Lopez	Lomong	01/01/1985	United States	1500 (m)	0
Priscilla	Lopes-Schliep	26/08/1982	Canada	100m Hurdles	05 07
Luis	López	03/06/1979	Colombia	20km Walk (m)	05 07
Cristina	López	19/09/1982	El Salvador	20km Walk (w)	05
Yeimer	López	28/08/1982	Cuba	800m (m)	03 05 07
Yaniuvis	López	01/02/1986	Cuba	Shot Put (w)	0
Patricia	Lossouarn	21/09/1972	France	Marathon (w)	0
Olive	Loughnane	14/01/1976	Ireland	20km Walk (w)	01 03 05 07
Stephan	Louw	26/02/1975	Namibia	Long Jump (m)	01
Chaunté	Howard Lowe	12/01/1984	United States	High Jump (w)	05
Josanne	Lucas	14/04/1984	Trinidad & Tobago	400m Hurdles (w)	05
Ion	Luchianov	31/01/1981	Moldova	3000m SC (m)	05
Mervyn	Luckwell	27/11/1984	Great Britain	Javelin (m)	0
Olexiy	Lukashevych	11/01/1977	Ukraine	Long Jump (m)	99 01 03 07
Fernando	Lumain	18/10/1989	Indonesia	100m (m)	0
Kou	Luogon	11/06/1984	Liberia	400m Hurdles (w)	05
Nataliia	Lupu	04/11/1987	Ukraine	800m (w)	0
Maksim	Lynsha	06/04/1985	Belarus	110m Hurdles	0
Tatyana	Lysenko	09/10/1983	Russia	Hammer (w)	05
Pavel	Lyzhyn	24/03/1981	Belarus	Shot Put (m)	03 05 07
Xuejun	Ma	26/03/1985	China	Discus (w)	07
Donna	MacFarlane	18/06/1977	Australia	3000m SC (w)	07
Giitah	Macharia	24/12/1979	Canada	Marathon (m)	0
Julia	Mächtig	01/01/1986	Germany	Heptathlon	0
Kazuhiro	Maeda	19/04/1981	Japan	Marathon (m)	07
Simon	Magakwe	25/05/1985	South Africa	100m (m)	0
Maurren Higa	Maggi	25/06/1976	Brazil	Long Jump (w)	99 01 07
Michael	Mai	27/09/1977	United States	Hammer (m)	0
Ibrahim	Maïga	14/03/1979	Mali	400m Hurdles (m)	03 05 07
Ulrike	Maisch	21/01/1977	Germany	Marathon (w)	03
George	Majaji	28/02/1978	Zimbabwe	Marathon (m)	0
Tomasz	Majewski	30/08/1981	Poland	Shot Put (m)	05 07
Andriy	Makarchev	15/11/1985	Ukraine	Long Jump (m)	0
Sergey	Makarov	19/03/1973	Russia	Javelin (m)	99 01 03 05 07
Taoufik	Makhloufi	29/04/1988	Algeria	1500 (m)	0
Isaac	Makwala	29/09/1986	Botswana	400m (m)	0
Piotr	Malachowski	07/06/1983	Poland	Discus (m)	07
Romana	Malácová	15/05/1987	Czech Republic	Pole Vault (w)	0
Zuzana	Malíková	02/08/1983	Slovakia	20km Walk (w)	07
Casey	Malone	06/04/1977	United States	Discus (m)	03 05
Hugo	Mamba-Schlick	01/02/1982	Cameroon	Triple Jump (m)	07
Svitlana	Mamyeyeva	19/04/1982	Ukraine	Triple Jump (w)	0
Durka	Mana	19/06/1988	Sudan	3000m SC (w)	0

Athlete Index

Forenames	Surname	Born	Country	Event(s)	Prev Apps
Pascal	Mancini	18/04/1989	Switzerland	4x100m (m)	0
Laurence	Manfredi	20/05/1974	France	Shot Put (w)	99 03
Beatriz	Mangue	02/04/1992	Equatorial Guinea	100m (w)	0
Asenate	Manoa	23/05/1992	Tuvalu	100m (w)	0
Nadjim	Manseur	08/06/1988	Algeria	800m (m)	0
Andra	Manson	30/04/1984	United States	High Jump (m)	03
Leonel	Manzano	12/09/1984	United States	1500 (m)	07
Marcin	Marciniszyn	07/09/1982	Poland	400m (m), 4x400m (m)	05 07
Luis Alberto	Marco	20/08/1986	Spain	800m (m)	0
Ida	Marcussen	01/11/1987	Norway	Heptathlon	07
Marina	Marghiev	28/06/1986	Moldova	Hammer (w)	0
Zalina	Marghieva	05/02/1988	Moldova	Hammer (w)	0
Hanna	Mariën	16/05/1982	Belgium	4x100m (w)	0
Adrian	Markowski	14/10/1978	Poland	Javelin (m)	0
Shani	Marks	24/08/1980	United States	Triple Jump (w)	07
Beatrice	Marscheck	23/09/1985	Germany	Long Jump (w)	0
Jenna	Martin	31/03/1988	Canada	4x400m (w)	0
Scott	Martin	12/10/1982	Australia	Shot Put (m)	07
Eliseo	Martín	05/11/1973	Spain	3000m SC (m)	99 01 03 05 07
Diana	Martín	01/04/1981	Spain	3000m SC (w)	07
Churandy	Martina	03/07/1984	Netherlands Antilles	100m (m), 200m (m)	03 05 07
Eugene	Martineau	14/05/1980	Netherlands	Decathlon	05 07
Víctor	Martínez	01/06/1975	Andorra	1500 (m)	99 01
Mayte	Martínez	17/05/1976	Spain	800m (w)	01 05 07
Guillermo	Martínez	28/06/1981	Cuba	Javelin (m)	05 07
José Manuel	Martínez	22/10/1971	Spain	Marathon (m)	99 01 03 05 07
Manuel	Martínez	07/12/1974	Spain	Shot Put (m)	01 03 05 07
Magdelín	Martínez	10/02/1976	Italy	Triple Jump (w)	01 03 05 07
Anita	Márton	15/01/1989	Hungary	Shot Put (w)	0
Moses Ndiema	Masai	01/06/1986	Kenya	10000m (m)	0
Linet Chepkwemoi	Masai	05/12/1989	Kenya	10000m (w)	0
Amos	Masai	16/02/1984	Uganda	Marathon (m)	07
Marina	Maslenko	03/07/1982	Kazakhstan	400m (w)	0
Lenka	Masná	22/04/1985	Czech Republic	800m (w)	0
Yousef Ahmed	Masrahi	31/12/1987	Saudi Arabia	400m (m)	0
Chauncy	Master	02/06/1985	Malawi	1500 (m)	07
Sachiko	Masumi	20/12/1984	Japan	Long Jump (w)	0
Richard Kipkemboi	Mateelong	14/10/1983	Kenya	3000m SC (m)	07
Michael	Mathieu	24/06/1984	Bahamas	400m (m)	0
Télie	Mathiot	25/05/1987	France	Pole Vault (w)	0
Sibusiso	Matsenjwa	02/05/1988	Swaziland	200m (m)	0
Tanith	Maxwell	02/06/1976	South Africa	Marathon (w)	07
Gerhard	Mayer	20/05/1980	Austria	Discus (m)	0
Maksym	Mazuryk	02/04/1983	Ukraine	Pole Vault (m)	07
Martial	Mbandjock	14/10/1985	France	100m (m), 200m (m), 4x100m (m)	07
Joshua	McAdams	26/03/1980	United States	3000m SC (m)	07
Lee	McConnell	09/10/1978	Great Britain	4x400m (w)	03 05 07
Danny	McFarlane	14/06/1972	Jamaica	400m Hurdles (m)	99 01 03 05 07
Roisin	McGettigan	23/08/1980	Ireland	3000m SC (w)	05 07
Katie	McGregor	02/09/1977	United States	10000m (w)	05 07
Ramone	McKenzie	15/11/1990	Jamaica	200m (m)	0
Nathaniel	McKinney	19/01/1982	Bahamas	200m (m), 4x400m (m)	0
Erica	McLain	24/01/1986	United States	Triple Jump (w)	05
Anneisha	McLaughlin	06/01/1986	Jamaica	200m (w)	0
Sally	McLellan	19/09/1986	Australia	100m Hurdles	07
David	McNeill	06/10/1986	Australia	10000m (m)	0
Jennifer	Meadows	17/04/1981	Great Britain	800m (w), 4x400m (w)	07
Mebam Carole	Kaboud	17/09/1974	Cameroon	400m Hurdles (w)	0
Teklemariam	Medhin	24/06/1989	Eritrea	5000m (m), 10000m (m)	0
Ben Yousef	Meité	11/11/1986	Ivory Coast	100m (m), 200m (m)	0
Mahiedine	Mekhissi-Benabbad	15/03/1985	France	3000m SC (m)	07
Deresse	Mekonnen	20/10/1987	Ethiopia	1500 (m)	07
Inés	Melchor	30/08/1986	Peru	5000m (w)	03
Irina	Meleshina	25/05/1982	Russia	Long Jump (w)	05 07
Melanie	Melfort	08/11/1982	France	High Jump (w)	05 07

Athlete Index

Forenames	Surname	Born	Country	Event(s)	Prev Apps
Lukáš	Melich	16/09/1980	Czech Republic	Hammer (m)	05
Karin Mey	Melis	31/05/1983	Turkey	Long Jump (w)	0
Luis Felipe	Méliz	11/08/1979	Spain	Long Jump (m)	99 01 03
Meselech	Melkamu	27/04/1985	Ethiopia	5000m (w), 10000m (w)	05 07
Hanna	Melnychenko	24/04/1983	Ukraine	Heptathlon	07
Stanislav	Melnykov	26/02/1987	Ukraine	400m Hurdles (m)	0
Olisdeilys	Menéndez	14/11/1979	Cuba	Javelin (w)	99 01 03 05
Aleixo-Platini	Menga	29/09/1987	Germany	200m (m)	0
Leon	Mengloi	24/04/1989	Palau	100m (m)	0
Aleksandr	Menkov	07/12/1990	Russia	Long Jump (m)	0
Imane	Merga	15/10/1988	Ethiopia	10000m (m)	0
Deriba	Merga	26/10/1980	Ethiopia	Marathon (m)	0
Aselefech	Mergia	23/01/1985	Ethiopia	Marathon (w)	0
Brigitte	Merlano	29/04/1982	Colombia	100m Hurdles	05 07
Aries	Merritt	24/07/1985	United States	110m Hurdles	0
LaShawn	Merritt	27/06/1986	United States	400m (m), 4x400m (m)	05 07
Tesfayohannes	Mesfin	24/11/1974	Eritrea	Marathon (m)	0
Romain	Mesnil	13/06/1977	France	Pole Vault (m)	99 01 03 07
Nzola	Meso Teresa	30/11/1983	France	Triple Jump (w)	07
Obinna	Metu	12/07/1988	Nigeria	100m (m), 200m (m)	0
Daniele	Meucci	07/10/1985	Italy	5000m (m)	0
Aksana	Miankova	28/03/1982	Belarus	Hammer (w)	03 07
Lukasz	Michalski	02/08/1988	Poland	Pole Vault (m)	0
Virginie	Michanol	18/06/1985	France	4x400m (w)	0
Kimberley	Mickle	28/12/1984	Australia	Javelin (w)	0
Vilius	Mikelionis	05/03/1985	Lithuania	20km Walk (m)	0
Andrei	Mikhnevich	12/07/1976	Belarus	Shot Put (m)	99 01 03 05 07
Natallia	Mikhnevich	25/05/1982	Belarus	Shot Put (w)	05
Marta	Milani	09/03/1987	Italy	4x400m (w)	0
Eric	Milazar	01/06/1975	Mauritius	400m (m)	99 01 03 05 07
Joel	Milburn	17/03/1986	Australia	400m (m), 4x400m (m)	0
Derek	Miles	28/09/1972	United States	Pole Vault (m)	03
Dmitrijs	Milkevics	06/12/1981	Latvia	800m (m)	05 07
Andrea	Miller	13/03/1982	New Zealand	100m Hurdles	0
Ramon	Miller	17/02/1987	Bahamas	400m (m), 4x400m (m)	0
Ildar	Minshin	05/02/1985	Russia	3000m SC (m)	0
Nastassia	Mironchyk	13/04/1989	Belarus	Long Jump (w)	0
Anna	Mishchenko	25/08/1983	Ukraine	1500 (w)	0
Galina	Mityaeva	29/04/1991	Tajikistan	Hammer (w)	0
Dickson Marwa	Mkami	09/03/1982	Tanzania	10000m (m)	07
Sabrina	Mockenhaupt	06/12/1980	Germany	Marathon (w)	03 05
Keith	Moffatt	20/06/1984	United States	High Jump (m)	07
Ofentse	Mogawane	20/02/1982	South Africa	4x400m (m)	0
Mustafa	Mohamed	01/03/1979	Sweden	3000m SC (m)	03 05 07
Mohamed Ali	Mohamed	11/11/1989	Somalia	5000m (m)	0
Zakia Mrisho	Mohamed	19/02/1984	Tanzania	5000m (w)	05 07
Malte	Mohr	27/06/1986	Germany	Pole Vault (m)	0
Godfrey Khotso	Mokoena	06/03/1985	South Africa	Long Jump (m)	05 07
Viktoriya	Molchanova	26/05/1982	Ukraine	Long Jump (w)	0
Antje	Möldner	13/06/1984	Germany	3000m SC (w)	0
Juan Manuel	Molina	15/03/1979	Spain	20km Walk (m)	05 07
Anne	Möllinger	27/09/1985	Germany	4x100m (w)	0
Grace Kwamboka	Momanyi	13/03/1981	Kenya	10000m (w)	0
Avard	Moncur	02/11/1978	Bahamas	4x400m (m)	03 07
Manuela	Montebrun	13/11/1979	France	Hammer (w)	99 01 03 05 07
Inês	Monteiro	18/05/1980	Portugal	10000m (w)	05
Ricardo	Monteiro	02/10/1985	Portugal	4x100m (m)	0
Amantle	Montsho	04/07/1983	Botswana	400m (w)	05 07
Tera	Moody	18/12/1980	United States	Marathon (w)	0
Sajad	Moradi	30/03/1983	Iran	800m (m)	05 07
Clara	Morales	10/03/1975	Chile	Marathon (w)	0
Patrizia	Morceli	11/07/1974	Switzerland	Marathon (w)	0
José Carlos	Moreira	28/09/1983	Brazil	100m (m), 4x100m (m)	07
Sara	Moreira	17/10/1985	Portugal	5000m (w), 3000m SC (w)	07
José	Moreira	05/05/1980	Portugal	Marathon (m)	0

Athlete Index

Forenames	Surname	Born	Country	Event(s)	Prev Apps
Johana	Moreno	15/04/1985	Colombia	Hammer (w)	0
Lyubov	Morgunova	14/01/1971	Russia	Marathon (w)	01 07
Koichiro	Morioka	02/04/1985	Japan	20km Walk (m), 50km Walk	05 07
Angela	Morosanu	26/07/1986	Romania	400m Hurdles (w)	07
Amaechi	Morton	30/10/1989	Nigeria	4x400m (m)	0
Ryan	Moseley	08/10/1982	Austria	100m (m)	0
Cydonie	Mothersille	19/03/1978	Cayman Islands	200m (w)	99 01 03 05 07
Mohamed	Moustaoui	02/04/1985	Morocco	1500 (m)	07
Cecile	Moynot	02/10/1976	France	Marathon (w)	0
Thuso	Mpuang	01/03/1985	South Africa	200m (m), 4x100m (m)	0
Carline	Muir	01/10/1987	Canada	4x400m (w)	0
Nedžad	Mulabegovic	04/02/1981	Croatia	Shot Put (m)	07
Mbulaeni	Mulaudzi	08/09/1980	South Africa	800m (m)	01 03 05 07
Norman	Müller	07/08/1985	Germany	Decathlon	07
Nadine	Müller	21/11/1985	Germany	Discus (w)	07
Stefan	Müller	20/09/1979	Switzerland	Javelin (m)	05 07
Ángel	Mullera	20/04/1984	Spain	3000m SC (m)	0
Steve	Mullings	28/11/1982	Jamaica	200m (m), 4x100m (m)	07
Prince	Mumba	28/09/1984	Zambia	800m (m)	01 05
Marina	Muncan	06/11/1982	Serbia	1500 (w)	07
Markus	Münch	13/06/1986	Germany	Discus (m)	0
Simon	Munyutu	27/12/1977	France	Marathon (m)	0
Julia Mumbi	Muraga	25/01/1985	Kenya	Marathon (w)	0
Yukifumi	Murakami	23/12/1979	Japan	Javelin (m)	05 07
Vyacheslav	Muravyev	14/07/1982	Kazakhstan	200m (m)	0
Fabiana	Murer	16/03/1981	Brazil	Pole Vault (w)	05 07
Emmanuel Kipchirchir	Mutai	12/10/1984	Kenya	Marathon (m)	0
Mark Kiprotich	Muttai	23/03/1978	Kenya	400m (m)	0
Gabriel	Mvumvure	23/02/1988	Zimbabwe	200m (m)	0
Carl	Myerscough	21/10/1979	Great Britain	Shot Put (m)	03 05
Gaute	Myklebust	29/04/1979	Norway	Discus (m)	05
Fabiano Joseph	Naasi	24/12/1985	Tanzania	5000m (m), 10000m (m)	03 05
Cédric	Nabe	16/06/1983	Switzerland	100m (m)	0
Racheal	Nachula	14/01/1990	Zambia	400m (w)	0
Beata	Naigambo	11/03/1980	Namibia	Marathon (w)	0
Yurika	Nakamura	01/04/1986	Japan	5000m (w), 10000m (w)	0
Yondan	Namelo	13/10/1989	Fed States of Micronesia	100m (m)	0
Abdallahi	Nanou	31/12/1989	Mauritania	1500 (m)	0
Kenji	Narisako	25/07/1984	Japan	400m Hurdles (m)	05 07
Elizna	Naude	14/09/1978	South Africa	Discus (w)	05
Goran	Nava	15/04/1981	Serbia	1500 (m)	0
Horacio	Nava	20/01/1982	Mexico	50km Walk	05 07
Franklin	Nazareno	24/04/1987	Ecuador	100m (m), 200m (m)	07
Dilshod	Nazarov	06/05/1982	Tajikistan	Hammer (m)	05 07
Natalya	Nazarova	26/05/1979	Russia	4x400m (w)	99 03
Maria Nicoleta	Negoita	06/12/1986	Romania	Javelin (w)	0
Tim	Nelson	27/02/1984	United States	10000m (m)	0
Adam	Nelson	07/07/1975	United States	Shot Put (m)	01 03 05 07
Steffi	Nerius	01/07/1972	Germany	Javelin (w)	99 01 03 05 07
Yulia	Nestsiarenka	15/06/1979	Belarus	4x100m (w)	05
Rosemar Maria	Neto	02/01/1977	Brazil	4x100m (w)	0
Brent	Newdick	31/01/1985	New Zealand	Decathlon	0
Coolboy	Ngamole	21/06/1977	South Africa	Marathon (m)	0
Samson	Ngoepe	28/01/1985	South Africa	800m (m)	0
Van Hung	Nguyen	04/03/1989	Vietnam	Triple Jump (m)	0
Yves	Niaré	20/07/1977	France	Shot Put (m)	01 07
Marek	Niit	09/08/1987	Estonia	200m (m)	07
Yevhen	Nikitin	09/01/1985	Ukraine	Decathlon	0
Minna	Nikkanen	09/04/1988	Finland	Pole Vault (w)	07
Cecilia	Nilsson	22/06/1979	Sweden	Hammer (w)	01 03 05 07
Pedro	Nimo	05/06/1980	Spain	Marathon (m)	0
Pauline	Niyongere	21/10/1988	Burundi	5000m (w)	0
Denis	Nizhegorodov	26/07/1980	Russia	50km Walk	03 07
Jean-Jacques	Nkouloukidi	15/04/1982	Italy	20km Walk (m)	0
Artur	Noga	02/05/1988	Poland	110m Hurdles	0

Athlete Index

Forenames	Surname	Born	Country	Event(s)	Prev Apps
Maryna	Novik	19/01/1984	Belarus	Javelin (w)	0
Roman	Novotný	05/01/1986	Czech Republic	Long Jump (m)	0
Iryna	Novozhylova	07/01/1986	Ukraine	Hammer (w)	0
Tiidrek	Nurme	18/11/1985	Estonia	1500 (m)	0
Selim	Nurudeen	01/02/1983	Nigeria	110m Hurdles	07
Martijn	Nuyens	18/11/1983	Netherlands	High Jump (m)	0
Sorina	Nwachukwu	21/08/1987	Germany	400m (w), 4x400m (w)	0
Ruth Bisibori	Nyangau	02/01/1988	Kenya	3000m SC (w)	07
Epiphanie	Nyirabarame	15/12/1981	Rwanda	Marathon (w)	03 05
Trond	Nymark	28/12/1976	Norway	50km Walk	99 01 03 05 07
Young Talkmore	Nyongani	02/09/1983	Zimbabwe	400m (m)	05 07
Carolin	Nytra	26/02/1985	Germany	100m Hurdles	0
Francine	Nzilampa	12/01/1982	Dem Rep of Congo	1500 (w)	0
Christina	Obergföll	22/08/1981	Germany	Javelin (w)	05 07
Francis	Obikwelu	22/11/1978	Portugal	4x100m (m)	97 99 03 05 07
Darlenis	Obregón	21/02/1986	Colombia	200m (w), 4x100m (w)	0
Christian	Obrist	20/11/1980	Italy	1500 (m)	03 07
Mikel	Odriozola	25/05/1973	Spain	50km Walk	99 01 03 05 07
Muizat Ajoke	Odumosu	27/10/1987	Nigeria	400m Hurdles (w), 4x400m (w)	07
Jennifer	Oeser	29/11/1983	Germany	Heptathlon	07
Ben	Offereins	12/03/1986	Australia	4x400m (m)	0
Egwero	Ogho-Oghene	26/11/1988	Nigeria	100m (m)	0
Amaka	Ogoegbunam	03/03/1990	Nigeria	400m (w)	0
Amaka	Ogoegbunam*	27/10/1987	Nigeria	400m Hurdles (w)	07
Andreea	Ograzeanu	24/03/1990	Romania	200m (w)	0
Jessica	Ohanaja	06/12/1986	Nigeria	100m Hurdles	0
Christine	Ohuruogu	17/05/1984	Great Britain	400m (w), 4x400m (w)	05 07
Blessing	Okagbare	09/10/1988	Nigeria	100m (w), Long Jump (w)	0
Tosin	Oke	01/10/1980	Nigeria	Triple Jump (m)	0
Eileen	O'Keeffe	31/05/1981	Ireland	Hammer (w)	05 07
Marilyn	Okoro	23/09/1984	Great Britain	800m (w)	07
Ezinne	Okparaebo	03/03/1988	Norway	100m (w)	0
Nuta	Olaru	28/08/1970	Romania	Marathon (w)	01 03 05 07
Ercüment	Olgundeniz	07/07/1976	Turkey	Discus (m)	99 07
Yavgeniy	Olhovsky	22/12/1983	Israel	Pole Vault (m)	0
Stanislavs	Olijars	22/03/1979	Latvia	110m Hurdles	99 03 05 07
Élodie	Olivarès	22/05/1976	France	3000m SC (w)	05 07
Manuel	Olmedo	17/05/1983	Spain	800m (m)	03 05 07
Csongor	Olteán	08/04/1984	Hungary	Javelin (m)	07
John Robert	Oosthuizen	23/01/1987	South Africa	Javelin (m)	07
Éva	Orbán	29/11/1984	Hungary	Hammer (w)	05
Johana	Ordóñez	12/12/1987	Ecuador	20km Walk (w)	0
Derval	O'Rourke	28/05/1981	Ireland	100m Hurdles	03 05 07
Yolanda	Osana	11/08/1987	Dominican Republic	400m Hurdles (w)	0
Oludamola	Osayomi	26/06/1986	Nigeria	100m (w), 200m (w), 4x100m (w)	07
Matic	Osovnikar	19/01/1980	Slovenia	100m (m)	03 05 07
Luvsanlkhundeg	Otgonbayar	13/07/1982	Mongolia	Marathon (w)	07
Kumi	Otoshi	29/07/1985	Japan	20km Walk (w)	0
Björn	Otto	16/10/1977	Germany	Pole Vault (m)	03 07
Yamna	Oubouhou	20/02/1974	France	Marathon (w)	99 01
Elodie	Ouédraogo	27/02/1981	Belgium	400m Hurdles (w), 4x100m (w)	07
Hanane	Ouhaddou	01/01/1982	Morocco	3000m SC (w)	07
Aziz	Ouhadi	24/07/1984	Morocco	100m (m)	0
Yoshimi	Ozaki	01/07/1981	Japan	Marathon (w)	0
Mikk	Pahapill	18/07/1983	Estonia	Decathlon	05
Song-Chol	Pak	10/11/1984	North Korea	Marathon (m)	0
Rolando	Palacios	03/05/1987	Honduras	100m (m), 200m (m)	05
Felipa	Palacios	01/12/1975	Colombia	4x100m (w)	97 99 01 07
Vita	Palamar	12/10/1977	Ukraine	High Jump (w)	01 03 05 07
Madara	Palameika	18/06/1987	Latvia	Javelin (w)	0
Hank	Palmer	16/03/1985	Canada	4x100m (m)	0
Babubhai	Panucha	10/08/1978	India	20km Walk (m)	0
Aléxandros	Papadimitríou	18/06/1973	Greece	Hammer (m)	99 01 03 05 07
Stilianí	Papadopoúlou	15/03/1982	Greece	Hammer (w)	05
Paraskeví	Papahrístou	17/04/1989	Greece	Triple Jump (w)	0

Athlete Index

Forenames	Surname	Born	Country	Event(s)	Prev Apps
Alexándra	Papayeoryíou	17/12/1980	Greece	Hammer (w)	03 07
Madeleine	Pape	24/02/1984	Australia	800m (w), 4x400m (w)	0
Krisztina	Papp	17/12/1982	Hungary	5000m (w)	0
Tae-kyong	Park	30/07/1980	South Korea	110m Hurdles	0
Chil-sung	Park	08/07/1982	South Korea	20km Walk (m)	07
Jae-myong	Park	15/12/1981	South Korea	Javelin (m)	0
Ho-sun	Park	17/11/1986	South Korea	Marathon (w)	0
Krisztián	Pars	18/02/1982	Hungary	Hammer (m)	05 07
Beatriz	Pascual	09/05/1982	Spain	20km Walk (w)	07
Miguel	Pate	13/06/1979	United States	Long Jump (m)	01 05 07
Courtney	Patterson	10/02/1985	US Virgin Islands	100m (w)	0
Kara	Patterson	10/04/1986	United States	Javelin (w)	0
Darvis	Patton	04/12/1977	United States	100m (m), 4x100m (m)	03
Elisabeth	Pauer	01/03/1983	Austria	Javelin (w)	0
Alberto	Paulo	03/10/1985	Portugal	3000m SC (m)	0
Igor	Pavlov	18/07/1979	Russia	Pole Vault (m)	05 07
David	Payne	24/07/1982	United States	110m Hurdles	05 07
Darya	Pchelnik	20/12/1981	Belarus	Hammer (w)	05
Fabiano	Peçanha	05/06/1982	Brazil	800m (m)	05 07
Taavi	Peetre	05/07/1983	Estonia	Shot Put (m)	05 07
Arismendy	Peguero	02/08/1980	Dominican Republic	400m (m), 4x400m (m)	05 07
Sladjana	Pejovic	26/03/1984	Montenegro	1500 (w)	0
Diosmely	Peña	12/06/1985	Cuba	4x400m (w)	0
Manuel Ángel	Penas	09/11/1977	Spain	10000m (m)	0
Eva	Pereira	22/03/1989	Cape Verde	1500 (w)	0
António	Pereira	10/07/1975	Portugal	50km Walk	07
Bianca	Perie	01/06/1990	Romania	Hammer (w)	07
Sandra	Perkovic	21/06/1990	Croatia	Discus (w)	0
Athanasía	Pérra	02/02/1983	Greece	Triple Jump (w)	05 07
Michelle	Perry	01/05/1979	United States	100m Hurdles	05 07
Ruggero	Pertile	08/08/1974	Italy	Marathon (m)	03 05
Pierre-Alexis	Pessonneaux	25/11/1987	France	4x100m (m)	0
Mario	Pestano	08/04/1978	Spain	Discus (m)	99 01 03 05 07
Sara	Petersen	09/04/1987	Denmark	400m Hurdles (w)	0
Tetiana	Petlyuk	22/02/1982	Ukraine	800m (w), 4x400m (w)	05 07
Bergur Ingi	Pétursson	05/10/1985	Iceland	Hammer (m)	0
Richard	Phillips	26/01/1983	Jamaica	110m Hurdles	0
Isa	Phillips	22/04/1984	Jamaica	400m Hurdles (m), 4x400m (m)	07
Dwight	Phillips	01/10/1977	United States	Long Jump (m)	01 03 05 07
Gerald	Phiri	06/10/1988	Zambia	100m (m), 200m (m)	0
Un Suk	Phyo	13/06/1980	North Korea	Marathon (w)	0
Alessandra	Picagevicz	20/02/1984	Brazil	20km Walk (w)	0
Elisa	Cusma Piccione	24/07/1981	Italy	800m (w)	05 07
Diana	Pickler	09/12/1983	United States	Heptathlon	07
Bayron	Piedra	19/08/1982	Ecuador	1500 (m), 5000m (m)	07
Anna	Pierce	31/03/1984	United States	1500 (w)	07
Tamla	Pietersen	03/06/1989	Zimbabwe	100m Hurdles	0
Emmilly	Pinheiro	03/11/1985	Brazil	4x400m (w)	0
Evans	Pinto	20/04/1984	Bolivia	800m (m)	0
Valery	Pisarev	30/06/1979	Kyrgyzstan	Marathon (m)	03
Bogdan	Pishchalnikov	26/08/1982	Russia	Discus (m)	05 07
Tero	Pitkämäki	19/12/1982	Finland	Javelin (m)	05 07
Leonor	Piuza	14/04/1978	Mozambique	800m (w)	0
Urszula	Piwnicka	06/12/1983	Poland	Javelin (w)	0
Joanna	Piwowarska	04/11/1983	Poland	Pole Vault (w)	07
Judith	Plá	02/05/1978	Spain	5000m (w)	0
Kjersti	Plätzer	18/01/1972	Norway	20km Walk (w)	99 01 03 07
Evgeniy	Plotnir	26/06/1977	Russia	Triple Jump (m)	0
Ronald	Pognon	16/11/1982	France	100m (m), 4x100m (m)	03 05
Aleksandr	Pogorelov	10/01/1980	Russia	Decathlon	03 05
Nataliya	Pohrebnyak	19/12/1988	Ukraine	100m (w), 4x100m (w)	07
Marie	Polli	28/11/1980	Switzerland	20km Walk (w)	07
André	Pollmächer	22/03/1983	Germany	Marathon (m)	0
Tatyana	Polnova	20/04/1979	Russia	Pole Vault (w)	05 07
Victoria	Poludina	29/06/1989	Kyrgyzstan	Marathon (w)	0

Athlete Index

Forenames	Surname	Born	Country	Event(s)	Prev Apps
Evgeniya	Polyakova	29/05/1983	Russia	100m (w), 4x100m (w)	07
Aliann	Pompey	09/03/1978	Guyana	400m (w)	01 03 05 07
Tiandra	Ponteen	09/11/1984	St Kitts & Nevis	400m (w)	05
Krishna	Poonia	05/05/1982	India	Discus (w)	07
Natalya	Popkova	21/09/1988	Russia	5000m (w)	0
Nikolai	Portelli	17/12/1981	Malta	200m (m)	0
Vera	Pospíšilová-Cechlová	19/11/1978	Czech Republic	Discus (w)	01 03 05 07
Wioletta	Potepa	13/12/1980	Poland	Discus (w)	05 07
Ana	Pouhila	18/10/1979	Tonga	Shot Put (w)	01 03 05 07
Asafa	Powell	23/11/1982	Jamaica	100m (m), 4x100m (m)	03 07
Ginnie	Powell	07/09/1983	United States	100m Hurdles	05 07
Adrienne	Power	11/12/1981	Canada	200m (w), 4x400m (w)	0
Phillip	Poznanski	13/12/1986	Marshall Islands	100m (m)	0
Thaissa	Presti	07/11/1985	Brazil	4x100m (w)	0
Martina	Pretelli	28/12/1988	San Marino	100m (w)	0
Petrina	Price	26/04/1984	Australia	High Jump (w)	0
Shara	Proctor	16/09/1988	Anguilla	Long Jump (w)	07
Andriy	Protsenko	20/05/1988	Ukraine	High Jump (m)	0
Jirina	Ptácniková	20/05/1986	Czech Republic	Pole Vault (w)	0
Balpreet Kaur	Purba	17/05/1990	Singapore	100m (w)	0
Oleksandr	Pyatnytsya	14/07/1985	Ukraine	Javelin (m)	0
Anna	Pyatykh	04/04/1981	Russia	Triple Jump (w)	03 05 07
Monika	Pyrek	11/08/1980	Poland	Pole Vault (w)	01 03 05 07
Qiang	Qin	18/04/1983	China	Javelin (m)	07
Tara	Quinn-Smith	19/09/1979	Canada	Marathon (w)	0
Jackson	Quiñónez	12/06/1980	Spain	110m Hurdles	03 05 07
Renny	Quow	25/08/1987	Trinidad & Tobago	400m (m)	07
Anastasiya	Rabchenyuk	14/09/1983	Ukraine	400m Hurdles (w), 4x400m (w)	07
Svetlana	Radzivil	17/01/1987	Uzbekistan	High Jump (w)	0
Eriks	Rags	01/06/1975	Latvia	Javelin (m)	99 01 03 05 07
Andres	Raja	02/06/1982	Estonia	Decathlon	07
Leyla	Rajabi	18/04/1983	Iran	Shot Put (w)	0
Judith	Ramírez	27/09/1974	Mexico	Marathon (w)	0
Jacob Mothsodi	Ramokoka	20/09/1983	South Africa	4x400m (m)	0
Ruben	Ramolefi	17/07/2008	South Africa	3000m SC (m)	05 07
Joseph-Berlioz	Randriamihaja	30/11/1975	Madagascar	110m Hurdles	01 03 05 07
Ilija	Ranitovic	06/02/1987	Montenegro	800m (w)	0
Kevin	Rans	19/08/1982	Belgium	Pole Vault (m)	05 07
Chandrika	Rasnayake	20/06/1987	Sri Lanka	400m (w)	0
Martina	Ratej	02/11/1981	Slovenia	Javelin (w)	0
Dana Abdul	Razak	03/01/1986	Iraq	100m (w)	0
Vira	Rebryk	25/02/1989	Ukraine	Javelin (w)	0
Joel	Redhead	03/07/1986	Grenada	200m (m)	0
Gary	Reed	25/10/1981	Canada	800m (m)	03 05 07
Brittney	Reese	09/09/1986	United States	Long Jump (w)	07
Aishath	Reesha	31/05/1989	Maldives	800m (w)	07
Julian	Reid	23/09/1988	Jamaica	Triple Jump (m)	0
Daniela	Reina	15/05/1981	Italy	800m (w), 4x400m (w)	07
Sorai Bella	Reklai	28/04/1992	Palau	100m (w)	0
Margrethe	Renstrøm	21/03/1985	Norway	Long Jump (w)	0
Jozef	Repcik	03/08/1986	Slovakia	800m (m)	07
Jennifer	Rhines	01/07/1974	United States	5000m (w)	01 05 07
Hyon U	Ri	30/09/1986	North Korea	Marathon (m)	0
Yainelis	Ribiaux	30/12/1987	Cuba	Javelin (w)	0
Sanya	Richards	26/02/1985	United States	400m (w), 4x400m (w)	03 05 07
Lukas	Rifesser	17/07/1986	Italy	800m (m)	0
Romary	Rifka	23/12/1970	Mexico	High Jump (w)	03 05 07
Elisa	Rigaudo	17/06/1980	Italy	20km Walk (w)	03 05 07
Michael	Rimmer	03/12/1986	Great Britain	800m (m)	07
Jeffrey	Riseley	11/11/1986	Australia	1500 (m)	07
Dathan	Ritzenhein	30/12/1982	United States	10000m (m)	07
Mélina	Robert-Michon	18/07/1979	France	Discus (w)	01 03 07
Gil	Roberts	15/03/1989	United States	400m (m)	0
Josef	Robertson	14/05/1987	Jamaica	400m Hurdles (m)	0
Muqimyar	Robina	03/07/1986	Afghanistan	100m (w)	0

Athlete Index

Forenames	Surname	Born	Country	Event(s)	Prev Apps
Khadevis	Robinson	19/07/1976	United States	800m (m)	99 01 03 05 07
Dayron	Robles	19/11/1986	Cuba	110m Hurdles	05 07
Michael	Rodgers	24/04/1985	United States	100m (m), 4x100m (m)	0
Snežana	Rodic	19/08/1982	Slovenia	Triple Jump (w)	05 07
Ángel David	Rodríguez	25/04/1990	Spain	100m (m), 200m (m)	07
Carol	Rodríguez	26/12/1985	Puerto Rico	100m (w), 200m (w)	07
Natalia	Rodríguez	02/06/1979	Spain	1500 (w)	01 03 05
Rosa	Rodríguez	02/07/1986	Venezuela	Hammer (w)	07
Dulce María	Rodríguez	14/08/1972	Mexico	Marathon (w)	01 05
Déborah	Rodríguez	02/12/1982	Uruguay	400m Hurdles (w)	0
Jeremy	Roff	22/11/1983	Australia	1500 (m)	0
Anna	Rogowska	21/05/1981	Poland	Pole Vault (w)	03 05 07
Sasha	Rolle	16/04/1982	Bahamas	4x400m (w)	0
Elena	Romagnolo	05/10/1982	Italy	3000m SC (w)	07
Sonja	Roman	11/03/1979	Slovenia	1500 (w)	07
Jarred	Rome	21/12/1976	United States	Discus (m)	01 03 05 07
Juan Carlos	Romero	15/12/1977	Mexico	10000m (m)	0
Daniel	Rono	13/07/1978	Kenya	Marathon (m)	0
Martyn	Rooney	03/04/1987	Great Britain	400m (m), 4x400m (m)	07
Chiara	Rosa	28/01/1983	Italy	Shot Put (w)	05 07
Joshua	Ross	28/07/1989	Australia	4x100m (m)	0
Anna	Rostkowska	26/07/1980	Poland	800m (w)	0
Jess	Rothwell	18/06/1989	Australia	20km Walk (w)	0
David Kimutai	Rotich	19/08/1969	Kenya	20km Walk (m)	0
Aaron	Rouge-Serret	21/01/1988	Australia	4x100m (m)	0
Brandon	Roulhac	13/12/1983	United States	Triple Jump (m)	0
Jurij	Rovan	23/01/1975	Slovenia	Pole Vault (m)	05
Shannon	Rowbury	19/09/1984	United States	1500 (w)	0
Sushmitha Singha	Roy	26/03/1984	India	Heptathlon	0
Ivana	Rožhman	14/07/1989	FYR Macedonia	100m (w)	0
Sandra	Ruales	30/05/1974	Ecuador	Marathon (w)	05
Denvil	Ruan	07/03/1989	Anguilla	100m (m)	0
Artem	Rubanko	21/08/1974	Ukraine	Hammer (m)	0
Giorgio	Rubino	15/04/1986	Italy	20km Walk (m)	07
David Lekuta	Rudisha	17/12/1988	Kenya	800m (m)	0
Galen	Rupp	08/05/1986	United States	10000m (m)	07
Natalia	Rusakova	12/12/1979	Russia	4x100m (w)	07
Greg	Rutherford	17/11/1986	Great Britain	Long Jump (m)	07
Adam	Rutter	24/12/1986	Australia	20km Walk (m)	0
Antti	Ruuskanen	21/02/1984	Finland	Javelin (m)	07
Deirdre	Ryan	01/06/1982	Ireland	High Jump (w)	0
Anatoliy	Rybakov	27/02/1985	Russia	10000m (m)	0
Yaroslav	Rybakov	22/11/1980	Russia	High Jump (m)	01 03 05 07
Viktoriya	Rybalko	26/10/1982	Ukraine	Long Jump (w)	07
Mariya	Ryemyen	02/08/1987	Ukraine	4x100m (w)	0
Olga	Rypakova	30/11/1984	Kazakhstan	Triple Jump (w)	07
Jefferson	Sabino	04/11/1982	Brazil	Triple Jump (m)	07
Peter	Sack	27/07/1979	Germany	Shot Put (m)	07
Philaylack	Sackpraseuth	30/04/1987	Laos	100m (w)	0
Natalya	Sadova	15/06/1972	Russia	Discus (w)	99 01 03 05
Konstantin	Safronov	02/09/1987	Kazakhstan	Long Jump (m)	0
Yukari	Sahaku	05/11/1988	Japan	10000m (w)	0
Eliane	Saholinirina	20/03/1982	Madagascar	1500 (w)	07
Jaysuma Ndure	Saidy	01/01/1984	Norway	100m (m), 200m (m)	03 05
Verena	Sailer	16/10/1985	Germany	100m (w), 4x100m (w)	07
Hitoshi	Saito	09/10/1986	Japan	200m (m)	0
Joy Nakhumicha	Sakari	06/06/1986	Kenya	400m (w)	0
Irving	Saladino	23/01/1983	Panama	Long Jump (m)	05 07
Munira	Saleh	18/05/1986	Syria	200m (w)	05
Silvia	Salis	17/09/1985	Italy	Hammer (w)	0
Mohamed Yusuf	Salman	26/07/1989	Brunei	Triple Jump (m)	0
Eemeli	Salomäki	11/10/1987	Finland	Pole Vault (m)	0
Kristina	Saltanovic	20/02/1975	Lithuania	20km Walk (w)	99 03 05
Nana Kofi	Samm	02/04/1986	Ghana	4x100m (m)	0
Roslinda	Samsu	09/06/1982	Malaysia	Pole Vault (w)	07

Athlete Index

Forenames	Surname	Born	Country	Event(s)	Prev Apps
Dani	Samuels	26/05/1988	Australia	Discus (w)	07
Jessica	Samuelsson	14/03/1985	Sweden	Heptathlon	07
Eder	Sánchez	21/05/1986	Mexico	20km Walk (m)	05 07
Jesús	Sánchez	23/03/1976	Mexico	20km Walk (m), 50km Walk	07
Felix	Sánchez	30/08/1977	Dominican Republic	400m Hurdles (m), 4x400m (m)	99 01 03 05 07
Sergio	Sánchez	01/10/1982	Spain	5000m (m)	0
Nicola	Sanders	23/06/1982	Great Britain	400m (w), 4x400m (w)	05 07
Shamar	Sands	30/04/1985	Bahamas	110m Hurdles	07
Leevan	Sands	16/08/1981	Bahamas	Triple Jump (m)	03 05 07
Savannah	Sanitoa	30/04/1987	American Samoa	100m (w)	0
Suwaibou	Sanneh	30/10/1990	Gambia	100m (m)	0
Idrissa	Sanou	12/06/1977	Burkina Faso	100m (m)	01 03 05 07
Vera	Santos	03/12/1981	Portugal	20km Walk (w)	03 05 07
Rolando	Saquipay	21/07/1979	Ecuador	20km Walk (m)	05 07
Evodie Lydie	Saramandji	03/08/1983	Central African Rep	400m (w)	0
Mayu	Sato	14/09/1982	Japan	4x400m (w)	0
Atsushi	Sato	08/05/1978	Japan	Marathon (m)	03
Tobias	Sauter	17/10/1983	Germany	Marathon (m)	0
Yargeris	Savigne	13/11/1984	Cuba	Triple Jump (w)	05 07
Mariya	Savinova	13/08/1985	Russia	800m (w)	0
Mykola	Savolaynen	25/03/1980	Ukraine	Triple Jump (m)	05 07
Daichi	Sawano	16/09/1980	Japan	Pole Vault (m)	03 05 07
Goldie	Sayers	16/07/1982	Great Britain	Javelin (w)	05 07
Daniel	Schärer	20/10/1985	Switzerland	Discus (m)	0
Robin	Schembera	01/10/1988	Germany	800m (m)	0
Fabrizio	Schembri	27/01/1981	Italy	Triple Jump (m)	0
Reto	Schenkel	28/04/1988	Switzerland	4x100m (m)	0
Zuzana	Schindlerová	25/04/1987	Czech Republic	20km Walk (w)	0
Carsten	Schlangen	31/12/1980	Germany	1500 (m)	0
Marc	Schneeberger	05/07/1981	Switzerland	200m (m), 4x100m (m)	07
Mike	Schumacher	21/05/1986	Luxembourg	800m (m)	0
Stefan	Schwab	29/05/1987	Germany	100m (m)	0
Christina	Schwanitz	24/12/1985	Germany	Shot Put (w)	05
Jillian	Schwartz	19/09/1979	United States	Pole Vault (w)	03 05 07
Helge	Schwarzer	26/11/1985	Germany	110m Hurdles	0
Lilli	Schwarzkopf	28/08/1983	Germany	Heptathlon	05 07
Roland	Schwarzl	10/12/1980	Austria	Decathlon	05
Alex	Schwazer	26/12/1984	Italy	50km Walk	05 07
Sharolyn	Scott	27/10/1983	Costa Rica	400m (w)	0
Jeremy	Scott	01/05/1981	United States	Pole Vault (m)	0
Salim	Sdiri	26/10/1978	France	Long Jump (m)	03 05
Jintara	Seangdee	18/05/1990	Thailand	4x100m (w)	0
Hassanine	Sebei	21/01/1984	Tunisia	20km Walk (m)	07
Roman	Šebrle	26/11/1974	Czech Republic	Decathlon	99 01 03 05 07
Gregory	Sedoc	16/10/1981	Netherlands	110m Hurdles, 4x100m (m)	03 05 07
Nikolay	Sedyuk	29/04/1988	Russia	Discus (m)	0
Allan	Segura	23/12/1980	Costa Rica	20km Walk (m)	03
Iryna	Sekachova	21/07/1976	Ukraine	Hammer (w)	03 05
Anis	Selmouni	15/03/1979	Morocco	5000m (m)	0
Mariem Alaoui	Selsouli	08/07/1984	Morocco	1500 (w)	07
Yevgen	Semenenko	17/07/1984	Ukraine	Triple Jump (m)	0
Oleksiy	Semenov	27/06/1982	Ukraine	Discus (m)	0
Caster	Semenya	07/01/1991	South Africa	800m (w)	0
Zinaida	Sendriute	20/12/1984	Lithuania	Discus (w)	0
Amr Ibrahim Mostafa	Seoud	10/06/1986	Egypt	200m (m)	07
Ola	Sesay	30/05/1979	Sierra Leone	Long Jump (w)	0
Marija	Šestak	17/04/1979	Slovenia	Triple Jump (w)	07
Martina	Šestáková	12/10/1978	Czech Republic	Triple Jump (w)	05
Katrina	Seymour	07/01/1993	Bahamas	4x400m (w)	0
Rozina	Shafqat	08/02/1982	Pakistan	400m (w)	0
Saif Saaeed	Shaheen	15/10/1982	Qatar	5000m (m)	03 05
Perri	Shakes-Drayton	21/12/1988	Great Britain	400m Hurdles (w)	0
Dzmitry	Shako	25/03/1979	Belarus	Hammer (m)	0
Mubarak Hassan	Shami	01/12/1980	Qatar	Marathon (m)	07
Viktor	Shapoval	17/10/1979	Ukraine	High Jump (m)	0

Athlete Index

Forenames	Surname	Born	Country	Event(s)	Prev Apps
William	Sharman	12/09/1984	Great Britain	110m Hurdles	0
Mohammed	Shaween	15/02/1986	Saudi Arabia	1500 (m)	07
Yury	Shayunou	22/10/1987	Belarus	Hammer (m)	0
Oleksiy	Shelest	27/03/1973	Ukraine	50km Walk	0
Dongpeng	Shi	06/01/1982	China	110m Hurdles	03 05 07
Masaya	Shimizu	12/11/1980	Japan	Marathon (m)	0
Ali Obaid	Shirook	13/10/1979	United Arab Emirates	400m Hurdles (m)	07
Svetlana	Shkolina	09/03/1986	Russia	High Jump (w)	0
Liliya	Shobukhova	13/11/1977	Russia	10000m (w)	05
Ekaterina	Shtepa	25/08/1987	Russia	100m Hurdles	0
Kuan Wong	Si	22/07/1982	Macau	Triple Jump (m)	0
Yelena	Sidorchenkova	30/05/1980	Russia	3000m SC (w)	0
Maksim	Sidorov	13/05/1986	Russia	Shot Put (m)	0
Soulisack	Silisavadymao	29/10/1987	Laos	100m (m)	0
Rui Pedro	Silva	06/05/1981	Portugal	10000m (m)	0
Rui	Silva	03/08/1977	Portugal	1500 (m)	99 01 03 05 07
Andrés	Silva	27/03/1986	Uruguay	400m (m), 400m Hurdles (m)	07
Vânia	Silva	08/06/1980	Portugal	Hammer (w)	01 03 07
Fernando	Silva	01/06/1980	Portugal	Marathon (m)	0
Andrea	Silvini	08/07/1983	Tanzania	Marathon (m)	0
Dzianis	Simanovich	20/04/1987	Belarus	20km Walk (m)	0
Lidia	Simon	04/09/1973	Romania	Marathon (w)	99 01 07
Jemma	Simpson	10/02/1984	Great Britain	800m (w)	07
Kenia	Sinclair	14/07/1980	Jamaica	800m (w)	05 07
Surendra Kumar	Singh	01/10/1978	India	10000m (m)	0
Eelco	Sintnicolaas	07/04/1987	Netherlands	Decathlon	0
Sibusiso	Sishi	22/06/1985	South Africa	4x400m (m)	0
Donatas	Škarnulis	21/10/1977	Lithuania	50km Walk	07
Lucie	Škrobáková	04/01/1982	Czech Republic	100m Hurdles	05
Austra	Skujyte	12/08/1979	Lithuania	Shot Put (w)	01 03 05 07
Elena	Slesarenko	28/02/1982	Russia	High Jump (w)	05 07
Gavin	Smellie	26/06/1986	Canada	200m (m)	0
Thomas	Smet	12/07/1988	Belgium	Javelin (m)	0
Roman	Smirnov	02/09/1984	Russia	200m (m)	0
Kimberley	Smith	19/11/1981	New Zealand	10000m (w)	05 07
Pieter	Smith	03/04/1987	South Africa	400m (m), 4x400m (m)	0
Oluseyi	Smith	21/02/1987	Canada	4x100m (m)	0
Maurice	Smith	28/09/1980	Jamaica	Decathlon	05 07
Tyrone	Smith	07/08/1984	Bermuda	Long Jump (m)	0
Andrew	Smith	09/07/1979	Canada	Marathon (m)	0
Trecia	Smith	05/11/1975	Jamaica	Triple Jump (w)	01 05 07
Anna	Söderberg	11/06/1973	Sweden	Discus (w)	99 03 05 07
David	Söderberg	11/08/1979	Finland	Hammer (m)	07
Pavel	Sofin	04/09/1981	Russia	Shot Put (m)	03 07
Vera	Sokolova	08/06/1987	Russia	20km Walk (w)	0
Elena	Sokolova	23/07/1986	Russia	Long Jump (w)	0
Igors	Sokolovs	17/08/1974	Latvia	Hammer (m)	07
Olexiy	Sokyrskiyy	16/03/1985	Ukraine	Hammer (m)	0
Pablo	Solares	22/12/1984	Mexico	800m (m)	0
Chris	Solinsky	05/12/1984	United States	5000m (m)	0
Bram	Som	20/12/1980	Netherlands	800m (m)	01 03 07
Wachara	Sondee	09/04/1983	Thailand	4x100m (m)	0
Aimin	Song	15/03/1978	China	Discus (w)	03 05 07
Yon	Soriano	02/11/1987	Dominican Republic	4x400m (m)	0
Arnold	Sorina	06/01/1988	Vanuatu	800m (m)	0
Rondell	Sorrillo	21/01/1986	Trinidad & Tobago	200m (m)	0
Mateo	Sossah	20/04/1988	France	Decathlon	0
Aïssata	Soulama	11/02/1979	Burkina Faso	400m Hurdles (w)	03 05 07
Myriam	Soumaré	29/10/1986	France	100m (w)	0
Maria Enrica	Spacca	20/03/1986	Italy	4x400m (w)	0
Raul	Spank	13/07/1988	Germany	High Jump (m)	0
Igor	Spasovkhodskiy	01/08/1979	Russia	Triple Jump (m)	01 03 05
Wallace	Spearmon	24/12/1984	United States	200m (m)	05 07
Kaliese	Spencer	06/05/1987	Jamaica	400m Hurdles (w), 4x400m (w)	07
Levern	Spencer	23/06/1984	St Lucia	High Jump (w)	05 07

Athlete Index

Forenames	Surname	Born	Country	Event(s)	Prev Apps
Silke	Spiegelburg	17/03/1986	Germany	Pole Vault (w)	07
Tania Regina	Spindler	10/04/1977	Brazil	20km Walk (w)	07
Grzegorz	Sposób	12/02/1976	Poland	High Jump (m)	01 03 05
Barbora	Špotáková	30/06/1981	Czech Republic	Javelin (w)	05 07
Linda	Stahl	02/10/1985	Germany	Javelin (w)	07
Vania	Stambolova	28/11/1983	Bulgaria	400m Hurdles (w)	05
Claudia	Stef	25/02/1978	Romania	20km Walk (w)	99 03 05 07
Konstadínos	Stefanópoulos	11/07/1984	Greece	50km Walk	07
John	Steffensen	30/08/1982	Australia	400m (m), 4x400m (m)	05 07
Pirrenee	Steinert	20/02/1985	Australia	4x400m (w)	0
Kamila	Stepaniuk	22/03/1986	Poland	High Jump (w)	0
Adonía	Steryíou	07/07/1985	Greece	High Jump (w)	07
Toby	Stevenson	19/11/1976	United States	Pole Vault (m)	03 05
Kerron	Stewart	16/04/1984	Jamaica	100m (w), 4x100m (w)	07
Monica	Stoian	25/08/1982	Romania	Javelin (w)	07
Nelson	Stone	02/06/1984	Papua New Guinea	400m (m)	0
David	Storl	27/07/1990	Germany	Shot Put (m)	0
Iva	Straková	04/08/1980	Czech Republic	High Jump (w)	03 05 07
Aryiró	Stratáki	03/08/1975	Greece	Heptathlon	03 05 07
Alexander	Straub	14/10/1983	Germany	Pole Vault (m)	0
Chandra	Sturrup	12/09/1971	Bahamas	100m (w), 4x100m (w)	03 05 07
Hrystyna	Stuy	03/02/1988	Ukraine	4x100m (w)	0
Leonel	Suárez	01/09/1987	Cuba	Decathlon	0
Alejandro	Suárez	30/11/1980	Mexico	Marathon (m)	03 05 07
Grzegorz	Sudol	28/08/1978	Poland	50km Walk	03 05 07
Mahau	Sugimachi	13/11/1984	Brazil	400m Hurdles (m)	0
Apinan	Sukaphai	21/08/1983	Thailand	4x100m (m)	0
Phaustin Baha	Sulle	30/05/1982	Tanzania	Marathon (m)	0
Weiwei	Sun	13/01/1985	China	Marathon (w)	07
Tadas	Šuškevicius	22/05/1985	Lithuania	50km Walk	0
Jane	Suuto	08/08/1978	Uganda	Marathon (w)	0
Sittichai	Suwonprateep	17/11/1980	Thailand	4x100m (m)	99 07
Yusuke	Suzuki	02/01/1988	Japan	20km Walk (m)	0
Takafumi	Suzuki	25/05/1987	Japan	Pole Vault (m)	0
Konstantin	Svechkar	17/07/1984	Russia	4x400m (m)	0
Monica	Svensson	26/12/1978	Sweden	20km Walk (w)	03 05
Petr	Svoboda	10/10/1984	Czech Republic	110m Hurdles	0
Patricia	Sylvester	03/02/1983	Grenada	Long Jump (w), Triple Jump (w)	0
Nick	Symmonds	30/12/1983	United States	800m (m)	07
Alexey	Sysoev	08/03/1985	Russia	Decathlon	05 07
Attila	Szabó	16/07/1984	Hungary	Decathlon	0
Tomasz	Szymkowiak	05/07/1983	Poland	3000m SC (m)	0
Kidane	Tadasse	01/01/1987	Eritrea	5000m (m), 10000m (m)	03 05 07
Zersenay	Tadese	08/02/1982	Eritrea	10000m (m)	03 05 07
Tareq Mubarak	Taher	01/12/1986	Brunei	3000m SC (m)	05 07
Bouabdellah	Tahri	20/12/1978	France	3000m SC (m)	99 01 03 05 07
Pia	Tajnikar	19/09/1985	Slovenia	100m (w)	0
Momoko	Takahashi	16/11/1988	Japan	100m (w), 200m (w), 4x100m (w)	07
Kensuke	Takahashi	30/05/1978	Japan	Marathon (m)	0
Shinji	Takahira	18/07/1984	Japan	200m (m), 4x100m (m)	05 07
Nooa	Takooa	10/03/1993	Kiribati	100m (m)	0
Jared	Tallent	17/10/1984	Australia	20km Walk (m), 50km Walk	05 07
Claire	Tallent	06/07/1981	Australia	20km Walk (w)	0
Luminita	Talpos	09/10/1972	Romania	Marathon (w)	03 07
Teddy	Tamgho	15/06/1989	France	Triple Jump (m)	0
Aleksander	Tammert	02/02/1973	Estonia	Discus (m)	99 01 03 05 07
Sonata	Tamošaityte	28/06/1987	Lithuania	100m Hurdles	0
Takayuki	Tanii	14/02/1983	Japan	50km Walk	05 07
Asami	Tanno	25/09/1985	Japan	400m (w), 4x400m (w)	05 07
Tasuku	Tanonaka	23/09/1978	Japan	110m Hurdles	07
Yoel	Tapia	11/09/1984	Dominican Republic	4x400m (m)	0
Tereapii	Tapoki	19/04/1984	Cook Islands	Discus (w)	05 07
Yuliya	Tarasova	13/03/1986	Uzbekistan	Heptathlon	0
Sónia	Tavares	21/03/1986	Portugal	100m (w)	0
Sandra-Helena	Tavares	29/05/1982	Portugal	Pole Vault (w)	0

Athlete Index

Forenames	Surname	Born	Country	Event(s)	Prev Apps
Jutamass	Tawoncharoen	21/12/1981	Thailand	4x100m (w)	0
Angelo	Taylor	29/12/1978	United States	400m Hurdles (m), 4x400m (m)	99 01 07
Daniel	Taylor	12/05/1982	United States	Shot Put (m)	07
Matthew	Tegenkamp	19/01/1982	United States	5000m (m)	07
Anay	Tejeda	03/04/1983	Cuba	100m Hurdles	05 07
Franklin	Tenorio	30/06/1969	Ecuador	Marathon (m)	01
Asuka	Terada	14/01/1990	Japan	100m Hurdles	0
Andrey	Tereshin	15/12/1982	Russia	High Jump (m)	05 07
Indira	Terrero	29/11/1985	Cuba	400m (w), 4x400m (w)	07
Brianne	Theisen	18/12/1988	Canada	Heptathlon	0
Jurgen	Themen	26/10/1985	Surinam	100m (m)	07
Paraskevi	Theodorou	15/03/1986	Cyprus	Hammer (w)	0
Zaw Win	Thet	01/03/1991	Myanmar	400m (m)	0
James Kibocha	Theuri	30/10/1978	France	Marathon (m)	0
Thi Nhung	Bui	21/01/1983	Vietnam	High Jump (w)	0
Amy Mbacke	Thiam	10/11/1976	Senegal	400m (w)	99 01 03 05 07
Marriam	Thole	24/12/1989	Malawi	5000m (w)	0
Dwight	Thomas	23/09/1980	Jamaica	110m Hurdles, 4x100m (m)	01 03 05
Charlene	Thomas	06/05/1982	Great Britain	1500 (w)	0
Reyare	Thomas	23/11/1987	Trinidad & Tobago	4x100m (w)	0
Tristan	Thomas	23/05/1986	Australia	400m Hurdles (m), 4x400m (m)	0
Donald	Thomas	01/07/1984	Bahamas	High Jump (m)	07
Richard	Thompson	07/06/1985	Trinidad & Tobago	100m (m), 4x100m (m)	07
Arasay	Thondike	28/05/1986	Cuba	Hammer (w)	07
Andreas	Thorkildsen	01/04/1982	Norway	Javelin	01 03 05 07
Linus	Thörnblad	06/03/1985	Sweden	High Jump (m)	05 07
Aretha	Thurmond	14/08/1976	United States	Discus (w)	99 03 05
Jonna	Tilgner	18/11/1984	Germany	400m Hurdles (w)	0
Okilani	Tinilau	02/01/1989	Tuvalu	100m (m)	0
Hanna	Titimets	05/03/1989	Ukraine	400m Hurdles (w)	0
Fatou	Tiyana	24/02/1987	Gambia	100m (w)	0
Robert	Tobin	20/12/1983	Great Britain	400m (m), 4x400m (m)	05 07
Aisea	Tohi	15/04/1987	Tonga	100m (m)	07
Svetlana	Tolstaya	09/08/1971	Kazakhstan	20km Walk (w)	99 01 03 05 07
Dragana	Tomaševic	04/06/1982	Serbia	Discus (w)	05 07
Christopher	Tomlinson	15/09/1981	Great Britain	Long Jump (m)	03 05 07
Dragutin	Topic	12/03/1971	Serbia	High Jump (m)	99 03 05 07
Biljana	Topic	17/10/1977	Serbia	Triple Jump (w)	0
Michel	Tornéus	26/05/1986	Sweden	Long Jump (m)	0
Martin	Toroitich	10/08/1983	Uganda	10000m (m)	0
Marestella	Torres	20/02/1981	Philippines	Long Jump (w)	05 07
Edwardo	Torres	22/08/1980	United States	Marathon (m)	0
Sheena	Tosta	01/10/1982	United States	400m Hurdles (w)	05 07
Matej	Tóth	10/02/1983	Slovakia	20km Walk (m), 50km Walk	05 07
Lívia	Tóth	07/01/1980	Hungary	3000m SC (w)	05
Chaima	Trabelsi	11/03/1982	Tunisia	20km Walk (w)	0
Saria	Traboulsi	05/02/1987	Lebanon	200m (w)	0
Terrence	Trammell	23/11/1978	United States	110m Hurdles, 4x100m (m)	01 03 05 07
Valentina	Trapletti	12/07/1985	Italy	20km Walk (w)	0
Petr	Trofimov	28/11/1983	Russia	20km Walk (m)	0
Malgorzata	Trybanska	21/06/1981	Poland	Triple Jump (w)	07
Loúis	Tsátoumas	12/02/1982	Greece	Long Jump (m)	03 05
Cathleen	Tschirch	23/07/1979	Germany	4x100m (w)	07
Samuel	Tsegay	24/10/1988	Eritrea	5000m (w)	0
Yemane	Tsegay	01/01/1984	Ethiopia	Marathon (m)	0
Dimítrios	Tsiámis	12/01/1982	Greece	Triple Jump (m)	07
Selloane	Tsoaeli	10/07/1977	Lesotho	200m (w)	07
Chi Ho	Tsui	17/02/1990	Hong Kong	100m (w)	0
Naoki	Tsukahara	10/05/1985	Japan	100m (m), 4x100m (m)	07
Mark	Tucker	15/08/1979	Australia	Marathon (m)	0
Dire	Tune	19/06/1985	Ethiopia	Marathon (w)	05 07
Andrew	Turner	19/09/1980	Great Britain	110m Hurdles	07
Laura	Turner	12/08/1982	Great Britain	4x100m (w)	07
Tamara	Tverdostup	17/07/1979	Ukraine	1500 (w)	0
Stephanie	Twell	17/08/1989	Great Britain	1500 (w)	0

Athlete Index

Forenames	Surname	Born	Country	Event(s)	Prev Apps
Karolina	Tyminska	04/10/1984	Poland	Heptathlon	07
Erik	Tysse	04/12/1980	Norway	20km Walk (m), 50km Walk	03 05 07
Yuichiro	Ueno	29/07/1985	Japan	5000m (m)	0
Ivan	Ukhov	04/04/1986	Russia	High Jump (m)	0
Steffen	Uliczka	17/07/1984	Germany	3000m SC (m)	0
Dorian	Ulrey	11/07/1987	United States	1500 (m)	0
Serafi Anelies	Unani	17/02/1989	Indonesia	100m (w)	0
Tobias	Unger	10/07/1979	Germany	100m (m), 4x100m (m)	01 03 05
Toriki	Urarii	25/10/1988	French Polynesia	110m Hurdles	0
Lisa	Urech	27/07/1989	Switzerland	100m Hurdles	0
Maris	Urtans	09/02/1981	Latvia	Shot Put (m)	07
Ainars	Vaiculens	21/01/1983	Latvia	Hammer (m)	0
Teresa	Vaill	20/11/1962	United States	20km Walk (w)	05 07
Atis	Vaisjuns	27/09/1982	Latvia	Decathlon	0
Dmitrij	Valukevic	31/05/1981	Slovakia	Triple Jump (m)	03 05 07
Cedric	Van Branteghem	13/03/1979	Belgium	400m (m), 4x400m (m)	03 05
Peter	Van der Westhuizen	21/12/1984	South Africa	1500 (m)	0
Krijn	Van Koolwijk	30/08/1981	Belgium	3000m SC (m)	05 07
Patrick	Van Luijk	17/09/1984	Netherlands	200m (m), 4x100m (m)	0
Kristof	Van Malderen	30/05/1983	Belgium	1500 (m)	0
Louis	Van Zyl	20/07/1985	South Africa	400m Hurdles (m), 4x100m (m)	05 07
Juan Gualberto	Vargas	12/07/1977	Mexico	Marathon (m)	05 07
Mailín	Vargas	24/03/1983	Cuba	Shot Put (w)	0
Andrus	Värnik	27/09/1977	Estonia	Javelin (m)	03 05 07
María	Vasco	26/12/1975	Spain	20km Walk (w)	99 01 03 05 07
Vadims	Vasilevskis	05/01/1982	Latvia	Javelin (m)	05 07
Álvaro	Vásquez	25/08/1984	Nicaragua	1500 (m)	0
Sabina	Veit	02/12/1985	Slovenia	200m (w)	0
Nallely	Vela	08/02/1986	Mexico	4x400m (w)	0
Jana	Veldáková	03/06/1981	Slovakia	Long Jump (w)	07
Dana	Veldáková	03/06/1981	Slovakia	Triple Jump (w)	05 07
Carlos	Véliz	12/08/1987	Cuba	Shot Put (m)	0
Teddy	Venel	16/03/1985	France	400m (m), 4x400m (m)	0
Venelina	Veneva-Mateeva	13/06/1974	Bulgaria	High Jump (w)	99 01 03 05
Niko	Verekauta	16/02/1987	Fiji	200m (m)	0
Vítezslav	Veselý	27/02/1983	Czech Republic	Javelin (m)	0
Maggie	Vessey	23/12/1981	United States	800m (w)	0
Sandro	Viana	26/03/1977	Brazil	200m (m), 4x100m (m)	07
Aaron	Victorian	11/03/1988	American Samoa	100m (m)	0
João	Vieira	20/02/1976	Portugal	20km Walk (m)	07
Sérgio	Vieira	20/02/1976	Portugal	20km Walk (m)	07
Bertrand	Vili	06/09/1983	France	Discus (m)	0
Valerie	Vili	06/10/1984	New Zealand	Shot Put (w)	03 05 07
Sunette	Viljoen	06/10/1983	South Africa	Javelin (w)	03
Aldy	Villalobos	20/04/1987	Nicaragua	1500 (w)	0
Eduard	Villanueva	29/12/1984	Venezuela	800m (m)	07
Paulo	Villar	28/07/1978	Colombia	110m Hurdles	01 05
Igor	Vinichenko	21/04/1984	Russia	Hammer (m)	0
Brigita	Virbalyté	01/02/1985	Lithuania	20km Walk (w)	0
Felipe	Vivancos	16/06/1980	Spain	110m Hurdles	01 05 07
Borja	Vivas	26/05/1984	Spain	Shot Put (m)	0
Nicola	Vizzoni	04/11/1973	Italy	Hammer (m)	99 01 03 05 07
Blanka	Vlašic	08/11/1983	Croatia	High Jump (w)	01 03 05 07
Miroslav	Vodovnik	11/09/1977	Slovenia	Shot Put (m)	03 05 07
Ekaterina	Volkova	16/02/1978	Russia	3000m SC (w)	05 07
Ingmar	Vos	28/05/1986	Netherlands	Decathlon	0
Christina	Vukicevic	18/06/1987	Norway	100m Hurdles	07
Maki	Wada	18/11/1986	Japan	4x100m (w)	0
Bettie	Wade	11/09/1986	United States	Heptathlon	0
Abdoulaye	Wagne	02/10/1981	Senegal	800m (m)	03 07
Marion	Wagner	01/02/1978	Germany	100m (w), 4x100m (w)	99 01
Štepán	Wagner	05/10/1981	Czech Republic	Long Jump (m)	0
Sunayna	Wahi	14/08/1990	Suriname	200m (w)	0
Brad	Walker	21/06/1981	United States	Pole Vault (m)	05 07
Melaine	Walker	01/01/1983	Jamaica	400m Hurdles (w)	01 05 07

Athlete Index

Forenames	Surname	Born	Country	Event(s)	Prev Apps
Shakeema	Walker-Welsch	10/11/1976	United States	Triple Jump (w)	0
Simon	Walter	13/03/1985	Switzerland	Decathlon	0
Ian	Waltz	15/04/1977	United States	Discus (m)	05 07
Tonny	Wamulwa	03/08/1989	Zambia	5000m (m)	07
Sofian Rayzam Shah	Wan	11/01/1988	Malaysia	110m Hurdles	0
Hao	Wang	16/08/1989	China	20km Walk (m)	0
Sangay	Wangchuk	01/01/1983	Bhutan	Marathon (m)	0
Jeremy	Wariner	31/01/1984	United States	400m (m), 4x400m (m)	05 07
Mayumi	Watanabe	06/06/1983	Japan	4x100m (w)	0
Rob	Watson	26/03/1983	Canada	3000m SC (m)	0
Mitchell	Watt	25/03/1988	Australia	Long Jump (m)	0
Cheryl	Webb	03/10/1976	Australia	20km Walk (w)	05
Lisa Jane	Weightman	16/01/1979	Australia	Marathon (w)	0
Silvia	Weissteiner	13/07/1979	Italy	5000m (w)	07
Hais	Welday	24/10/1989	Eritrea	1500 (m)	0
Saul	Welgopwa	14/06/1984	Nigeria	400m (m), 4x400m (m)	05 07
Scott	Westcott	25/09/1975	Australia	Marathon (m)	05
Angela	Whyte	22/05/1980	Canada	100m Hurdles	01 03 05 07
Rosemarie	Whyte	08/09/1986	Jamaica	4x400m (w)	0
Nicklas	Wiberg	16/04/1985	Sweden	Decathlon	0
Rafal	Wieruszewski	24/02/1981	Poland	4x400m (m)	07
Maurice	Wignall	17/04/1976	Jamaica	110m Hurdles	01 03 05 07
Lauryn	Williams	11/09/1983	United States	100m (w), 4x100m (w)	05 07
ChaRonda	Williams	27/03/1987	United States	200m (w)	0
Monique	Williams	23/09/1985	New Zealand	200m (w)	0
Meritzer	Williams	01/01/1989	St Kitts & Nevis	200m (w), 4x100m (w)	0
Tameka	Williams	31/08/1989	St Kitts & Nevis	200m (w), 4x100m (w)	0
Shericka	Williams	17/09/1985	Jamaica	400m (w), 4x400m (w)	05 07
Conrad	Williams	20/03/1982	Great Britain	4x400m (m)	0
LaToy	Williams	28/05/1988	Bahamas	4x400m (m)	0
Kimberly	Williams	03/11/1988	Jamaica	Triple Jump (w)	0
Rhys	Williams	27/02/1984	Great Britain	400m Hurdles (m)	05
Jonathan	Williams	29/08/1983	Belize	400m Hurdles (m)	07
Tiffany	Williams	05/02/1983	United States	400m Hurdles (w)	07
Novlene	Williams-Mills	26/04/1982	Jamaica	400m (w), 4x400m (w)	05 07
Simeon	Williamson	16/01/1986	Great Britain	100m (w), 4x100m (w)	0
Caitlin	Willis-Pincott	18/12/1982	Australia	4x400m (w)	0
Nickiesha	Wilson	28/07/1986	Jamaica	400m Hurdles (w)	07
Nils	Winter	27/03/1977	Germany	Long Jump (m)	03 05
Teemu	Wirkkala	14/01/1984	Finland	Javelin (m)	07
Joanna	Wisniewska	25/05/1972	Poland	Discus (w)	99 01 05 07
Yvonne	Wisse	06/06/1982	Netherlands	Heptathlon	07
Johan	Wissman	02/11/1982	Sweden	400m (m)	03 05 07
Anita	Wlodarczyk	08/08/1985	Poland	Hammer (w)	0
Sean	Wroe	18/03/1985	Australia	400m (m), 4x400m (m)	07
Christin	Wurth-Thomas	11/07/1980	United States	1500 (w)	07
Dylan	Wykes	06/06/1983	Canada	Marathon (m)	0
Limei	Xie	27/06/1986	China	Triple Jump (w)	07
Evaggelía	Xinoú	22/11/1981	Greece	20km Walk (w)	0
Faguang	Xu	17/05/1987	China	50km Walk	0
Shaoyang	Xu	09/02/1983	China	Discus (w)	0
Olha	Yakovenko	01/06/1987	Ukraine	20km Walk (w)	0
Yuki	Yamazaki	16/01/1984	Japan	50km Walk	05 07
Mingxia	Yang	13/01/1990	China	20km Walk (w)	0
Yawei	Yang	16/10/1983	China	20km Walk (w)	0
Nevin	Yanit	16/02/1986	Turkey	100m Hurdles	07
Khalid Kamal	Yaseen	10/10/1982	Brunei	Marathon (m)	07
Viktor	Yastrebov	13/01/1982	Ukraine	Triple Jump (m)	05 07
Iryna	Yatchenko	31/10/1965	Belarus	Discus (w)	99 01 03 07
Antonina	Yefremova	19/07/1981	Ukraine	4x400m (w)	03 05
Alfred Kirwa	Yego	28/11/1986	Kenya	800m (m)	05 07
Claudine	Yemalin	07/08/1986	Benin	400m (w)	0
Mounir	Yemmouni	12/10/1983	France	1500 (m)	05 07
Yekaterina	Yevseyeva	22/06/1988	Kazakhstan	High Jump (w)	0
Jing	Yin	23/05/1988	China	110m Hurdles	0

Athlete Index

Forenames	Surname	Born	Country	Event(s)	Prev Apps
Dejene	Yirdaw	21/08/1978	Ethiopia	Marathon (m)	0
Geuntae	Yook	14/03/1987	South Korea	Marathon (m)	0
Kazuaki	Yoshida	31/08/1987	Japan	400m Hurdles (m)	0
Lyudmyla	Yosypenko	24/09/1984	Ukraine	Heptathlon	0
Justin	Young	25/07/1979	United States	Marathon (m)	0
Rabah	Yousif	11/12/1986	Sudan	400m (m)	0
Mhadjou	Youssouf	05/06/1990	Comoros	100m (m)	0
Nailiya	Yulamanova	06/09/1980	Russia	Marathon (w)	07
Sun Suk	Yun	28/05/1972	South Korea	Marathon (w)	01
Sniazhana	Yurchanka	01/08/1984	Belarus	20km Walk (w)	0
Rachel	Yurkovich	10/10/1986	United States	Javelin (w)	0
Valeriya	Zabruskova	29/07/1975	Russia	Javelin (w)	03
Aleksey	Zagornyi	31/05/1978	Russia	Hammer (m)	03 07
Anne	Zagre	13/03/1990	Belgium	4x100m (w)	0
Mariánna	Zaharíadi	25/02/1990	Cyprus	Pole Vault (w)	0
Artsiom	Zaitsau	04/03/1984	Belarus	High Jump (m)	0
Luminita	Zaituc	09/10/1968	Germany	Marathon (w)	07
Aziz	Zakari	02/09/1976	Ghana	100m (m), 4x100m(m)	01 03 05
Svetlana	Zakharova	15/09/1970	Russia	Marathon (w)	01 03
Antonin	Žalský	07/08/1980	Czech Republic	Shot Put (m)	07
Milama Paulette	Zang	06/06/1987	Gabon	100m (w)	07
Magno Mesías	Zapata	08/01/1981	Ecuador	50km Walk	0
Yuliya	Zarudneva	26/04/1986	Russia	3000m SC (w)	0
Sergey	Zassimovich	11/03/1986	Kazakhstan	High Jump (m)	07
Olga	Zaytseva	10/11/1984	Russia	200m (w)	0
Oksana	Zbrozhek	12/01/1978	Russia	1500 (w)	0
Omar	Zepeda	08/06/1977	Mexico	50km Walk	01 05 07
Anter	Zerguelaine	04/01/1985	Algeria	1500 (m)	05 07
Yingying	Zhang	04/01/1990	China	10000m (w)	0
Wenxiu	Zhang	22/03/1986	China	Hammer (w)	01 03 05 07
Chengliang	Zhao	01/06/1984	China	50km Walk	05 07
Chunxiu	Zhou	15/11/1978	China	Marathon (w)	05 07
Yafei	Zhu	05/09/1988	China	20km Walk (m)	0
Xiaolin	Zhu	20/02/1984	China	Marathon (w)	07
Moacir	Zimmermann	30/12/1983	Brazil	20km Walk (m)	0
Iwona	Ziólkowska	10/10/1980	Poland	4x100m (w)	0
Szymon	Ziólkowski	01/07/1976	Poland	Hammer (m)	99 01 05 07
Nataliya	Zolotukhina	04/01/1985	Ukraine	Hammer (w)	05 07
Vincent	Zouaoui-Dandrieaux	12/10/1980	France	3000m SC (m)	07
Linda	Züblin	21/03/1986	Switzerland	Heptathlon	07
Ieva	Zunda	20/07/1978	Latvia	400m Hurdles (w)	99 03
Wodage	Zvadya	07/09/1973	Israel	Marathon (m)	05 07
Ellina	Zvereva	16/11/1960	Belarus	Discus (w)	99 01

www.ingramcontent.com/pod-product-compliance
Lightning Source LLC
Chambersburg PA
CBHW081131170426
43197CB00017B/2827